Outline Plan
of
HILLSDALE Co.
MICHIGAN.
Scale 2 Miles to the Inch

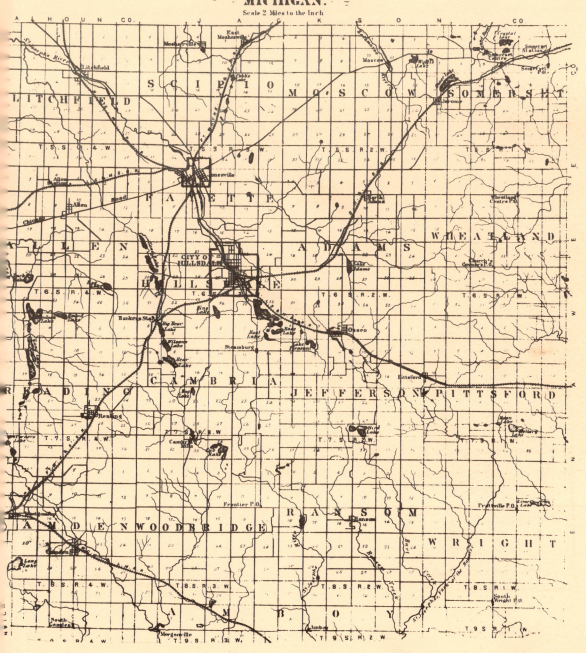

THE

BEAN CREEK VALLEY.

INCIDENTS OF ITS EARLY SETTLEMENT.

COLLECTED FROM THE MEMORIES OF ITS EARLIEST SETTLERS, NOW LIVING, AND
VERIFIED BY REFERENCE TO OFFICIAL DOCUMENTS.

BY JAMES J. HOGABOAM.

HUDSON, MICH.
JAS. M. SCARRITT, PUBLISHER.
1876.

The reproduction of this book has been
made possible through the sponsorship
of the Lenawee County Historical Society,
Adrian, Michigan.

A Reproduction by
UNIGRAPHIC, INC.
1401 North Fares Avenue
Evansville, Indiana 47711
nineteen hundred and eighty

TO THE PIONEERS

OF THE

BEAN CREEK COUNTRY,

AND

TO THEIR CHILDREN,

THIS BOOK IS RESPECTFULLY DEDICATED.

PREFACE

Pioneer "land lookers" chose to settle along a creek which they named "Bean Creek" because of a profusion of locust trees which grew along its banks. The trees produced bean-type pods which in springtime were resplendent with pink-red blossoms.

In pioneer times the Creek was referred to as the "Tiffin River," a name that still exists for the Ohio portion of the waterway.

The Lenawee County Historical Society has chosen to reprint this rare historical volume as a way to keep alive the heritage of the early settlers of the western part of Lenawee and the eastern part of Hillsdale Counties.

The new edition contains the complete text of Mr. Hogaboam's original 1876 edition, but it also contains a few significant additions.

For readibility the size of the print has been enlarged, and we have added maps on the endpapers to help locate the many places mentioned in the text. The Hillsdale map was obtained from the *1872 Atlas of Hillsdale County*, and the Lenawee map came from the *1874 Atlas of Lenawee County*. We are grateful to the Bentley Historical Library of the University of Michigan for permission to reprint the Hillsdale map.

Special illustrations by the Tecumseh artist, Janet Trowbridge, depict incidents from the book and enrich it further.

Finally, the Genealogical Committee and other members of the Lenawee County Historical Society have prepared a complete index to the work.

Those involved in the preparation of the work include:

Patricia Lamb	Doris Trowbridge	Elizabeth Kurtz
Wayne Carpenter	Veda Jaqua	C & K Lindquist
Thelma Frayer	Gail Kellum	Gordon Brown
Kim Carr	Doris Frazier	Janet Trowbride

INTRODUCTION.

By the term, "Bean Creek Country," would ordinarily be understood the country drained by the Bean and its tributaries. Bean creek, or Tiffin river, as it is called on the early maps, rises in Devil's lake, situate on sections two, three, four, nine and ten in the township of Rollin, and sections thirty-four and twenty-seven in the township of Woodstock, said townships being the two most northerly townships in the west tier of Lenawee county. The creek flows from the western extremity of the lake, on section four in Rollin, a little north of west, to the east and west quarter line of section thirty-two in Woodstock, bends southward, flows through the western part of Rollin and along the west line of Hudson, leaves the county on section thirty, makes a bend on sections twenty-five and twenty-six in the township of Pittsford, Hillsdale county, returns to Lenawee county at the northwest corner of section thirty-six, flows southeasterly across the southwest part of Hudson, northeast corner of Medina, and southwest corner of Seneca township, crosses into the State of Ohio near the southeast corner of section six, township nine south of range one east, and then taking a southwesterly course, empties into the Maumee river at Defiance.

Only that part of the Bean Valley situate north of the south line of Michigan is to be treated of in these sketches. That part of the valley is quite narrow, but embraces portions of two counties, Hillsdale and Lenawee. The township of Woodstock contributes the most of her waters to swell the Raisin; Somerset divides hers between the Kalamazoo, the Raisin and the Bean; the western borders of Wheatland drain into the St. Joseph, of Lake Michigan, and the eastern borders of Rollin into the Raisin; Pittsford and Wright divide their waters between the Bean and the St. Joseph of the Maumee; Seneca divides between the Bean and the Raisin, and even Hudson sends her compliments to the Raisin on the ripples of her Bear creek. Medina township, only, lies entirely within the valley of the Bean, but for the purposes of this book we shall consider the valley of the Bean as including the townships of Woodstock, Rollin, Hudson, Medina and Seneca in Lenawee county, and Somerset, Wheatland, Pittsford and Wright in Hillsdale county.

On the banks of the Bean, within the territory mentioned, are the villages of Addison, Rollin, Hudson, Tiffin, Medina, Canandaigua and Morenci. But as a history of the Bean Creek Country would be incomplete if it did not make mention of all the territory, the trade of which has contributed to the prosperity of the Valley, we shall include in these brief outlines of history the territory lying at the headwaters of the Kalamazoo and the two St. Josephs, comprising the townships of Moscow, Adams, Jefferson, Ransom and Amboy, in the county of Hillsdale.

I am aware that in writing the early history of the country the difficulties to be overcome are very great ; that in some of the townships the early records are lost, and in all they are very meager; that many of the early actors have passed away, and the memories of all are failing—but I have endeavored to collect my material from the most trustworthy sources, have verified them, when possible, by reference to contemporaneous records, and have endeavored to digest, write and arrange with an unbiased mind, only solicitous to discover and record the true history of the country and the times. How well I have succeeded I submit to the candid judgment of the old pioneers, than whom more noble and generous men and women never existed in any country.

The question may be asked, Why did you not wait until more facts and incidents had been accumulated? The answer is, "Procrastination is the thief of time," and while we have been talking and waiting many persons whose supervision would have been desirable have died, and in the course of human life nearly all the old pioneers will pass away in the course of the next five years. It is, therefore, every way desirable that the material accessible should make its appearance, and be submitted to criticism before all the competent critics shall have passed away.

The facts and incidents here related were mostly gathered by myself, from interviews with old people and a careful comparison of official records; but I desire to acknowledge valuable aid from newspaper articles prepared by several of the old settlers, among which I would specially name the Hon. Robert Worden, Hon. Orson Green, Hon. George W. Moore, and Beriah H. Lane, esq., of the Bean Creek Country and A. L. Millard and Samuel Gregg, esqs., of Adrian.

It was the original design of the Pioneer Society of Bean Creek Country that sketches prepared by members should be deposited with the Secretary, and that a book should be published by subscription, but no such material has been contributed. All the matter prepared by its members has been given to the public through the newspapers, no manuscripts have been deposited, and the interest appears to be dying out. At this juncture the publisher of the Hudson Post proposed to pay for a part of the labor of collecting material and writing it up. Believing it to be the only way in which such a book could at present be published, I accepted the proposition and commenced the work. It has been a hard task, but if it shall in any way serve to preserve the history of pioneer times, I shall be satisfied.

Truly yours,.

Hudson, Mich., Oct. 1, 1876.   THE AUTHOR.

I. MICHIGAN.

SCRAPS OF ITS EARLY HISTORY—INDIAN TREATIES—SURVEYS—SETTLEMENT—DIS-
PUTED BOUNDARIES—GERM OF THE TOLEDO WAR—MISCHIEVOUS
OFFICIAL REPORT, ETC.

The word Michigan is probably derived from two Chippewa words—Mitchaw, great, and Sagiegan, lake—Great Lake.

The territory of Michigan was visited by the French Jesuits, Fathers Chas. Rymbault and Isaac Jogues, at the Sault St. Mary, in July, 1641.

Father.Mesnard spent the winter of 1660-61 on one of the bays of Lake Superior.

In 1665 Father Claude Allonez founded a Mission at La Point, Lake Superior.

In 1668 Father Marquette founded a Mission at Sault St. Mary, and in 1671 founded a mission near Mackinaw. In the latter year an agent of the King of France took formal possession of all the country between Montreal and the South Sea. At that time Michigan for the most part was occupied by Ottawas and Chippewas. There were some Pottawatomies and Miamies in the south part, and some Sacs and Foxes along the southern shore of Lake Superior.

In 1686 Fort St. Joseph and Fort Detroit were built, the former where Fort Gratiot now stands, at the outlet of Lake Huron; the site of the latter is not known. Both were soon after abandoned.

Detroit, now the city of Detroit, was founded in 1701 by De La Motte Cadillac. He landed on the 24th day of July, and on the same day commenced the erection of Fort Pontchartrain. In 1761 the number of inhabitants in the Detroit settlement was estimated at 2,500. In 1763 France ceded her dominion over Michigan to England. In 1774, by act of Parliament, Michigan became a part of the province of Quebec, and Col. Henry Hamilton was appointed "Lieutenant Governor and Superintendent of Detroit." It was here that during the Revolutionary war Indian incursions against the infant settlements of Western Pennsylvania, Virginia and Kentucky, were organized.

Michigan was surrendered to the United States in 1796, and became a part of the Northwestern Territory, Gen. St. Clair, Governor. On the eleventh of August of that year Wayne county was organized, and included all of Michigan, the northern part of Ohio and Indiana and a part of Illinois and Wisconsin. The county elected delegates to the first Territorial legislature, which met at Cincinnati September 16th, 1799.

The State of Ohio was organized by act of Congress April 30th, 1802, and by the same act the Territory of Indiana was formed, and of it Michigan formed a part. Gen. William Henry Harrison was Governor of the Territory. The ordinance of 1787, by which the Northwest Territory was organized, provided that "Congress shall have authority to form one or two States out of the territory which lies north of an east and west line drawn through the southerly bend or extreme of Lake Michigan." The act of April 30th, 1802, organizing the State of Ohio, fixed for its northern boundary "an east and west line drawn through the southerly extreme of Lake Michigan," but the Constitution adopted by the people of Ohio described as the northern boundary of the State a line running "from the southern bend of Lake Michigan to the northerly cape of Maumee Bay." Congress admitted Ohio without taking any notice of the discrepancy, in matter of northern boundary line, between the State Constitution and the enabling act and the ordinance of 1787. By the line described in the ordinance and enabling act Toledo would be in Michigan; by the line described in the Ohio State Constitution it would be in Ohio. The unwarranted departure of the Constitutional Convention of Ohio from the express terms of the ordinance and enabling act laid the foundation for that affair known in history as the "Toledo war."

On the 11th day of January, 1805, Congress passed an act organizing the Territory of Michigan and by it the legislative power was vested in the Governor and Judges. On the 26th day of February Gen. Wm. Hull was appointed Governor of the Territory, and reached Detroit on the first day of July, but between the date of his appointment and arrival, that is to say, on the eleventh day of June, Detroit was entirely consumed by fire; not a house was left standing; nothing but ashes marked the site of the recent town.

On the second day of July, 1805, the government of the Territory of Michigan was organized, and the legislature commenced its session. The territory at that time comprised the Lower Peninsula only, and the Indians claimed title to and were in possession of nearly all of that. By the treaty concluded by Gen. Clarke at Fort McIntosh in 1785, the Indian title was extinguished to a belt of territory six miles in width, extending along the Detroit river from the river Raisin to Lake St. Clair. Aside from this strip of country, the Indians claimed title to the whole of Michigan. South of the river Raisin the Indian country extended to and bordered the waters of Lake Erie, so that the settlements of the young territory were completely cut off from the settled portions of Ohio.

On the seventeenth day of November, 1807, the United States government concluded a treaty with the Chippewas, Ottawas, Wyandottes and Pottawatomies, by which the Indian title to the following described tract of land was extinguished, viz : "Beginning at the mouth of the river Miami of the Lakes (Maumee), running thence up the middle of said river to the mouth of the great Auglaize river; thence running due north one hundred and thirty-two miles, until it intersects a parallel of latitude to be drawn from the outlet of Lake Huron, which forms the river St. Clair; then northeast the course will lead in a direct line to White Rock, Lake Huron; thence due east until it intersects the boundary line between the United States and Upper Canada; thence southerly, following said boundary line down said lake, through the river St. Clair, Lake St. Clair, and the Detroit river, into Lake Erie, to a point due east of the Miami river; thence to the place of beginning." This tract included that part of the State of Michigan lying east of the principal meridian of the Monroe survey, and south of a line drawn from near the village of Ovid northeasterly, diagonally intersecting the counties of Shiawasse, Saginaw, Tuscola, Sanilac and Huron, to White Rock, on the eastern shore of Lake Huron.

The Territory of Michigan was surrendered to the British by General Hull on the seventeenth day of August, 1812, and was put under martial law. On the twenty-ninth day of September, 1813, the Territory was evacuated by the British, and on the thirteenth day of October following, Colonel Lewis Cass was appointed Governor.

By proclamation of the Governor, Wayne county was re-organized November first, 1815; and on the fourteenth day of July, 1817, the county of Monroe was organized, also by Executive proclamation.

On the fourth day of September, 1817, William Woodbridge, Secretary and acting Governor of the Territory, issued a proclamation organizing the township of Monroe. The preamble recites, "*Whereas*, It appears by the report of John Anderson and Wolcott Lawrence, Esquires, appointed to examine and report in the premises, that a part of the farm of Joseph Loranger, and some adjacent ground on the borders of La Riviere aux Raisins, constitute the most eligible portion thereof. * * * *

"*Now, therefore*, I, the above named William Woodbridge, do by the power and authority in me for the time being vested, constitute the whole of that certain tract and parts of tracts described in the aforesaid reports, * * * * into a township for the permanent seat of justice in and for said county of Monroe, to be known and called by the name of the town of Monroe. * * * * * "

In 1819 Governor Cass concluded a treaty with the Chippewas, of Saginaw, by which the Indian title to a tract of country, beginning at a point near the site of the village of Kalamazoo, and extending to the head of Thunder Bay river; thence by the course of the river to its mouth was extinguished.

During the years 1818 and 1819 the Monroe survey was made. It included the State of Michigan, and that portion embraced in Lenawee county was surveyed by Joseph Fletcher during 1819. President Monroe issued a proclamation, dated March 15th, 1820, declaring the public domain then recently surveyed subject to entry from and after the first Monday in July of that year.

In the year 1821, Governor Cass and Judge Sibley, of Detroit, negotiated a treaty with the Indians, by which the Indian title was extinguished to all that portion of the territory lying west of the cession of 1807, and also to that portion lying west of the cession of 1819, south of Grand river. This cession included the present counties of Hillsdale, Branch, St. Joseph, Cass, Berrien and Van Buren, the south part of Jackson and Calhoun, the south and west portion of Kalamazoo, the south part of Ottawa and Kent, and the southwest portion of Ionia. The treaty was held at Chicago. To reach that point, the commissioners descended the Detroit river, crossed the head of Lake Erie to Maumee bay, ascended the Maumee river to its source, crossed the intervening country to the Wabash, descended that river to the Ohio, the Ohio to the Mississippi, ascended the Mississippi to the mouth of the Illinois, and the Illinois to Chicago.

On the tenth day of September, 1822, Governor Cass issued a proclamation altering and defining the boundaries of the counties of Wayne, Monroe, Macomb, Oakland and St. Clair, and laying out the counties of Lapeer, Sanilac, Saginaw, Shiawasse, Washtenaw and Lenawee. The boundaries of Lenawee county are therein thus defined: "Beginning on the principal meridian, where the line between the townships numbered four and five south of the base line intersects the same; thence south to the boundary line between the Territory of Michigan and the State of Ohio; thence with the same, east, to the line between the fifth and sixth ranges east of the principal meridian; thence north to the line between townships numbered four and five south of the base line; thence west to the place of beginning." By the same proclamation the county of Lenawee was attached to the county of Monroe. At the date of its formation the county did not contain a single white inhabitant; but, although the Indian title had been extinguished for fifteen years, the county contained quite a numerous Indian population. The Indian title to that portion of Michigan lying west of the principal meridian had been extinguished by the treaty of Chicago, concluded on the twenty-ninth day of August, 1821, but the Indians remained in partial possession of the southern portion of the State until about the year 1839.

Sometimes wonder has been expressed that Michigan should have settled so slowly and remained so long under a Territorial government. For some reason the climate and soil of the Territory were strongly misrepresented; and so late as 1836 Michigan was spoken of in the East as the land of savages, venomous snakes and beasts, where all manner of fell diseases lay in wait to make skeletons of foolhardy adventurers.

In 1812 Congress directed that 2,000,000 acres of Michigan land should be surveyed and set apart for soldiers in the war with Great Britain, to the end that each soldier should have one hundred and sixty acres of land fit for cultivation. A like amount was also set apart in the Territories of Louisiana and Illinois. The lands were surveyed in the latter Territories, but concerning the lands of Michigan, the Surveyor General reported:

The country on the Indian boundary line from the mouth of the great Auglaize river, and running thence for about fifty miles, is (with some few exceptions) low, wet land, with a very thick growth of underbrush, intermixed with very bad marshes, but generally very heavily timbered with beech, cottonwood, oak, etc.; thence continuing north and extending from the Indian boundary eastward, the number and extent of the swamps increases with the addition of numbers of lakes, from twenty chains to two and three miles across. Many of the lakes have extensive marshes adjoining their margins, sometimes thickly covered with a species of pine called "tamarack," and other places covered with a coarse, high grass, and uniformly covered from six inches to three feet (and more at times) with water. The margins of these lakes are not the only places where swamps are found, for they are interspersed throughout the whole country, and filled with water as above stated, and varying in extent. The intermediate land between these swamps and lakes, which is probably nearly one-half of the country, is (with a very few exceptions) a poor, barren, sandy land, on which scarcely any vegetation grows, except small, scrubby oaks. In many places that part which may be called dry land is composed of little short sand hills, forming a kind of deep basins, the bottoms of many of which are composed of a marsh similar to that above described. The streams are generally narrow and very deep compared with their width, the shores and bottoms of which are (with a very few exceptions) swampy beyond description; and it is with the utmost difficulty that a place can be found over which horses can be conveyed in safety.

A circumstance peculiar to that country is exhibited in many of the marshes, by their being thinly covered with a sward of grass, by walking on which evinced the existence of water or a very thin mud immediately under their covering, which sinks from six to eighteen inches from the pressure of the foot at every step, and at the same time rising before and behind the person passing over. The margins of many of the lakes and streams are in a similar condition, and in many places are literally afloat. On approaching the eastern part of the military lands, toward the private claims on the *straights* and lakes, the country does not contain so many swamps and lakes, but the extreme sterility and barrenness of the soil continues the same. Taking the country altogether, so far as has been explored, and to all appearances, together with the information received concerning the balance, is so bad there would not be more than one acre out of a hundred, if there would be one out of a thousand, that would in any case admit of cultivation.

The consequence of such a report being made was that the act locating the 2,000,000 acres of military land was repealed, and Michigan escaped the misfortune of having her best lands long kept out of the market for the benefit of land speculators.

Upon the appearance of this report, Governor Cass at once set on foot numerous explorations throughout the interior, and when he had become thoroughly convinced of the falsity of the report, and had collected sufficient evidence of such falsity, he at once used all the means in his power to correct the mischievous impression made by the report. It is a trite saying that "a lie will travel faster than the truth," but it was verified in this instance, for it was more than twenty years before Michigan recovered from the effects of the false impression caused by that unjust official report.

II. LENAWEE COUNTY.

1823 TO 1833.

In the summer of 1823 Musgrove Evans, of Brownsville, Jefferson county, in the State of New York, came into the Territory of Michigan to find for himself and family a home. He formed the acquaintance of Austin E. Wing, of Monroe, a man of considerable prominence in the territory, who afterwards represented it in Congress. Wing informed Evans of a desirable location on the Raisin, within the county of Lenawee, and represented the advantages the county possessed as a farming country, and the wonderful hydraulic advantages offered by the Raisin and a tributary, which united their waters at this place, in such glowing terms that Evans was induced to visit the place, and an agreement was entered into between Wing and Evans to organize a company for the improvement of the almost unrivaled water power. Evans returned to the State of New York to enlist others in the enterprise, and during his absence Wing purchased of the United States the west part of section twenty-seven and the east part of section twenty-eight, in township five south of range four east, which included the water power, and that part of Tecumseh now known as Brownsville, and the tributary stream received the cognomen of Evans' creek.

Musgrove Evans was a native of Pennsylvania, but had then recently been an inhabitant of the State of New York. He belonged to the Society of Friends, and was educated. He possessed a well-balanced mind and untiring perseverance, and the survivors of those days agree that he was a noble man. Mr. Evans returned to his home in New York, to enlist others in the enterprise, and secure a few good colonists with which to start the settlement of the new country. He succeeded in inducing his brother-in-law, Joseph W. Brown, also of Brownsville, Jefferson county, New York, to become a partner in the enterprise, and several others to accompany them to their new home in the then far west.

Evans and Brown secured the old schooner Erie to bring their colony across Lake Erie. The company consisted of Musgrove Evans, wife and five children, Joseph W. Brown, Ezra F. Blood, Turner Stetson, Nathan Rathbone, Peter Lowery, and perhaps one or two others. They arrived at Detroit in the month of April, 1824. Here Evans left his family, and the men procured a Frenchman, with pony and cart, to carry their packs, until they struck the Raisin a little above where the village of Clinton now stands, and there shouldering their packs, they traveled to the proposed site of the new colony at the mouth of Evans' creek. Of course the first thing to do was to prepare temporary shelter for the men, and then immediately the work of organization commenced. A co-partnership was formed between Wing, Evans and Brown, the north half of section thirty-four entered, and a saw mill commenced. They brought forty men from the village of Monroe, thirty-three miles distant, to assist in raising the frame of the mill. Having prepared a rude log house, with bark roof and floors, Evans brought his family from Detroit, and took possession of the mansion house of the county on the second day of June, 1824. Peter Benson and wife, in the employ of Wing, Evans & Brown, occupied the house with them. The Evans family was the first white family in Lenawee county, and Mrs. Evans and Mrs. Benson were the first white women to set foot within the boundaries of Lenawee county.

Early in the summer of 1824 a village was platted and named Tecumseh, in honor of the renowned Shawaneese warrior, who had often, tradition says, visited that locality and sat in council around the fires of the resident tribes. As soon as the settlement was fairly commenced,—a village platted and named,—then a movement was put on foot to establish the seat of justice for the county at this, its only settlement, and in its only village of one log house. A petition unanimously signed, no doubt, was sent to Governor Cass, who, in accordance with the territorial statute in such case provided, appointed commissioners to examine, select and report a location for the seat of justice of Lenawee county. They decided to locate it at Tecumseh, and it is related that when the commissioners stuck the stake to mark the site for the court house, the company present, among whom were the proprietors of the village, swung their hats and gave three hearty cheers. Mr. Wing, in the ardor of his enthusiasm, swung his hat with such emphasis that at the last whirl it flew away, leaving in his hand a piece of the brim about as large as a silver dollar. This, perhaps, was prophetic of the early flight of the "seat of justice" to a more southern site.

Upon receipt of the commissioners' report, the Legislative Council passed "An Act to establish the seat of justice in Lenawee county," although at that time the county was unorganized, being attached to the county of Monroe. The act was approved June 30th, 1824, and is as follows:

Be it enacted by the Governor and Legislative Council of the Territory of Michigan, That the seat of justice in the county of Lenawee be, and the same is hereby established on the northwest quarter of section number thirty-four, in township five south, range four east, in the said county of Lenawee, on lands owned by Messrs. Wing, Evans & Brown, agreeable to the plan of a town or village, situated on said northwest quarter section, and recorded in the Register's office, in the county of Monroe, the twenty-sixth day of June, one thousand eight hundred and twenty-four.

About the latter part of June a post-office also was established, and Musgrove Evans appointed postmaster. About the first day of July, 1824, Mr. Brown returned to Jefferson county, N. Y., for his family. An extract from a letter, written him by Mr. Evans, will shed some light on the condition of things in this young settlement. The letter bears date "Tecumseh, 8 M., 8th, 1824." After acknowledging the receipt that morning of Brown's letter "of the 6th ult.," the latter says:

"The articles thee mentions will be good here, particularly the stove, as it takes some time always in a new place to get ovens and chimneys convenient for cooking. We have neither yet, and no other way of baking for twenty people but in a bake kettle and the fire out at the door."

The saw mill was completed and commenced operations in the fall of 1824, and building thenceforth became possible. In the month of June, 1824, Jesse Osburn visited the infant settlement, and selected and purchased a tract of land near where Judge Stacy now resides. In the month of August, that year, he removed his family to the wilds of Michigan. He came by schooner to Detroit; from thence Mr. Osburn drove his own team to Monroe, over the old River road, and his was the first team driven over the route subsequent to the war of 1812. They found bridge frames and stringers, but none were planked. The covering had been removed by the contending armies, and since the return of peace the traffic of Detroit had been carried on by the lake craft. There was but little need of a highway between Detroit and Monroe, as their intercourse could be carried on by way of the lake much cheaper and more easily, and for years the road was traveled only by the French pony trains, the animals carrying about four hundred pounds each.

Mr. Osburn brought to the territory two plows of diverse pattern, and one of them deserves, perhaps, a few words of description. Cast iron plows had been made in the the latter part of the 18th century, but were not used by farmers until after Mr. Wood patented his improvement in 1819. The plow in general use before that time was a wooden plow, with a wrought iron share or point, and had received the cognomen of "bull plow." The introduction of cast iron plows met with great opposition from the farmers of the east. They argued they would spoil the land; that land plowed with them would not produce as good crops as that plowed with the old bull plow, "for," said they, "it turns a furrow too flat, and does not leave the ground as loose and light as the bull plow does." To express their contempt for it, they dubbed the Wood plow the pot-metal plow. When Mr. Osburn was preparing to come to the Territory of Michigan he purchased a Wood's plow. His neighbors looked at him with astonishment. "What," said they, "you going to use a pot-metal plow; why, you can't do anything with it among stones." "That's just it,"said Mr. Osburn, "I am going to Michigan, where they don't have any stones." But although Mr. Osburn brought an iron plow to Michigan, he never entirely lost his prejudice against the pot-metal affair. He brought the share of his old bull plow with him, re-wooded it here, and as long as he could find a blacksmith that understood sharpening it, he would plow with no other, and the probabilities are that the first crop of wheat raised in Lenawee county was sowed on land plowed with a bull plow. Mr. A. C. Osburn, of Woodstock, preserves the remains of his father's bull plow, and as the younger readers have, probably, never seen such a plow, a description will be attempted.

The component parts of this plow are the "chip," the share, mouldboard, beam, and handle. The "chip" was made out of a round piece, two sides dressed at right angles, so as to present a smooth side on the bottom and to the land; the forward end was formed to fit into the share, and the other was mortised to receive the handle. The "share" resembles the forward part of an iron plow, including the point, and forward portions of mouldboard and landside. To this share and chip was fitted a wooden mouldboard, usually rived out of a piece of timber having the proper wind. The beam was of wood, but little larger than a corn cultivator beam, and was tenanted to receive the handle. A single bolt, which had its flattened head let into the bottom of the chip, and had a nut at its upper end, on top of the beam, fastened the chip and share to the beam forward, while the handle—only one—fitting on to the tenant of the beam and into the mortise of the chip, fastened the beam to the chip behind. The rectangular sides of the chip, measuring not more than two inches, formed the bottom and landside. The share was of wrought iron, and was sharpened by being drawn out at a smith's forge.

A school house was built by Evans and Brown, of tamarack logs, and was twelve feet square. In that house Mrs. George Spafford taught school in the winter of 1824-5. The Evans' house this winter sheltered Mr. and Mrs. Evans and five children, Mr. and Mrs. Brown and five children, Mr. and Mrs. Geo. Spafford, and from ten to twelve work hands employed at the mill and about the business of the mill firm.

On the third day of May, 1824, William Kedzie, of Delhi, N. Y., purchased of the United States government a tract of land in the township of Blissfield, but he did not settle on it until October, 1826. In the month of June, 1824, Mr. Hervey Bliss purchased a tract of land in that township, and moved on it in the month of December following. Mr. Bliss came to this county from Raisinville, Monroe county, He settled in the village of Monroe in 1816, a year later he moved thirteen miles up the Raisin, and settled on government land, but it proved to be on the "Macon reservation." He was driven off by the Indians in 1819, and settled in the township of Raisinville, Monroe county, where he resided until he removed to Lenawee county, as heretofore stated. He built a log house, which he and his family occupied for about twelve years. Mr. Gideon West settled on section twenty-nine in January, 1825.

In the spring of 1825 Mr. Bliss lost one of his oxen, and had no means to buy another, but his new neighbor, a Mr. Harrison, being about to return to Massachusetts for his wife, loaned him a pair of young steers. With these he managed to log and drag a small field for spring crops. He had to go to Monroe to mill, and had no team he could drive on the road. He drove his ox to the township of Raisinville, yoked him with a borrowed ox, hitched the pair to a borrowed cart, returned to his residence, took in sixteen bushels of corn, and drove to Monroe. The grist ground, the whole distance had to be again traveled over in reverse order. To get that grist ground it cost him eight days' time and one hundred and forty miles travel. He found this milling so expensive that he burned a hollow in the top of a stump, of sufficient size to contain a half bushel of grain, and with a pestle attached to a spring pole, he pounded his corn for bread until he was enabled to procure another team.

With the opening of the spring of 1825 busy scenes recurred, and before autumn large accessions had been made to the population of Lenawee county. In that year the people of the Tecumseh settlement were principally engaged in making sure the progress of the preceding eventful year, in preparing dwellings for those on the ground and those arriving, and in clearing off ground for cultivation. Mr. Brown built a frame building and opened it as a public house, the first and then the only public house west of the village of Monroe. Mr. Jesse Osburn, in the fall of that year, sowed the first wheat in Lenawee county, on the ground a little north of the present residence of Judge Stacy, and James Knoggs built and opened a store. The elder Osburn spelled his name with a *u;* his son uses an *o* instead.

In the summer of 1825 Mr. Darius Comstock, of Niagara county, N. Y., purchased a tract of land in the present township of Raisin, in what is known as "The Valley," about midway between Tecumseh and Adrian. His son, Addison J. Comstock, purchased of the government, on the seventh day of September, 1825, four hundred and eighty acres of land, on which he afterwards laid out the village of Adrian. Of the elder Comstock we quote the eulogistic words of Francis A. Dewey, esq.: "Of the early pioneers no one is more worthy of special notice than our late friend, Darius Comstock, with his ample means and generous ways. He located his lands in the valley four miles south of Tecumseh; there he made himself and family a beautiful home, where his declining years were spent with good will to all. For many years past these lands and stately buildings have been in the hands of trustees, and have become one of the best literary institutions in the country. It was largely through the efforts of Darius Comstock that the first meeting house in the county was erected, and it now stands a monument to his memory. Thousands of the Friends persuasion yearly assemble in it to worship the true and only God." The younger Comstock, after entering his lands, returned to the State of New York, where he remained during the winter of 1825-6.

In the spring of 1826 Wing, Evans & Brown built a grist mill at Tecumseh, the settlers having agreed to pay two hundred dollars towards the cost of its erection. Turner Stetson was the builder. The dam was ready built, the building and water-wheel easily built, but it was extremely difficult to provide the mill-stones. A pair of French burr stones would cost a large sum at the east, and then it would have been difficult, not to say impossible, to transport them over Michigan mud, through Michigan forests, to the metropolis of Lenawee county. It has been said "necessity is the mother of invention," and these pioneer mill builders were not to be discouraged by difficulties. A granite rock was found lying on the ground about two miles from the mill building. It had been broken into two pieces by the falling of a tree across it. The services of Sylvester Blackmar, a practical miller, were called into requisition, and the pieces prepared, the smaller for the upper and the larger for the nether mill-stone, and with them for several years the grain of Lenawee county was ground.

The people had determined to celebrate Independence Day this year, and great preparation was made for the first Fourth of July celebration in Lenawee county. The mill was ready for business, the wheat sowed by Jesse Osburn the fall before had ripened, been harvested and threshed, and on this auspicious Fourth of July morning Jesse Osburn carried some wheat to the mill, Sylvester Blackmar ground it into flour, and Mrs. Brown made the cake and biscuit for the celebration of that day. The performance of this feat is vouched for by living witnesses.

On the fourteenth day of February, 1826, Addison J. Comstock was married to Miss Sarah S. Dean, of Phelps, Ontario county, N. Y., and in the early spring returned, with his bride, to Lenawee county, accompanied also by Mr. John Gifford and wife. Mr. Gifford had been employed by Mr. Comstock to assist him in the clearing of his land and the erection of suitable buildings. The women were left at the Valley until suitable houses could be erected on the Comstock tract.

While the houses were being built, that is to say on the twenty-eighth day of June, 1826, John Gifford purchased of the United States eighty acres of land, now constituting a portion of the second ward of the city of Adrian. Mr. Gifford occupied the house built for him on the tenth day of August, and Mr. Comstock moved into his a few days later, and thus Mrs. Gifford became the first white woman inhabitant of the future Adrian. Mr. Comstock's house was situated in an oak grove on the bank of the river, south side of Maumee street, nearly opposite the Gibson House. Mr. Comstock built a saw mill this year, and had it completed in the month of November. It was the second saw mill in the county.

December 26th, 1826, Elias Dennis purchased of the United States eighty acres of land, now known as L. G. & A. S. Berry's Southern Addition to the city of Adrian.

In October of this year Mr. William Kedzie, who as before stated, purchased land in Blissfield in May, 1824, settled on his land. The winter was spent in cutting down, with the help of two brothers, Nathan and Benjamin Tibbits, the timber on about thirty acres of land, and in the following spring ten acres were logged and planted to corn.

November 20th of this year (1826) the Legislative Council passed an act organizing the county of Lenawee, to take effect from and after the 31st day of December of that year. The terms of the County Court were fixed on the first Mondays of June and January in each year, and by this act, " All the country within this territory to which the Indian title was extinguished by the treaty of Chicago shall be attached to and compose a part of the county of Lenawee." The territory thus attached to Lenawee county comprised a belt of country extending from the meridian line, the west line of the county, to Lake Michigan, including the present counties of Hillsdale, Branch, St. Joseph, Cass, and Berrien.

November 23d the first wedding, or rather pair of weddings, occurred in the township of Blissfield—Mr. Samuel Buck and Miss Margaret Frary and Mr. George Stout and Miss Delight Bliss. Loren Marsh, a Monroe county justice, was imported to perform the ceremony.

In the fall of 1826 Musgrove Evans was employed by the United States government to superintend the construction of the Chicago Road from Detroit to Clinton. It had been surveyed by the United States in 1825, and established as a military road between Detroit and Chicago. It is two hundred and fifty-four miles long, extends from Detroit through Ypsilanti and Saline, enters Lenawee county a little to the northeast of Clinton village, passes through the village of Clinton and along the northern boundary of Lenawee county, through Hillsdale, Branch and St. Joseph counties, and crosses the corner of Berrien into the State of Indiana. It was the thoroughfare to other States along which emigrants flocked in almost countless numbers. Blois' Gazetteer of the State of Michigan, published in 1838, speaking of the Chicago Road, said: "The travel on this road is immense, equal to, if not more, than on any other in the United States of the same length."

By an act of the Legislative Council, approved April 12th, 1827, it was provided that all that part of the county of Lenawee containing the surveyed townships numbered five south of the base line, in ranges one, two, three, four and five east of the principal meridian, be a township by the name of Tecumseh: all that part of said county containing the surveyed township numbered six, in ranges one, two, three, four and five, be a township by the name of Logan; and that all that part of the country containing the surveyed townships seven, eight and nine, in ranges one, two, three, four and five, be a township by the name of Blissfield. But by another act of the Legislative Council, approved the same day, all the foregoing was repealed, and the county was divided into townships as follows: Township numbered five and the north half of township numbered six south, in ranges one, two, three, four and five east, to be a township named Tecumseh, first township meeting to be held at the house of Joseph W. Brown; the south half of townships numbered six and townships numbered seven south, in ranges numbered one, two and three east, to be a township by the name of Logan, the first township meeting to be held at the house of Darius Comstock; and townships numbered seven, in ranges four and five, and townships numbered eight and nine south, in ranges numbered one, two, three, four and five east, to be a township named Blissfield, the first township meeting to be held at the house of Hervey Bliss.

According to the division which became and remained the law, Tecumseh township comprised the present townships of Macon, Tecumseh, Clinton, Franklin, Cambridge, Woodstock, and the north half of the townships of Rollin, Rome, Adrian, Raisin and Ridgeway. The township of Logan comprised the south half of the present townships of Ridgeway, Raisin, Adrian, Rome and Rollin, and all of the townships of Hudson, Dover and Madison—an odd shaped township, truly; the township of Blissfield comprised the present townships of Palmyra, Blissfield, Deerfield, Riga, Ogden, Fairfield, Seneca and Medina.

By the same Legislative Act, "All that district of country situated west of the said county of Lenawee, and which is attached to said county, and to which the Indian title was extinguished by the treaty of Chicago," was formed into a township named St. Joseph, the first township meeting to be held at the house of Timothy S. Smith.

The first township meeting in the township of Logan was held on the 28th day of May. Elias Dennis was Moderator of the meeting; Darius Comstock was elected Supervisor; Addison J. Comstock, Town Clerk; Noah Norton, Warner Ellsworth and Cornelius A. Stout, Commissioners of Highways; Patrick Hamilton and Abram West, Overseers of the Poor.

The first township meeting in the township of Blissfield was held on the 28th day of May. William Kedzie was elected Supervisor, and Ezra Goff Town Clerk. That the county had settled rapidly since the advent of its first family, in 1824, may be seen by the following extract from a letter, written by Mr. Brown, under date of January 14th, 1827: "The Legislative Council have organized three new counties this winter, and in none of them was there a white inhabitant in the year 1823, and in ours not till June, 1824. This is the youngest and smallest of the three, and we have more than six hundred inhabitants."

This year, 1827, Dr. Caleb N. Ormsby erected the first frame dwelling within what is now the city of Adrian. The first birth and death in the A. J. Comstock settlement occurred this year—Leander, infant son of A. J. and Sarah L. Comstock. He was born August 9th, and died October 8th.

October 23d, Mr. James Whitney purchased of the United States four hundred acres of land, on the west side of the river, Adrian.

The original plat of the village of Adrian was laid out by Addison J. Comstock, and recorded April 1st, 1828. It consisted of two streets only, Main and Maumee, of equal length, crossing each other at right angles. There were forty-nine lots in all.

In June, 1828, James Whitney returned to Adrian with his family, and built a log house on his farm. He resided here until 1833. when the place becoming too thickly settled for him, he sold his land and removed to a newer country.

July 4th, 1828, Independence Day was celebrated in the village of Adrian. The stand was erected under a white oak tree, near where W. S. Wilcox's store now stands. A national salute was fired, a blacksmith's anvil having been prepared for that purpose. Amidst the booming of the extemporized cannon the people assembled. Addison J. Comstock read the Declaration of Independence, and Dr. C. N. Ormsby delivered the oration, which ended, the Marshal of the Day, Noah Norton, formed the procession and marched through streets fringed with hazel brush, to the residence of A. J. Comstock, where the ladies of the village had prepared dinner. Mr. Norton and Eleazer Baker had one pair of shoes between them, and they belonged to Baker. A bare-footed marshal would never do, so Norton wore the shoes and Baker remained at home.

In the summer of 1828 Isaac Dean commenced building the "Exchange," a public house which for many years occupied the site of the Lawrence house, and was the principal hotel of the village.

In the winter of 1828-9 Miss Dorcas Dean taught the first school in Adrian, in the house of Noah Norton. During the year 1829 a frame school house was built on the west side of South Main street.

The subject of religion was not forgotten by the busy pioneers of Lenawee county.

The Rev. Noah M. Wells preached at Tecumseh in 1825. In 1827 the Rev. John Janes preached at the house of Noah Norton, in Adrian. In April, 1828, the Rev. Alanson Darwin organized the Presbyterian church in Tecumseh. Daniel Smith and Elijah Brownell often preached the word to the Friends of the Valley. In August, 1828, the Rev. John A. Baughman, of Monroe, preached the first sermon in the township of Blissfield.

August 5th, this year, William Kedzie, of Blissfield township, died. Mr. Kedzie purchased the first land sold by the Government in the township of Blissfield, settled on it in October, 1826, and was elected first Supervisor of the township in 1827. He possessed a robust constitution, was seldom sick, and was always a hard-working man. He had sowed a crop of wheat in the fall of 1827, and in July, 1828, he harvested it; but while it still stood in shock, he was prostrated on a bed of sickness, and died in a few days. He left a widow, five boys and two girls, to grapple unaided with the hardships of pioneer life. On the marble slab at the head of his grave is chiseled the story of his life:—"WILLIAM KEDZIE. A native of Roxboroshire, Scotland, who departed this life Aug. 5, 1828, aged 47 years, 6 mo. and 5 days. A useful citizen; a true friend; a loving and faithful husband; an affectionate parent; and a sincere christian."

In June of this year, the Legislative Council laid out a Territorial road from "Port Lawrence," (Toledo) "in the county of Monroe," through "Blissfield and Logan, and also through the village of Adrian, in the county of Lenawee, to intersect the Chicago road on the most direct and eligible route; and Anthony M'Kee, of said county of Lenawee, and Eli Hubbard and Seneca Allen, of the county of Monroe, are hereby appointed commissioners to lay out said road." The act was approved June 23d, 1828, and the reader will perceive that at this time the Territory of Michigan was exercising jurisdiction over the region bordering on the Maumee, and that the site of the city of Toledo was then considered a part of the county of Monroe.

In 1829 Governor Cass organized the militia of Lenawee county, and appointed the following officers: Col., John W. Brown; Lieut. Col., William McNair; Maj., Davis Smith.

In December, 1828, or early in January, 1829, a post-office was established at the village, and Addison J. Comstock was commissioned post-master. Of this post-office Mr. Comstock, in a document prepared by him several years since, says:

"The conditions of establishing the office were that the contractor should take the net revenue of the office for transporting the mail from Adrian to Monroe. The whole receipts of the first quarter, ending March 31, 1829, was $8.60¾. The net revenue to the contractor, after paying expense of office, 90¾ cents. It should be remarked that the carrying of the mail was not expensive, as the post-master took advantage of the ox teams that made regular trips to Monroe, and so obtained the mail about every week, as a trip to Monroe and back could be performed in about five days when they had good luck."

It was during this year Dr. E. Conant Winter settled in Adrian. He opened a dry goods store on the southwest corner of Maumee and Winter streets, and Addison J. Comstock and Isaac Dean built the red flouring mill.

June 2d, 1829, Abijah Russell purchased of the general government about thirty-five acres of land within the present limits of the city of Adrian.

During the year 1829 Cornelius Millspaw settled in Woodstock, and Silas Benson entered land in the township of Moscow.

In October, 1829, the Legislative Council laid out the township of St. Joseph into the counties of Hillsdale, Branch, St. Joseph, Cass, and Berrien; and by act of the Council, approved November 4th, 1829, the counties of St. Joseph and Cass were organized; Hillsdale was attached to Lenawee; the counties of Branch, Kalamazoo, Calhoun, Barry and Eaton were attached to the county of St. Joseph; and the counties of Berrien and Van Buren were attached to the county of Cass. By an act approved November 5th, the townships of White Pigeon, Sherman and Flowerfield, in the

B

county of St. Joseph, and the townships of Pokagon, LaGrange and Ontwa, in the county of Cass, were organized. These townships, as then organized, comprised several surveyed townships; and from them, from time to time, other townships have been organized, until each only comprised one surveyed township.

In 1830 the United States census was taken, and for the purpose of taking that census within Lenawee county, Musgrove Evans, of Tecumseh, was made assistant United States marshal. Hillsdale county was at that time attached to Lenawee county, and Mr. Evans' returns show the population to be as follows: Hillsdale, 75; Tecumseh, 771; Logan, 500; Blissfield, 145. Total, 1,491.

It will be remembered that Logan, as then constituted, embraced the south half of Ridgeway, Raisin, Adrian, Rome and Rollin, and the townships of Madison, Dover and Hudson. The following is said to be a complete list of heads of families in Logan township: Darius Comstock, Catharine Fay, Alpheus Hill, Cornelius A. Stout, George Scott, Allen Chaffee, Jonathan Harnard, Elijah Brownell, Anson Howell, Samuel Todd, Cary Rogers, James Whitney, John Wood, Pliney Field, Addison J. Comstock, Charles Morris, Hannah Gifford, Robert Smith, Josiah Shumway, Patrick Hamilton, John Walsworth, Daniel Smith, Milo Comstock, D. Torrey, Davis D. Bennett, John Powers, Anson Jackson, Lyman Pease, Silas Simmons, Lewis Nickerson, Nelson Bradish, William Edmonds, Curren Bradish, Levi Shumway, Daniel Gleason, Samuel Davis, Stephen Fitch, Aaron S. Baker, William Foster, Elias Dennis, Nathan Pelton, Turner Stetson, William Jackson, John Arnold, Nathan Comstock, Betsy Mapes, Joseph Pratt, Abram West, Thomas Sachrider, Daniel Odell, William H. Rowe, Moses Bugby, Samuel Weldon, Jeremiah Stone, David Wiley, Noah Norton, Asher Stevens, Samuel Burton, John Comstock, Joseph Beals, John Murphy, Samuel S. L. Maples, David Bixby, Charles Haviland, Benjamin Mather, John Chapman, Jacob Brown, Jacob Jackson, Job S. Comstock, Elijah Johnson. Samuel Carpenter, Cassander Peters, William Brooks, Josiah Baker, Seth Lammon, N. W. Cole, Reuben Davis, John Fitch, Daniel Walsworth, Nehemiah Bassett, Ephriam Dunbar, Isaac Dean and C. N. Ormsby.

In the fall of 1830 Isaac French came to Adrian and built a hotel on the corner now occupied by Crane & Mason. In 1836 he sold it to Pomeroy Stone.

In the year 1831 Turner Stetson built the Hotel now known as the Gibson House, but for many years kept by Sampson Sammons as the Mansion House. Hiram Kidder, of Ontario county, New York, settled in what is now known as the Valley, midway between Tecumseh and Adrian, where he entered land for his brother, Nathan B. Kidder. Dr. Bebee settled in Adrian, and the next year died of small-pox. Joseph H. Cleveland opened a store on the north side of Maumee street, near the river.

During 1831 James D. Van Hoevenburgh and Charles Blackmar entered, and soon afterwards Van Hoevenburgh settled on lands within the limits of the township of Somerset as at present organized; and Samuel Aiken, Peter Benson and Pontius Hooper entered lands within the limits of Moscow.

Charles Blackmar settled in the township of Cambridge in 1829 and died of cholera in August, 1834.

The year 1832 was a stirring year in the annals of our young county. In the spring, Black Hawk, with a band of warriors, crossed the Mississippi river and advanced through the settlements. He was attacked by a body of Illinois militia, and then the Indians broke up into small parties and began an indiscriminate massacre of the inhabitants, still constantly advancing toward Chicago, which seemed their common objective point. Chicago was then an insignificant trading post, protected by a fort; but the probabilities were, if that post should fall, the Indians, encouraged by its fall, would advance through the infant settlements of Northern Indiana and Southern Michigan to the Canada line. Word came to the infant settlements of the southern tier of counties that the Indians were advancing, and along with it the call of the Indian Agent at Chicago for military assistance. There were enough Indians within these counties to cut the throats of the white inhabitants, if aroused, and perhaps the best way to defend their own homes was to meet the enemy beyond the borders of the Territory. Col. John W. Brown had been promoted to the command of the third brigade of Michigan militia, and without waiting for orders from the Governor, he ordered his brigade to rendezvous at the village of Niles. The eighth (Lenawee) regiment, then commanded by Col. William McNair, responded nobly to the call, and was in the shortest possible time ready for the order to march.

The regiment was composed of two companies from Tecumseh, one from Adrian, and one from the village of Clinton, which had sprung into existence since the completion of the Chicago road. Gen. Brown's order required Col. McNair to take only volunteers. Said the order: "Take no man with you who is not a volunteer. Let the timid return to their homes." When the regiment was drawn up into line, the order was read, and all who desired to return home were ordered to step four paces to the front; but not a man advanced. The regiment took up its line of march by the way of the Chicago road for Niles, the place appointed for the brigade rendezvous.

The reader can hardly appreciate the feelings of mothers and children as they saw every able bodied man move off to battle with the Indian foe, hundreds of miles away. It is true the danger was then distant, but their minds were keenly alive to the terrors of Indian warfare. It was then not twenty years since the horrible massacre at the river Raisin, only a few miles off, the details of which were all too well remembered to beget a feeling of security. The Indians living in their midst were friendly, it is true, but such was the known treachery of the Indian character that they lived in dread lest even these friendly Indians should suddenly go upon the war path, and fall upon them in their unprotected condition. But the Indians remained friendly, and before the brigade left Niles, the regular army, under Gen. Atkinson, defeated the hostile Indians and captured Black Hawk. The troops were sent home with the thanks of the commanding general for the spirit displayed in their prompt response to the call of their country.

In the winter of 1831-2 Congress made an appropriation to build a turnpike road from LaPlaisance bay to the Chicago road, through Tecumseh, and in the fall of 1832 Musgrove Evans, of Tecumseh, was employed to survey the route. The jobs were let in the spring of 1833, and the road was completed during the summer of 1835.

Mr. A. C. Osborn says Cornelius Millspaw was the first settler in township five south, of range one east, now called Woodstock, and he thinks Millspaw settled there in 1829; but a reference to the tract book shows that Millspaw entered his land October 27th, 1832. He may, however, have "squatted" on his land, and been unable to enter it sooner than 1832; but however that may be, Mr. Jesse Osburn was either the first or second settler, and his family award the post of honor to Millspaw. Jesse Osburn sold his land in Tecumseh, and August 27th, 1832, entered land in Woodstock, and probably moved on it that fall. John Gilbert located land in that township in 1825, but tradition says he was only a speculator and held his land for that purpose only.

In June, 1832, the Legislative Council organized two townships in Branch county—Coldwater and Prairie River,—and in March, 1833, organized township five south, in ranges one, two and three east, Lenawee county, into a new township, and named it Franklin. The first township meeting was held at the house of Hiram Reynolds. By act approved March 7th, 1834, townships eight and nine and fractional township ten south, in ranges one, two and three east, were erected into the township of Fairfield. It will be observed that in this act also the Territorial Legislature asserted its authority over the strip of territory which afterwards was *casus belli* of the Toledo war. Townships seven south, in ranges one, two and three east, were erected into a new township and named Lenawee. The first township meeting was held at the school house one mile east of William Edmonds, in said township. Township six south, in range four east, was organized into a township and named Raisin. The first township meeting was held at the house of Amos Hoeg. Townships seven, eight, nine, and fractional township ten, in range four, east, were organized into a township, and named Palmyra, first township meeting to be held at the house of Caius C. Robinson; and townships five and six south, in range five east, were made into a township named Macon, first township meeting to be held at the house of Henry Graves. All that part of Tecumseh comprised in the north half of township six south, in ranges one, two and three east, being the north half of the present townships of Rollin, Rome and Adrain, was detached from Tecumseh and attached to the township of Logan. This statement of the organization of townships in 1834 is here made out of its chronological order because with this chapter this historical sketch of the settlement of eastern Lenawee will close. For the same reason another enterprise which had its inception in 1833, but was carried out later, which exerted a large influence in the settlement of the western part of the county, deserves to be noticed here.

By an act of the Legislative Council of the Territory of Michigan, approved April 22nd, 1833, the Erie and Kalamazoo Railroad Company was incorporated, with a nominal capital stock of one million dollars, in shares of fifty dollars each, and when one thousand shares were subscribed for, the corporators thereby and thenceforth became a ' body corporate and politic." Stephen B. Comstock, Benjamin F. Stickney, David White, Caius C. Robinson, Darius Comstock, Asahel Finch, E. Conant Winter, Seth Dunham, Silas Holbrook, Stephen Vickery and Edwin H. Lothrop were the corporators, and were authorized to build a railroad, with single or double track, from Port Lawrence through or as near as practicable to the village of Adrian, and thence on the most eligible route to such point on the Kalamazoo river as they may deem most proper and useful. The corporators were to begin the road within three years, finish it to Adrian in six years, one-half of it in fifteen years, and the whole road within thirty years. That part of the road beyond Adrian was afterwards abandoned. At the time of the inception of this project there not only was no railway west of Lake Erie, but none in New England. There was a railroad between Albany and Schenectady operated with horse power and stationary engines, and a few short routes in Pennsylvania, but American railroad building had just begun. The subscription books for the Erie and Kalamazoo Railroad Company were opened March, 1834, and the first $50,000 of stock was subscribed and the Company fully organized before the end of May. The work was immediately commenced. It was designed to use horse power only on the road, and therefore the road was built with wooden rails. It was so far finished that cars commenced to run in 1836. It was run by horse power until June, 1837, when the road was ironed with strap rail and a locomotive was purchased. The successful completion of this enterprize shortened routes and cheapened fares and freight so materially as to mark a new epoch in the history of the county.

III. BEAN CREEK VALLEY.

1833 TO 1836.

The beginning of the year 1833 found the Bean Creek country an unbroken wilderness. Nine years had elapsed since the first settlement was made within the county limits, and although considerable encroachments had been made on the dense forests, yet comparatively but little had been done. From Tecumseh, as a center, settlers had made their way through the township of Franklin and some settlements had been made in Cambridge. The principal part of the settlers were in the region of country between the two principal points, Tecumseh and Adrian. From Adrian settlers had ventured as far west in Dover as Robert and Bart White's, who lived on either side of the road where the Raisin crosses the line between sections two and eleven. Settlers had occupied the most eligible lots in Madison, and commenced on the two northerly tier of sections in Fairfield, but the southern part of Dover, the townships of Seneca, Medina, Hudson and Rollin were yet untouched by the pioneer hand, and but one or two families had settled in Woodstock. The Government had made a military road, —the Chicago,—leading from Detroit to Chicago, which passed through the extreme north part of the county. It was surveyed in 1825 and built in the succeeding years, probably before 1830, but for years it was but little better than a quagmire. The road followed the old Indian trail along the highest lands, but a single belt six rods in width, through interminable forests, afforded the sun but little opportunity to dry the soil, and it required but little travel to make the newly plowed road almost impassible. But there are some men possessed of such adventurous spirits that their courage seems to rise with increased and increasing difficulties. A few such men as these had scattered themselves along the Chicago road, built themselves log cabins, and commenced keeping hotel, ministering to the wants of adventurous emigrants and thirsty savages. There were perhaps two such within the limits of Woodstock, one such in Somerset, and one in Moscow; but none of these were properly within the valley of Bean Creek. In 1832 the General Government surveyed another military road, from La Pleasance Bay to the Chicago road in the township of Cambridge. This road was not finished until 1835, but its completion afforded a valuable route to the westward bound emigrant. In 1828 the Legislative Council appointed commissioners to lay out a territorial road "from Port Lawrence (Toledo) in the county of Monroe, running in the most direct and eligible route through Blissfield and Logan, and also through the village of Adrian, to intersect the Chicago road on the most direct and eligible route." This road was surveyed soon after to pass through the townships of Rome and Woodstock, just touching the corner of Rollin, but the westerly portion of it was not completed until 1835. This road passed to the north-eastward of Devil's Lake, and thus it will be seen all the northerly lines of travel led the emigrant by and around the Bean Creek country.

In the year 1832 the Legislative Council of the territory established a road commencing at Vistula, (Toledo,) in the town of Port Lawrence, running on the most eligible route to the forks of the Ottawa river, thence westerly in towns nine, south on the most eligible route to the eastern boundary line of the State of Indiana. There was but little done on this road until 1834 and 1835, and there was not then enough done on it to make it in any sense a thoroughfare.

Thus matters stood in 1833. The valley of the Raisin had been sparsely settled, while beyond to the westward, half of Lenawee and all of Hillsdale counties was an interminable forest. On the 4th of June, 1831, Ira Alma, of Seneca county, New York, had entered the west half of the northwest quarter of section twenty in the township of Rollin, and on the tenth day of May, 1832, Addison J. Comstock entered the east half of the northeast quarter of section thirty-two, in the same township, but nothing was done towards effecting a settlement in either of those years. Hiram Kidder settled in "the valley" in 1831, and early in the year 1833 visited the Bean creek country, and on the sixth day of February entered the southwest quarter and west half of the southeast quarter of section six and the northwest fractional quarter of section seven, town seven south, range one east, now the township of Hudson. This land he entered in the names of Daniel Hudson, Nathan B. Kidder and William Young, all of Ontario county, New York.

About the first day of April, 1833, Joseph Beal and his son William, equipped for a land hunt, departed from the village of Adrian, and taking a southwesterly course, reached Bean creek in the vicinity of where Morenci now stands. They then proceeded up the creek until they reached the bend in the southerly part of town seven south (Hudson), and then taking their bearings by the aid of a pocket compass, they proceeded through the wilderness on a straight line as near as possible for Devil's Lake, the headwaters of the Bean. They came out on the banks of Round Lake. After considerable explorations thereabouts they returned to Adrian through town six south, range two west (Rome). At that time, April, 1833, the north half of towns seven south in ranges one and two east (Rollin and Rome) formed a part of the township of Tecumseh, and the south half of those towns formed a part of the township of Logan. Several other exploring parties visited the region of the lakes during that month, and the result of such explorations was, that May 1st David Steer entered seven or eight lots, and on May 3d William Beal and Erastus Aldrich entered their land, all in the township of Rollin, as now constituted. During the early part of May, say about the sixth, seventh or eighth days, the Hon. Orson Green visited Devil's Lake, and slept under the blue vault of heaven on the land he afterwards entered and now owns. At that time, says Mr. Green, there were no inhabitants save Indians in all this country, from the Chicago road to and into the States of Ohio and Indiana.

At this time Charles Ames and his brothers and brothers-in-law were contemplating emigrating to Michigan. They had arranged to come to the house of a friend living in the vicinity of Detroit, and to explore the country from there. Nathan B. Kidder, Esq., learning of their intentions, described to them in glowing terms the advantages of the Bean creek country, as he had learned them from his brother Hiram, then already an inhabitant of Lenawee county, and advised Mr. Charles Ames and Thomas Pennock, whom it had been arranged should look land for the party, to proceed at once to the house of his brother Hiram who would, he said, show them the loveliest county under the sun. They acted on his advice, and in the month of May, 1833, visited Lenawee county and under the lead of Mr. Hiram Kidder explored the Bean creek country. Mr. Kidder was a practical surveyor, and was well acquainted with the country. He had deliberately selected land in what he deemed the most eligible part of the country. He intended to locate there and desired neighbors, and it is not strange, therefore, that he should convince the land lookers sent by his brother that their best interests would be subserved by locating in his neighborhood.

Charles Ames, on the 20th day of May, 1833, entered the east half of the southwest quarter of section seven. His brother-in-law, Thomas Pennock, entered the west half of the southwest quarter of section seven. On the 7th day of June Charles Ames entered the southeast quarter of section one and the northeast quarter of section twelve, in town seven south of range one west, now the township of Pittsford, and Thomas Pennock the southeast quarter of the southeast quarter of the same section and township. Having made these purchases, Ames and Pennock returned to the East to prepare their families for removal.

On the 16th day of June, Hiram Kidder entered the east half of the southeast quarter, and the west half of the north part of the northwest fractional quarter of section eight, town seven south, range one east (Hudson), in the name of his brother, Nathan.

B. Kidder, and on the 27th day of July entered the west half of the northeast quarter of section seven, same town, in the names of Hudson, Kidder and Young.

In the month of May, 1833, Ebenezer Gay, of the State of New Hampshire, an old man and a widower, came to Michigan and stopped at the house of Cornelius Mills-paw, on the Chicago road near the northwest corner of town five south, of range one east (now Woodstock). According to Father Gay there was only one other house near, and that was the house of James D. Van Houvenburgh, also on the Chicago road, and within the limits of the present township of Somerset. He busied himself in the month of May looking land. While thus engaged, a man named Richard L. Lewis came there and joined him in his journeying through the wilderness. They passed quite through town five south, one west, into town six south now called Wheatland. They came to a piece of land having a large spring on it. Gay said "I will enter that," and took its description. They both reached the land office in Monroe the same day, but Lewis just enough in advance to enter Gay's spring lot. That day was the seventh day of June, and it is quite remarkable that the first land purchased in Wheatland and the first in Pittsford were entered at the land office the same day. Gay entered land in both towns five and six south (Somerset and Wheatland), but Lewis in only the latter. Mr. Gay having secured his land, imme-mediately wrote his son Timothy, who was then living in Albany, to come on and make himself a home in the wildernsss.

On the first day of June, 1833, Stephen Lapham bought land on section four, in town six south, one east (Rollin), and immediately built a shanty and moved a man into it. The man's name was Levi Thompson, and to him must be accorded the fame of being the first settler in the Valley of the Bean. Erastus Aldrich settled, in August, on section nine, and in the month of October Joseph Beal and his son Porter settled on section ten.

Samuel Gregg, then of Adrian, piloted a party of mill men into the Bean creek country in search of water power. They left Adrian July 4th, 1833, going by the way of Mudge's Corners and Samuel Jordan's, this last near the south bend of the Raisin, which was, Gregg says, the "very verge of civilization in that direction." They fol-lowed an old Indian trail, until they reached the creek on what is now the site of the village of Canandaigua. It was dark when they arrived. They passed the night in an old Indian wigwam. In the morning they took their bearings and found they were at the southeast corner of section one, town eight south, range one east. They resumed their journey, and followed Bean creek to a little stream just below where the village of Morenci now stands, since called Silver creek. They did not find water power to suit, and returned to Adrian. Gregg was so pleased with the country he wrote his brother-in-law, William Cavender a glowing description. Cavender visited Michigan in August of that year, and selected lands on section six in town eight south, range two east, and on section one town eight south, range one east, compris-ing the site of the village of Canandaigua and lands adjoining. The land was entered at the land office the second day of September, the Seneca lands in his own name, the Medina land in the name of Samuel Jordan. But this latter was afterwards deeded to Cavender, according, no doubt, to an agreement entered into at the time the land was taken up.

On the 14th day of August, 1833, Mr. Hiram Kidder took with him from the Valley, George Lester and Henry C. Western, proceeded to his Bean creek purchase, and rolled up the body of a log house and put a roof on it. This, the first log house within the limits of Hudson, was twenty-five feet square, and in the fall was finished off in the heighth of style, with chinked and mudded cracks, stick chimney, and puncheon floor.

Yielding to the solicitations of his father, on the last day of August, 1833, Timothy Gay, wife and three children, left Albany, in the State of New York, and arrived at the house of James Van Houvenburgh, in Somerset, on the night of the 18th day of September, 1833. The old gentleman wrote them to stop at Cornelius Millspaw's, where he boarded, but the house was passed in the night without being observed. The same vessel that brought the family across Lake Erie, brought also several stage coaches to be put on a line in the State of Illinois. At Detroit, the agent proposed to Timothy Gay and the other men westward bound that if they would lend a hand in putting the coaches together he would give them a free passage to their destination. The proposition was acceded to, and very soon the company were wallowing in the mud of the Chicago road. The journey was a tedious one. Every house on the road was a tavern, and it was well it was so, for the progress was so slow that many houses of entertainment were necessary. Mrs. Gay and her children had lived in the city, and to them the emigrant's fare seemed poor enough, and on the journey out they nearly starved. At Osborn's they inquired how far it was to Millspaw's. " Two miles," was the answer. It was nearly dark, but the company pushed on, the Gays proposing to end their journey that night. Mrs. Gay called out to the man in charge of the extra horses to go ahead and have the chickens cooked, and away he went. At the foot of a steep hill they were told they could save the ascent by taking a woods road around. The horses were reined into the by-road, but when the woods were fairly entered, the darkness was so great that the men had to lead the horses to keep them in the road. When they emerged from the woods, night had set in, in earnest, and they floundered on in the mud and darkness, the two miles seeming interminable. At last they were encouraged by the sight of a light, and soon were at the door of a log house. A man ran out, looked into the coach, and asked, "Is this Mr. Gay and family ?" "Yes." "Come right in." It was the good Mr. Van Houvenburgh making his future neighbors welcome. In the darkness they had passed Millspaw's unwittingly, and traveled three instead of two miles. But here, too, they found their messenger. He stopped at Millspaw's, but finding the house full, without revealing who the passengers were, had pushed on and ordered supper at Van Houvenburg's. And a royal good supper it was, too. In the morning old Mr. Gay came over to see who the strangers were, and to his surprise and delight found his son and family. "Well, Nancy," said the old man, "you have got along at last. I don't know but we will all starve to death." The old man had ague-bleached until he seemed to have no blood in his veins, and it was no wonder he felt gloomy. The old man had procured a little piece chopped, and very soon a log house was ready for occupancy, although for years it had but one window, with a single six-lighted seven-by-nine sash. Until winter there was no chimney in the house. Mrs. Gay did the cooking for her family of eight to ten persons over an out-door fire. She had neither oven or bake-kettle, but in lieu thereof baked her bread in a deep spider, that had a can-topped cover fitted to it. Late in the fall, a stone hearth and a stick chimney were built. The house was not large, and had two outside doors on opposite sides. When building the stone hearth they had to use large rocks, as flat stones could not be procured in sufficient quantities. They loaded the stones on a stone-boat, drew it near the door, and then taking the oxen around, passed the chains through the house and drew the rocks in. This occasioned Mrs. Gay to write her Albany friends: " We have our house nearly done. They are now drawing the stones into the house with two yoke of oxen." It was twenty years before her friends solved the mystery. The Gays cleared a small piece of land and sowed it to wheat. Several families had moved into the township between the arrival of Ebenezer Gay and the arrival of Timothy and family. Heman Pratt, Horace White and David Harrington came in June 8th, Elias Branch, June 1st, and Elias Alley came in December 8th.

In October Hiram Kidder moved his family from the Valley to Bean creek. They arrived on the evening of Tuesday, the 29th. The family consisted of Mr. and Mrs Kidder, their children, Harriet, Calista, Addison, Maria and Nathan, and two men who assisted them in moving. The house was yet unfinished, and indeed it had no floors, doors nor windows. To the eastward it was twelve miles to the nearest abode of civilized man. Near the shores of Devil's Lake there was a solitary cabin, and there were a few houses along the Chicago road from fifteen to twenty miles distant, but all to the westward and southward was one vast wilderness. At about sunset on the first day of November, 1833, the Ames family arrived at the Kidder habitation. The party consisted of Charles Ames and wife, Miss Ball, a sister of Mrs. Ames, Elizabeth Ames, since Mrs. James Sprague, Henry, William, and Ezra Ames, and Alpheus Pratt. Mr. Pratt had left his wife and child at the house of Mr. Lyman Pease, about one mile west of Adrian, where they remained about one week, resting from the fatigues of the journey. The night before the most of the party had lodged at the house of Stephen Perkins, about four miles west of Adrian, and all that day had wended their way through the wilderness intervening between there and Bean creek. There was about four inches of snow on the ground. A wagon way had been underbrushed among the trees, but covered with snow, it could only be followed by the "blazed" trees which marked its course. Mrs. Charles Ames had a seven-weeks old babe and was compelled to ride, but the girls, Miss Ball and Elizabeth Ames, walked nearly all the way, sitting down occasionally on a log by the roadside, they wrung the water from their stockings, and then proceeded on their journey until it became necessary to repeat the operation. They found Mr. Kidder's house yet unfinished; it lacked doors, windows and chimney. The new comers were welcomed and treated to the best the house afforded, a supper and a bed upon the floor. The next morning, one of the party relates, it was necessary to unload a barrel of pork before breakfast could be prepared. The barrel slipped from their hands and rolled away, about six rods down the hill. Charles, worn out by the journey, and worried because of the illness of his wife and babe, sat down on the barrel at the foot of the hill, and wished himself and family back to Buffalo. Vain wish! Buffalo was more than a thousand miles to the eastward, over the frozen lake. No railways, or even wagon roads, for many a mile between the actual and longed-for place of location. Sitting on and around that pork barrel, the prospects of the new colony were discussed, and an agreement reached to remain together five years, and then if the prospects were no better, they should be at liberty to divide and separately try their fortunes elsewhere. Indeed it was a time to try men's souls—in a wilderness, at the beginning of winter, twelve miles from the nearest house, dependant on their present store for subsistence through a long winter, without any means of securing help from friends without. It needed stout hearts and firm resolves to master the situation. After breakfast it was determined to first finish the house they had. Henry was a carpenter, and he proceeded to make the windows and doors; the others prepared the chinks and the sticks for the chimney, Hiram Kidder taking the general supervision of the whole matter. In a few days the house was made quite comfortable, but the party was so large a part of the cooking had to be done out of doors, which, on account of the cold weather, proved disagreeable business for the ladies of the colony.

While the Ames party were at Clinton, on their way in, they were accosted by a trapper and hunter with the query where they were going. They told him of the Bean Creek Country, whither they were traveling, and enlarged upon the quality of land and quantity of game. Jesse Smith, for that was the hunter's name, said that he was land-looking, and if there was any good country out there he would see it. He threw his traps into one of the wagons, shouldered his gun, and marched on. He skirmished around the party, frequently making them calls, until they reached the house of Stephen Perkins, on the last day of October. From there he went on a hunting excursion, and a few days after the arrival of the party at the Creek he came in, and believing he had found the country for which he had been looking, he started for Monroe. As was usual with him, he took a free course through the woods and the first night encamped alone in the woods in the vicinity of Devil's Lake. The next morning he visited a temporary Indian camp near by, and after that visited the house of Mr. Thompson, who had settled near the lake, where he breakfasted. The next night he lodged at the house of a Mr. Taylor, on the east side of Round Lake. The morning after, Smith sent his baggage on to Adrian by a teamster and proceeded on foot toward the same place. In the vicinity of the Raisin he met a party of land-lookers, who were on their way to the lakes. He described to them the advantages of the Bean Creek Country. They were inclined to turn that way, and asked Mr. Smith to pilot them in. Two of the party were Oliver Purchase (a bachelor brother of the late William Purchase) and Samuel Vangauder. In two or three days Mr. Purchase had made his selection, and leaving Vangauder to take and keep possession, Messrs. Smith and Purchase started for the land office at Monroe. There they arrived on the sixth of November. Mr. Purchase entered his land on the same day, but for some as yet unexplained reason Mr. Smith's was not entered until the 15th of that month—about the time he thinks he arrived home at Albion, New York. Mr. Purchase returned to his land and immediately built a cabin, in which he and Vangauder wintered.

But to return. As soon as Mr. Kidder's house had been made comfortable, the Ames family looked out a site for a house of their own. A spot on the bank of Hillsdale creek was selected, and the clearing of the ground and the cutting of logs commenced. The work had progressed but little when the provisions gave out, and Alpheus Pratt and Ezra Ames were sent to Adrian for a supply, distance eighteen miles. They accomplished the round trip in five days, having slept one night under their wagon in the "twelve mile woods." The wolves all night long howled for their entertainment a soul-stirring chorus, that, to use the words of one of the party, made their hair stand on end. They reached home in safety, however, bringing with them eight hundred pounds of provisions. By the time the party returned from Adrian the logs were prepared for the house, and the work of drawing them in and laying them up commenced; but it was a new kind of work and moved slowly. In about five weeks, however, the house was so far completed that the Ames people moved into it.

As soon as the Ames mansion was completed, Alpheus Pratt and Henry Ames looked about for places to build houses for themselves. Pratt selected land on section thirteen, town seven south, one west (Pittsford), since known as the Bush farm, and Ames selected the west sub-division of the northwest fractional quarter of section eighteen, town seven south, range one east (Hudson), the farm on which the venerable Clark Ames now lives. They entered their land at the Monroe land office December 5th, 1833, and before the first day of January following, Pratt had a house far enough advanced to be inhabited.

On the ninth day of November, 1833, Francis H. Hagaman and Gershom Bennett purchased of the United States lands on section 31, in Dover, and section 6, in Seneca, and the same month erected a log house near the northwest corner of the township of Seneca. Samuel Gregg, desirous of opening a road to his brother-in-law's new purchase, induced the Highway Commissioners of the township of Blissfield to lay out the angling road leading northeasterly from Canandaigua. The surveying party went to Cavender's purchase, in the month of November, to commence the survey of the road. Mr. Gregg says they found Hagaman and Bennett there, having arrived the day previous and commenced building a house. The surveying party encamped on the ground that night. The next morning there was several inches of snow on the ground, and the survey was postponed for a while, but was executed and the road established during the winter of 1833 and '34.

Late in the fall or in the early part of the winter, Silas Moore came to the house of Timothy Gay, on the Chicago road, and desired to be piloted to some land of his in town seven south, range one west (Wheatland). He had purchased the land of Lewis and was moving on it. Timothy Gay underbrushed a road for him to his land and helped him cut logs and roll up the body of a log house. They succeeded in getting the upper floor beams in position, but had not help enough to roll up the logs above the beams. They heard, a little way off, the sound of Indians chopping. Mr. Gay said he would go and get the Indians to help roll the logs. The others laughed at the idea of an Indian rolling logs; but away went Gay to find the Indians. They were chopping a bee tree after the usual Indian style of hacking around and around. Mr. Gay made known his wants as well as he could, and they showed him the tree was

"The wolves all night long howled for their entertainment a soul-stirring chorus,
that, to use the words of one of the party, made their hair stand on end." (p. 26)

"I have seen Mrs. Kidder picking her way over the heads and toes of this pavement of sleeping men, women and children, early in the morning, to get things started for breakfast . . . " (p. 27)

about to fall, and promised to help him as soon as it should fall. He waited patiently until the tree fell, and then, after a brief examination to see that the honey was not wasting, they accompanied Mr. Gay and afforded valuable assistance in rolling the logs on to the building. This done, Mr. Moore brought out his jug and treated the Indians to a drink of whisky. The Indians went away, but soon returned with a large quantity of very nice honey and in turn treated the white men. The jug again went around, and the white men and Indians parted very good friends. The precise date of the coming of Mr. Moore into the Valley cannot now be ascertained. He entered some land in his own name November 23d, but whether that occurred before, at the time, or subsequent to his settlement does not appear.

Beside those already named, the following persons purchased land in the Valley during 1833:

In town five south, one east (Woodstock)—John T. Comstock, William Western, George F. Comstock, George Barnum, Philip Kennedy and George W. Clark.

In town six south, one east (Rollin)—John Skane, George F. Comstock, Richard Robinson, Jonathan Birdsall, Sands Brownell, James Hathaway, Hiram Beal, Gamaliel Beal, Joseph C. Beal, Patience Comstock and Isaiah C. Miller.

In town seven south, one east (Hudson)—Charles Van Court, Henry Hayward, Oliver Purchase, Simeon Van Akin, Caleb N. Ormsby and Addison J. Comstock.

In town five south, one west (Somerset)—Heman Pratt, June 8th; Horace White, June 8th; Elias Branch, June 1st; Elias Alley, December 3d; and David Herrington, June 8th.

In town six south, one west (Wheatland)—Ebenezer Gay, June 7th; Mahlon Brown, Jacob Brown and Edmund B. Brown, June 6th.

In town seven south, one west (Pittsford)—Thomas Hurdsman, Oct. 30th; Jesse Smith, Nov. 15th; William and Elizabeth Ames, Dec. 5th; Curren White, Sept. 24th; Stephen Wilcox, Nov. 20th; John Gustin, Dec. 5th and 6th; William Flowers, Oct. 30th; Isaac French, Dec. 10th.

In town five south, two west (Moscow), a settlement had already been commenced. Peter Benson had settled on the Chicago road, within the limits of that township, some time during the year 1831, but he remained only a short time. Land was also entered that year by, or for, the following named persons: Samuel Aiken, July 23d; Osmond B. Blackmar, July 23d; and Pontius Hooper, July 2d.

In 1832 Samuel Aiken settled on his land, and Lyman Blackmar, father of Osmond B. Blackmar, settled on the land entered in his son's name the year previous. At first he had only eighty acres of land, but by frequent purchases he became the owner of more than one thousand acres of choice land. He had one of the handsomest farms in the county. Judge Blackmar lived on his farm until his decease, which occurred in the spring of 1874, forty-two years after his advent to the peninsula of Michigan. Benjamin Fowle entered land in the township July 3d.

In 1833 Charles Fowle settled on his land, and the following named persons entered lands: David Hiller, Jan. 25th; Thomas Watts, July 15th; John Simmons, June 1st; Tompkins C. Dellivan, Charles T. Dellivan, Lucius Lyon, Alonzo Kies and Charles Stock, June 1st.

Winter had now fairly settled down upon the settlements in the Valley; but the settlers were not idle. Aiding land-lookers, hunting the deer and wolf, and felling the forests, they were a busy set of men. Mrs. C. R. Beach, a daughter of Mr. Hiram Kidder, thus writes of the scenes or that winter:

"The excitement of this first winter was an ever changing drama; the land-lookers, the wolf trappers and deer hunters. I remember a manner of sleeping in those days that would hardly do in these modern times. It was a sort of general bed that covered the entire floor of the house. I have seen Mrs. Kidder picking her way over the heads and toes of this pavement of sleeping men, women and children, early in the morning, to get things started for breakfast that she might be able to supply the demands of all for breakfast. And every night brought a new set of lodgers."

And now, reader, let us imagine ourselves ensconsed beside one of those old fire-places, filled with burning logs, and listen to some of the tales of those days.

"An adventurer (one of the kid gloved kind), dressed in broadcloth, with beaver hat and calf boots, anxious to become a land speculator, started on foot from Adrian to the Bean Creek Country. In the evening one of the children reported to Mrs. Kidder that something white out in the bushes kept flopping its wings. Observing it for a moment, the object left the brush and came to the door. Mrs. Kidder was much surprised to find it a man. Our would-be speculator had been thrown down so many times by his long-toed boots that, fearing his fine clothes would be spoiled, he had changed his habit by putting his white cotton-flannel under-clothes on over his broadcloth, and thus became the white fowl that flopped its wings to the terror of the children."

"Mr. Kidder was awakened one night by the squealing of some hogs in an enclosure near by. A bear had entered the enclosure, killed one hog, and, seating himself on the carcass, proceeded to hold the other hog in fond embrace until it, too, was dead."

"One night Mr. Kidder was absent, having gone out that morning with some land-lookers. Mrs. Kidder put the children in bed, and laid down too, hoping at least to get a little rest. She thought of wolves, bears and Indians until she fell asleep. Soon after she was awakened by a noise like the gnawing and crunching of bones. She arose in terror to see which of her darlings had become a prey to the beasts. She went quickly to the fire-place, and taking a fire brand, turned toward the door. She found a horse in the doorway; the blanket which had served as a door now served as a head-dress for the horse. The horse was neither in the house nor out of doors. There was no floor on that side of the house, and as he rested across the log that served as a door-sill his feet could not reach the ground. He could neither advance or retreat. In this dilemma he had seized a tin pan and was biting it, which made the peculiar noise that had alarmed Mrs. Kidder."

One morning a stranger appeared at Mr. Kidder's door and introduced himself as Francis H. Hagaman, Mr. Kidder's nearest neighbor, living only twelve miles away.

But few remain of those who called the Kidder settlement home in 1833-34. Mrs. Kidder, the first white woman settler in the Valley of the Bean south of Devil's Lake, still lingers among us. Then she was in the vigor of early womanhood. The following description of that young wife and mother as she appeared amidst the scenes of the October evening when she first gazed on a sunset from her pioneer cabin door, is quoted from a paper prepared by Mrs C. R. Beach, once before quoted in these pages. It is a daughter's fond recollection of her mother's early loveliness, but it will be none the less interesting on that account: "A log cabin on the brow of a hill; at its base a little stream whose ripple could be heard at its summit. It was sunset. From the aperture left for a doorway the view is obstructed by dense forests. Before us, on the right hand, on the left hand, all around us on every side, were deep, dark forests. The departing sun gilded for awhile the beautiful canopy of brown, crimson and yellow leaves, and then the shades of night drew on and all were wrapped in im-penetrable gloom. At this moment another home, with its vacant places beside the cheerful fireside, the school and college days, with well remembered class-mates, all came back on memory's wings to add intensely to home-sick feelings, which, despite strong endeavor, came over the spirit of that young wife and mother as, standing there with head uncovered but wreathed in golden curls, she views her future home. Those golden locks are silvered now; those strong arms are palsied by the lapse of years; but her heart seems as young and blithe as ever." Yes, the kind-hearted pioneer woman is in the sere and yellow leaf of life, but some of her associates of 1833 remain to call her blessed. Alpheus Pratt, Henry, William and Ezra Ames and Jesse Smith remain, all, too, save Ezra, in the autumn of life, waiting to be sum-moned over the river. Old Uncle Simeon Van Akin, himself more feeble than Mrs. Kidder, exclaimed, not long since: "Why, there's Mrs. Kidder; she kept us from starving!"

The following story is told as illustrative of Mrs. Kidder's kindness of heart: "She had one child—a daughter—in delicate health. one day a party of twenty-six persons arrived at her house. They had been lost in the woods and were very hungry. The last provisions had been cooked, Mr. Kidder had gone for a supply, and it was hoped these would last the family until his return. It took several days to go to market then, and the day of return was by no means certain; but Mrs. Kidder could not resist the appeals of hungry fellow-beings. Her entire store was placed before the hungry crowd. Still they were not satisfied, and one woman bemoaned her fate in bitter terms. Soon one of the boys came in and said: 'Mamma, is there not something Maria can eat?' 'No,' said Mrs. Kidder. Soon he came again. 'Ain't there some potatatoes that Maria can have? Was not some dropped around the hole whence they were taken?' No, my son; there are none.' Soon after, Maria fainted. 'Why! how long is it since that child has had anything to eat?' asked the lady who was making such a fuss. 'None since morning,' said Mrs. Kidder. 'God bless the child!' went up in chorus from twenty-six voices. 'Why!' said the lady, I have just had something to eat, and I am repining while the child is starving.' Just then the signal gun announced the arrival of Mr. Kidder on the hill, east of the creek, and summoning aid to descend the dangerous declivity. It was ten o'clock when the wagon reached the door that night, but supper had to be prepared for the family and the guests before sleep was thought of."

Besides the exciting scenes incident to land explorations, it became necessary for our settlers to become acquainted with their Indian neighbors. The Indians here were the Potawatomies, who had been crowded by the settlement of the eastern portion of the State into this then unbroken forest. They had a village or camping ground in the southwest part of the township known as Somerset, and another in the southwestern part of Pittsford. Of these villages Meteau and Bawbeese were the chiefs. The principal Indian trail extended from Detroit to Chicago, nearly where the Chicago road now is. A trail left this in the northeastern part of the county, and lead off, through the townships of Dover and Medina, to Defiance. Another left the main trail near Silver Lake, skirted Devil's Lake, passed near the Kidder settlement, to Squawfield, in southwestern Pittsford. Another connected the Indian villages; and still another, leaving the main trail at Jonesville, passed through Squawfield, Medina and Morenci, and terminated at the rapids of the Maumee. These were the Indian thoroughfares, and into them came, and from them went many lesser trails, all as well known to an Indian as our roads are to the present denizens of the land. It was desirable they should be friends; it was quite possible they might on acquaintance develop into enemies. Mrs. Gay relates that at first a single native visited her house. He stayed all day, but not a word would he speak, and the family concluded he could neither speak nor understand English. Mr. Timothy Gay was from home. Old Mr. Gay, a hired man and the children composed the family that day. Mrs. Gay resolved that no hindrance should be placed in the way of amicable relation, so when dinner was ready she, by signs, asked the Indian to sit at the table and eat dinner with the family. He accepted the invitation and behaved in a very orderly manner. During the meal conversation, among the circle, turned upon the Indians,—their character and doings,—and the Indians were fully discussed. Mrs. Gay had recently come from the State of New York, and had heretofore lived at a great distance from the Indians. Her ideas of Indian character had been formed by reading the opinions of philanthropic minds, and she was in full sympathy with poor "Lo." The other members of the family did not agree with her notions and instanced the many acts of cruelty committed by them as arguments against the Indian character, but Mrs. Gay defended them on the ground that they had first been ill treated by the whites. Notwithstanding the discussion was very free, the harshest expression against the Indians was made by Mr. Gay in summing up his case: "Well, they are cruel cusses anyway." The Indian carried himself as stoically as if he really did not understand a word of what was said. At evening the Indian went away. But Mrs. Gay was very much surprised the next day when another Indian made his appearance at her house unannounced. He was a tall man of noble bearing, and was dressed, as for a State occasion, in blue frock coat, pants and vest, and had three gold medals on his breast. He was evidently a man of some distinction among his people. He seated himself without speaking a word, and soon after the Indian visitor of the previous day made his appearance. There the two sat, close observers of all that passed, but speechless. Once during the forenoon Mrs. Gay went to the hearth to look at her yeast, which was being prepared for her baking. As she uncovered the yeast vessel she was surprised to hear the ejaculation, "Turnpike!" She looked up and found both the Indians peering over her head at the yeast. Smiling, to reassure the natives and to draw them out, she asked, "What you call him?" but not a word could she get out of either of them. Their presence at the dinner table again this day brought up the subject of yesterday's conversation, and again Mrs. Gay assumed the task of defending the Indians, and, as some excuse for their conduct, instanced the fact that Michigan land had been purchased of them at two and a-half cents an acre, "and now," said Mrs. Gay, "the Government is selling to settlers for one dollar and a quarter an acre." The Indians ate as though they heard not, and resumed their waiting and watching attitude of the forenoon and day previous. Along towards night the babe became restless and cried a considerable. Mrs. Gay tried in vain to quiet him, and at last she said, "If you don't be still I will have this Indian carry you off." The child continuing to cry, she said, "Here, Indian, carry this baby off." "Where to, mam?" said the Indian, in pretty good English. Mrs. Gay was startled, but she determined not to appear alarmed, so she said, "O, anywhere." "I don't know," said the Indian. At night the two Indians withdrew, but on their next visit, and ever after, were talkative enough, and seemed to have no difficulty in speaking or understanding English; and the tribe ever after were the fast friends of Mr. Gay's family. One of Mrs. Gay's two visitors was named She-gau-ken and the other Kesus.

We shall have occasion to refer to two other Indians frequently—Mag-in-a-swot and Me-mag-in-a-swot. Mag-in-a-swot was the brother-in-law of Meteau. He was a noble man and so peaceful in his disposition that he had received the sobriquet of the Peace Chief. Me-mag-in-a-swot was a good-for-nothing, drunken Indian, possessing a wonderful faculty for getting into difficulty and making himself disagreeable generally.

The reader has already, perhaps, guessed what the Indians meant by the ejaculation, "Turnpike." They had seen the builders of the Chicago road heap up the dirt in oval form, and had been told it was a turnpike, and when they saw the light yeast in the same form they named it turnpike.

She-gau-ken was young, good-looking, and very playful. One day, being at the house and in one of his playful moods, he turned the yeast over, and Mrs. Gay took up a stick and chased him out of doors. He stuck his head in at the door and said: "Squaw Nancy plenty mad?" He went to the shop and told William (the Indians always called Timothy, William) "Squaw Nancy plenty mad." Mr. Gay asked: "What did you do?" "Me spill turnpike."

Indians like fair dealing, and will not trade with those who prove to be dishonest, either with them or with other white people. A story in point is told by Mrs. Gay. One day a trade was pending between one of the Indians and herself, but she had not the right change. The neighbors were unable to change her money, and she had applied to the shopkeeper, but was told he had no change. The Indian visited the store and came back in a great rage. He said, "Him plenty cheat; he have heap of shuniah." The shopman had offered to purchase his stuff, and to induce him to trade had shown him a handful of coin.

One day She-gau-ken brought a lot of their wares to trade with Mrs. Gay. She told him she would give him so much napinah (flour) and so much shuniah (money). "Good squaw Nancy, give whisky?" "No; Indian must not drink whisky." "Ah, good squaw Nancy, give little whisky." "No, She-gau-ken, no whisky." A woman happening to be there said, "Take them to my house; I'll give whisky." "No," said She-gau-ken; "plenty cheat." Mr. Branch, who lived some three miles west on the Chicago road, was in the other part of the house, used as a store. He called to the Indian, "Take them to my house; I give whisky." "No; me no take to Branch house; plenty water whisky. Good Squaw Nancy, give whisky." After teasing Mrs. Gay awhile, She-gau-ken said, "Good Squaw Nancy, take 'em."

1834.—THE KIDDER SETTLEMENT.

Charles and William Ames were absent from the settlement during the winter, working at their trade (shoemaking) in Detroit.

On the 23d day of January, Charles, the six-year-old son of Alpheus Pratt, was lost in the woods. Mr. Pratt was chopping not very far from his house. The little boy had gone to his father to call him to supper. Mr. Pratt coming in soon after, was asked where Charley was. He had not seen Charley, and fears were at once entertained that he was lost. Mr. Pratt at once returned to the woods and searched until dark, but could not find the child. He returned to the house for his lantern, to continue the search. Mrs. Pratt went alone, on foot, nearly a mile through the woods, to the house of Charles Ames, and informed Henry and Ezra Ames of the affair, and they, immediately procuring the assistance of Kidder and Tabor, joined in the search. The father had found the boy's track. This they attempted to follow, but as there was a crust on the snow, they found it a difficult task. They continued the search for a long time, until they became tired, cold and discouraged, and concluding the boy could not be found, the assistants gave up the search and built a fire to warm themselves, also to serve as a protection against wild beasts. The father, intent on finding his child, paid no attention to their proceedings, but went forward, calling, "Charley! Charley!" and soon heard the answering voice of little Charley. Clasped in the arms of a grateful father, the boy was taken to the fire. He was benumbed and his feet were frozen. The child told of having seen dogs in the woods, and no doubt was entertained but that the boy had been visited in his wilderness wanderings by wolves, which, for some unexplained reason, did not harm him. Who will say he was not providentially preserved? To reach home was the object next to be attained, but their whereabouts was only a matter of conjecture. They supposed themselves to be west and south of the settlement, and accordingly they directed their course towards the northeast as well as they could, having only the north star for a guide. After some hours' traveling, they struck the well-known Indian trail about three miles west of Charles Ames' house. They arrived home about sunrise, and restored the boy to the arms of an almost despairing mother. The party were unable to tell where they found the boy, but suppose it to have been a little south of the village of Pittsford.

In the month of February Thomas Pennock, being at Jackson, undertook to make the Kidder settlement. He reached the settlement on the Chicago road since called Gambleville all right, and hired a man to pilot him through the woods to the the Kidder settlement. But shortly after starting it commenced snowing, and the driving snow so blinded and confused the guide that he became lost, and our travelers, after wandering about all day, were obliged to stay in the woods all night, and that, too, without any fire, for they were without the means of kindling one. They were wet and thoroughly chilled, and soon after night set in, the guide, saying he could stand it no longer, laid down in the snow to die. Pennock cut a switch and by frequently switching him briskly kept him up on his feet and saved his life. During the night the storm abated, and the next morning was bright. The cheerful rays of the sun revived courage in their hearts, and taking the track, they followed it as best they could, and reached Gambleville about three o'clock in the afternoon, tired, faint and hungry,

Pennock staid there that night, and the next morning found an Indian who said he knew where the white *Chemkeman,* or white black-haired man—Kidder—lived on the *Nebish,* where there were two wigwams all alone. Committing himself to the guidance of the red man, they followed an Indian trail to Devil's Lake, and thence on a trail leading to Squaw-field, in Pittsford, the camping ground of the tribe of which Meteau was chief. They crossed the Kidder road a little east of Kidder's house. Here the Indian stopped and said to Pennock, "Go on this road and you will find two wigwams on the Nebish." This tribe called water *nebish,* but here used the term to signify the creek. Pennock gave his guide a silver dollar, and he turned back towards the lake, while Pennock proceeded to the settlement, where he arrived about the middle of the afternoon, sick and weary from the effects of travel and exposure. Pennock afterwards became satisfied that the night he spent in the woods snow-bound, he staid somewhere in the vicinity of the present village of Rollin.

By an act of the Legislative Council, approved March 7th, 1834, several changes were made in the townships of Lenawee county, Towns seven south, in ranges one, two and three east (Madison, Dover and Hudson), were organized into a separate township and named Lenawee; towns eight, nine, and fractional ten south, in ranges one, two and three east (Fairfield, Seneca and Medina in Michigan, and Royalton, Chesterfield and Gorham, now in Ohio), were organized into a township named Fairfield; and "all that part of the township of Tecumseh comprised in townships six south, in ranges one, two and three east," (the north half of Rollin, Rome and Adrian,) "was attached to the township of Logan."

In the month of March, 1834, Sylvenus Estes came to the Bean Creek Country, and the 15th day of that month entered land on section ten, town seven south, one west (Pittsford), in the name of his wife, Ruth Estes. During the same month his brother, Rufus Estes, came in and assisted his brother in chopping a piece for spring crops.

In the same month also, March, 1834, Reuben Davis located the middle sub-division of the southwest fractional quarter of section eighteen, town seven south, one east (Hudson) and commenced building a log house. That lot of land now forms a part of the village of Hudson, it being that portion lying north of Main street and between Church and High streets. The house he commenced stood in the vicinity of Market street, between Main street and the railroad.

On the 7th day of April, 1834, the first township meeting of the township of Lenawee was held. Calvin Bradish was moderator, and N. D. Skeels was clerk of the election. Officers were elected as follows: Supervisor, Garret Tenbrooke; Township Clerk, Isaac A. Colvin; Assessors, John Hitchins, Patrick Hamilton and Levi Shumway; Collector, Ezra Washburn; Overseers of the Poor, Nehemiah Bassett and Elijah Johnson; Commissioners of Highways, Jacob Jackson, Samuel Bayless and Moses C. Baker; Constable, Ezra Washburn; Commissioners of Schools, Lyman Pease, Isaiah Sabens and John Power; School Inspectors, Curran Bradish, Thomas F. Dodge, William Edmunds and Isaac A. Colvin.

The township meeting voted to pay three dollars for every wolf slain within the township, and one dollar and fifty cents for each wolf whelp. During the year Bart White was paid bounty on six wolves, and William Winslow a bounty on one wolf.

In the latter part of April, Jesse Smith, accompanied by his family,—a wife and five children,—started for their possessions in the Bean Creek Country. At Buffalo they shipped on the steamboat William Penn for Monroe. The steamboats of that period were clumsy affairs. It was early in the season, and their progress was necessarily slow. At Monroe he hired two teams to bring his family and goods to Adrian. Here it became necessary to dispose of some boots and shoes, and a new wagon which he was bringing into the country. From his sales he realized twenty-seven bushels of wheat and ten dollars in money. The wheat, except enough to feed the teams on the road, was left at the Adrian mill to be ground. With the money, Mrs. Smith having sold feathers to pay their tavern bill, Mr. Smith hired two more teams, and with his wife and three children started for Kidder's. His two older boys and

William Purchase, who was coming to his brother Oliver, had gone on foot in advance. The first day they traveled four miles. The next day one of the teams gave out about noon; the goods were unloaded and piled up by the roadside, and the team sent back. With the remaining team and load they toiled on through the afternoon, but at dark were compelled to camp in the woods, a little south of Posey Lake. Two of the children were put in bed in the wagon. Mrs. Smith sat up all night and held the babe in her arms. The next morning they resumed their journey, and soon after they were met by their sons, Lorenzo and William, who had been through to the settlement and reported the approach of the family. The boys were accompanied by Mr. Vangauder with a yoke of oxen, which enabled them to double teams. Vangauder and the boys managed the teams, while Mr. Smith, with the babe in his arms, trudged along on foot. They reached Kidder's about noon, where dinner was waiting for them.

Here the Smith family were at last—in the Michigan woods, with but fifty cents in pocket. Messrs. Purchase and Vangauder were bachelors. The house they had built and wintered in was tendered to Mr. Smith, and here he sheltered his family until the 20th day of August, when they moved into a house of their own. Mr. Purchase had chopped the timber down on quite a large piece of ground around his house; this he offered to Smith for a corn-field. Mr. Smith and sons logged and burned it off, and planted it to corn and potatoes. On this ground they raised fifty bushels of corn and forty bushels of potatoes. These two articles were important factors in their next winter's subsistence. The lakes and streams were filled with fishes, there was an abundance of game in the woods, and stores of honey deposited in convenient hollows by the ever busy bee; these Mr. Smith knew how to capture and bring in, and, with his corn and potatoes, sufficed for the sustenance of his family and numerous adventurers, none of whom were ever turned from his door hungry. Mr. Smith was accounted—and no doubt justly—a great hunter, as it is said he spent the greater part of his time at that business; but there are boys of that period who will not admit that he was a better shot than Rufus Estes; indeed, they called Mr. Estes the crack shot of the Bean Creek Valley. Both these worthy men are still living. For some years Mr. Smith has been blind, but Mr. Estes yet does six days' work in a week.

Early in the spring Henry Ames returned to the Eastern States for his wife, who had been left behind on account of feeble health. He returned to Michigan with his wife in September, reaching the Creek on the 30th.

On the first day of May Hiram Kidder commenced work on mill-race, and preparing timber for a saw mill. On the first day of June Samuel O. Coddington, mill-wright, of Geneva, New York, commenced work on the mill.

In the month of May Beriah H. Lane and his brother Erastus came to the Bean Creek Country. Beriah selected the first sub-division of the northwest fractional quarter of section nineteen. Upon going to the land office he found it had already been entered by Harvey Cobb. He returned to the Bean Creek and selected the west and middle sub-divisions of the southwest fractional quarter of section nineteen, which he afterwards entered. Almost immediately after, he traded the south part of the tract to Reuben Davis for his land, and sold the north half to Sylvester Kenyon. The land he bought of Davis had a log house partly finished and about one and a half acres chopped. Mr. Lane also purchased of Jesse Kimball the south half of the west sub-division of the south-west fractional quarter of section eighteen, or that part of the village of Hudson north of Main street and west of Church street.

The Messrs. Lane determined to build up a village, and immediately set about building a saw-mill in order that they might be able to compete with the Kidder settlement, which was already putting on village airs. They hired a mill-wright and helpers and set them at work. Reuben Davis remained in their house and boarded the men. Mr. Davis also drew the timber on to the ground and did such other work as the Lanes required.

c

During the latter part of May, 1834, Robert Worden, Dudley Worden and Samuel Day arrived at the Creek. The two Wordens started from Fairport, Monroe county, New York, in a covered wagon, about the first of April, 1834. The party consisted of Dudley Worden, wife and one child, and Robert Worden, wife and one child. On, the way they fell in company with the family of Mr. Samuel Day, traveling in the same way and intending to settle in Ohio. The two parties traveled along together, and after a while Mr. Day concluded to come to Michigan with the Wordens. They arrived at the Creek, as before stated, in the latter part of May. Their lands were entered at the land office on the 29th day of the month. Their last day's journey was from Adrian to the Creek, eighteen miles, twelve of which—from Bart White's, west —were in a dense wilderness. When night set in the party were about five miles from Kidder's, in the thick woods. To proceed farther with the wagons that night vas impossible, and they could not encamp as they were unprovided with the means to start a fire. The horses were unhitched from the wagons and the party attempted to make their way on foot, but the horses were in constant trouble, running against trees and into the brush. So the party formed themselves in single file. Mrs. Worden wore a white skirt and was placed in the rear to pilot the driver of the horses. In this manner they marched until they reached Kidder's house, late in the evening. The next day they found their land and commenced building a house. Mr. Robert Worden thus describes the house he built: "I built me a house without a single board, except what was made with an ax. I split logs for a floor. The chamber floor was bark peeled from elm logs. Our roof was bark, as was also the gables or ends. Our door was plank made with an ax, two inches thick, pinned to wooden hinges and fastened to the logs so it would swing inside. With an auger a hole was made in the logs so it could be pinned on the inside to protect us from the bears and wolves, of which there were a plenty. We had a window hole cut out for a six-lighted window, but had no window to put in it. The principal light came down the chimney hole. One night the wolves commenced to howl. There were so many of them and so near I became frightened. We were sleeping on the floor, not having even a Michigan bedstead. We got up, went up the ladder with our bed, pulled the ladder after us, made our bed on the bark, and should have considered ourselves secure from the wolves only that we were fearful that the bark would give way and let us fall." And all this fear of the wolves within two miles of two villages. One village had double the number of houses the other had, and that had two."

Of Mr. and Mrs Day, a writer in the Hudson *Post*, of March 26th, 1874, wrote:

"Mr. Samuel Day died in 1856. He was a man who made his mark in this new country, will be remembered as a stock man, and who could show the finest stock in the Valley of the Bean. Coming here when Hudson was a vast forest, with five boys at his command, much of the improvement in this vicinity was made through his influence. But he has laid by his armor and passed over the River with others who were his associates here, to be employed in higher and nobler spheres than earth can offer.

"Mrs. Day is one of those noble women who first settled this Bean Creek Valley, when in its native state. May, 1834, found her coming down Bean Creek hill at ten o'clock at night, she having walked from Adrian the same day. She crossed the Bean upon a log, and came up to Mr. Kidder's log house, where the family stopped for the night, and until they could find some house to stop at or until they could build themselves. This they did in the month of May, having to cut a wagon road from Bush's Corners up to where their house now stands. The house was built without a single board; the roof was covered with bark, and the floor made of split logs. There was not a tree cut west of Bush's Corners; the wolf and deer were all that inhabited that region. Mrs. Day was a woman of strong constitution, always working with a will, having a large family of her own to provide for, in a new country, with all the settlers in like circumstances. But she worked on with her neighbors, every one feeling dependent upon each other for things to keep soul and body together. Mr.

and Mrs. Day having lived in a dairy country East, and been brought up in that branch of farming, as soon as the country would warrant, commenced making butter and cheese in the Valley of the Bean, which, in addition to her other work, employed all the powers of body she possessed. She is now quite feeble, not able to go out, but with her cane can walk about the house. Her sight is good; she can sew without spectacles. She is very glad to have old friends come in and talk over the hardships gone through by the early settlers in opening up this tier of counties, which has far exceeded what she expected to see. She brought apple seeds from the East, and when they planted them she said, 'I shall never live to eat fruit of this orchard.' "

In the early part of June Hiram Kidder platted the village of Lenawee, and June 13th the plat was acknowledged by the proprietors, Daniel Hudson and Nathan B. Kidder, and recorded in the Register's office of Lenawee county. On the next day four village lots were sold.

Sometime during the summer Dudley Worden, having built a house in the village of Lenawee, opened a little store, and, as was the custom of those days, a part of his stock consisted of whisky,—an article as necessary for Indian traffic as for home consumption.

On the first day of July, 1834, the mill irons for the Kidder mill were brought from Adrian by ox teams, and on the 14th day of the same month the frame was raised. The mill commenced sawing October 1st, and was completed the same month. The cost of the mill to its starting was $983.17; its total cost was $1,441.31. One of the boys of that period tells that the first board made at the mill was taken upon the shoulders of the men, carried to the grocery and the whisky "set up" on that notable occasion.

About the first of July Mr. Beriah H. Lane returned to Massachusetts for his family. On the 18th day of August he left Enfield to return to Bean Creek. He brought with him his wife and two children, his father and mother, and his widowed sister (Mrs. M. K. Douglass) and her two children. They traveled by team to Troy, by canal "line boat" to Buffalo, steamboat to Cleveland, and team to Bean Creek. They were yet five miles out when darkness settled down, and would have had to camp in the woods, but his brother Erastus, having heard of their approach, met them with a lantern. He found the mill frame up and the work was progressing finely. They immediately commenced work on the dam, and completed the mill in December following; but a freshet carried the dam away, and it was not repaired until the following spring.

In the fall of this year Mr. Simeon Van Akin and family came to the settlement. He had visited the country in the month of November, 1833, and located his land. He says that when coming in, November 9th, 1833, he met Mr. Pratt, with his ox team, going after another load of goods. According to Mr. Pratt's recollection, he was going for Mrs. Pratt and their boy, whom he had left at the house of Lyman Pease, one mile west of Adrian. Besides his own family Mr. Van Akin was accompanied by William H. H. Van Akin, then quite a young man. They at once commenced building themselves a house. Alpheus Pratt drew the logs together with his ox team, and Mr. Lane and his mill hands helped roll the logs up. That house was built on the east side of the creek, near the southwest corner of Main and High streets, about where the new engine house now stands. While excavating for the foundation walls of that building one of the logs of the old house was exhumed.

In December of that year John Davenport and family settled in Lanesville. The house he built and occupied was built on or near the east bank of the Bean, and just north of Main street, on a half acre of land reserved by Reuben Davis when he sold to the Lanes. In excavating for the railroad, the north part of the house was undermined, and soon afterwards was removed.

Mrs. Davenport, in a letter written February 15th, 1875, describes the first bridge across Bean Creek at Lanesville. She says:

"Forty years and two months have passed since I came with my husband and five little ones to the wilderness, now the thriving village of Hudson. On our arrival there we found the following named settlers: Mr. Simeon Van Akin (a widower) and his mother (Grandma Van Akin, as she was called by all until her death), two children (Margaret and Lydia Ann), and a younger brother (Harrison Van Akin). Also, Beriah H. Lane, his wife and his father (Nathaniel), two children (Anna and Nathaniel, Jr.), also a widowed sister (Mrs. Douglass) and her two children. These, with my own family, composed the population of Hudson proper. Mr. Davenport had the little log house built upon the east bank of Bean Creek, but on the arrival of the family we were met by Mr. Van Akin and taken to his mansion, which was of the same style and finish as our own. We received such a welcome as pioneers know how to give. The following morning the wagons were unloaded and we commenced in earnest a pioneer life. The few that may be present well know what it means,— the toil, the privations and the hardships.

"The first bridge built was by Grandma Van Akin and myself. The society of the three families was much sought after by each other, and finding that Bean Creek was a barrier to full social enjoyment,—Mrs. Lane, living on the west side, was unable to cross on the sapling that had fallen across the creek some distance away,—we determined to have a better way of crossing; so, finding two benches that had been used to chink and daub the walls of Mr. Van Akin's house, Grandma and I carried them down and waded into the stream and placed them in position, then went to Mr. Davis' saw mill, carried planks and laid them from the bank to the bench, and so over to the opposite bank. This was in the spring of 1835, and it remained until the freshet of the following spring, when no trace of it longer remained."

During the year 1834, besides those already named, John Rice, John Davenport, Sylvester Kenyon and Silas Eaton settled in town seven south, one east; and William Champlin, Lewis Gillett, Ozen Keith and Jesse Maxson, R. H. Whitehorn, Ruth Estes, Urias Treadwell and Lawrence Rheubottom settled in town seven south, range one west.

The following named persons, not elsewhere mentioned, purchased land this year, in this township (Hudson): Moses Bennett, Joseph Hagaman, William Chapman, Frederick Corey, Dexter Smith, Ruth Haines, John C. Emery, Peries Lincoln, Mary P. Todd, Gabriel H. Todd, Robert Huston, James Maloney, Michael Dillon, B. Newton, Erastus W. Starkweather, A. Sagar, Harman Whitbeck, Samuel F. Davis, Buckley Newton, Erastus Lane, Ira Jewett, Chauncey Whitney, Seba Murphy, Laban King, David E. Wiscott, Isaac Freeman, Daniel Featherly, John Rice, Harvey Cobb, Hiram Van Akin, M. Sherman, J. Kimball, Philo Tracey, Seth Fletcher, Robert Kinney, Randall Mills, Samuel Bayless, Eliza Bayless, Polly Potter, Abel Gibbs, John Beard, Samuel Skinner, William N. Stockwell, Truman Bown.

In Pittsford, Lewis Gilbert, Curran White, James DeGraph, Hannah DeGraph, Lorenzo Church, David Fish, Peter Potter, William Purchase, Benjamin Bassett, Dolly Bassett, William Cular, Lewis Dillon, Walter Culver, Guiles Sage, Matthew Dillon, Aaron Aldrich, Asahel Dolbear, Marcus Hawley, Jesse Treadwell, Ira L. Mills, Joseph Barnhart, John Davenport, Dudley Worden, Merrit Sherman, James McLain, Levi Thompson, Buckley Newton, Nathan Birdsall, Nathaniel J. Redfield, Israel Loomis, Daniel Loomis, Richard Britton, Eldad B. Trumbull, Jesse Kimball, William Burnham, Richard Butler, Nicholas Fratts, Samuel Cole, Horace P. Hitchcock, Warren Burnham, Jesse Maxson, Ezra A. Washburn, James B. Marry, Cyrus Robinson, N. Wood, John Munger, Truman Bishop.

Some of these parties settled on their land that season and others in subsequent seasons, but some of them entered their land for speculative purposes only and never settled on it.

Christmas day, 1834, occurred the first wedding in this part of the Valley. Mr. James Sprague and Miss Elizabeth Ames were united in marriage at the house of

Mr. Alpheus Pratt, by the Rev. Mr. Willey, a Methodist clergyman of Adrian. The following named persons composed the wedding party: Alpheus Pratt, wife and son, Charles Ames, wife and two sons, Henry Ames, wife and son, Jesse Kimball, wife and daughter, and Miss Martha Redfield.

Mr. Robert Worden, writing of this year's experience in a new country, said:

"We were a community of many wants from the outside world. The article of currant-roots, or sprouts, were in great demand. The undersigned went out to the settlement to obtain some sprouts, and all I could get were ten pieces of sprouts about eight inches long each, and felt myself fortunate and thankful. I got them of Richard Kent, a little north of the city of Adrian, and from the sprouts I obtained at that time I have bushes on my farm now, and have supplied very many new beginners from them with roots.

"The first settlers had an enemy in what is called the deer-mouse. They were numerous, would crawl through an incredible small hole, and were very destructive. Before we were aware of it they had got into our trunks and seriously injured our clothing. We had no place of security for anything they wanted. My wife had brought with her some starch done up in a paper. One day, wanting to use some, she found the paper that contained the starch, but no starch. It had been carried off by the mice, and it could not be replenished short of a trip of twenty miles; but some time after we had occasion to use an empty bottle stowed away, and in the bottle we found our starch, put there by the mice; it was not possible for them to get into the bottle. We were in great want of a house-cat to destroy the mice, and they were very scarce in this section of the Territory. I took a bag and started for Adrian on foot to procure a cat, if possible. I could find none in Adrian, but heard of some kittens three miles south of Adrian, at Col. Bradish's. I went to Col. Bradish's, but was a little too late—they had let the last one go the day before. I then started for home, came about two miles this side of Adrian and stopped over night with a family of English people. I told the lady of the house of my unsuccessful efforts to find a cat. She sympathized with me, and said they had been similarly situated. When morning came and I was about to start for home the lady said: 'I have been thinking of your troubles through the night; I have but one cat, a great nice one, and I have concluded to lend it to you until I shall want it.' I took the cat in the bag and started for home—on foot, of course—and before I got home with it I thought it a very heavy cat. We kept the cat but a few weeks; it was killed by the wild-cats, which were quite plenty at the time."

But, hark! While the last paragraph was being written (August 21st, 1876), a church bell has begun to toll the departure of a pioneer of 1834. Silas Eaton has passed away; life's toils and pains, its joys and blessings are over. Mr. Eaton was born at Duanesburg, Montgomery county, New York, on the 22d day of February, 1798. When he was twelve years old his father removed to the Genesee country and settled at Perrington, Monroe county. On the 18th day of November, 1819, he inter-married with Miss Eliza Simmons, of Victor, Ontario county. Mr. and Mrs. Eaton lived in various localities in the State of New York, until the year 1834. While residing in that State the happy couple had five children born unto them, one of whom had died. Those remaining were Harriet Newell (since the wife of Joseph M. Johnson), Stephen A., Constantine S. and Hervey U. In 1834 Mr. Eaton began seriously to think of making his home in the West. He came to Michigan in the month of June, that year, and entered the west half of the northwest quarter of section eight, town seven south, one west—the farm now occupied by Silas L. Allen, Esq. He returned home, and in October of that year removed his family to Michigan and settled on his farm, where he remained nearly three years. In the year 1837 he removed to the village of Keene, where he had built himself a frame house; there he remained until the spring of 1840, laboring at his trade—that of a carpenter and joiner. While there he was appointed postmaster under Van Buren's administration. He held the office until his removal, when he was succeeded by Henry Ames. In the spring of 1840, the Southern

Railroad having been located through Lanesville, Mr. Eaton removed to the latter place, moving not only his family and personal effects, but his house as well. In this village he resided all the rest of his life. He was Supervisor of the township in 1848 and 1849, and was postmaster eight years—during the administration of Pierce and Buchanan. Politically, Mr. Eaton was a Democrat of the straightest sect, and during his active life was held in high esteem in the councils of that party. In all his acts, social, business, political, and religious, Mr. Eaton was ever governed by strong conscientious convictions, and if he erred it was an error of judgment rather than affections. In early life, the winter of 1821-2, Mr. Eaton was made a Free and Accepted Mason in a lodge at Pittsford, Ontario county, N. Y. He was a charter member of Morning Star lodge, Hudson, Mich., at its organization on Monday, the 19th day of June, 1848; was the first senior warden, and for several years held official positions. He was also a charter member of Warren Lodge, organized September 24th, 1863, and was made an honorary member in 1871. He was made a Royal Arch Mason in Hudson chapter No. 28. His funeral on the 22d was largely attended by members of the craft, and his remains were consigned to the tomb with mystic rites. As a mark of respect and honor to the worthy dead—for one so early and so long identified with the moral and material progress of this community—places of business were generally closed during the moving of the procession and the funeral exercises, which were held in the M. E. church. The services consisted of the reading of portions of scripture by Rev. Mr. Roberts, of the Wesleyan Methodist church, prayer by the Rev. Mr. Frazer, of the Methodist Episcopal church, sermon by the Rev. Mr. Gibbs, of the Universalist church of Manchester, and appropriate singing by the Congregational and Methodist choirs—the large auditorium being filled with sorrowing relatives and friends, brothers, neighbors and citizens, "who a last tribute would pay to a good man passed away." The Hudson *Post*, a Republican newspaper, closed an appreciative obituary with these words: "Mr. Eaton leaves a widow (the companion of his youth), two sons and one daughter, many grandchildren, and a host of friends to mourn his departure:

" 'But why weep ye for him, who having won
    The bound of man's appointed years, at last,
Life's blessings all enjoyed, Life's labors done,
    Serenely to his final rest has passed;
While the soft memory of his virtues yet
Lingers like twilight hues when the bright sun is set?' "

Warren Lodge, No. 147, Free and Accepted Masons, adopted the following resolutions:

WHEREAS, Our esteemed brother, Silas Eaton, has, at the ripe age of seventy-eight years, been called to exchange an earthly for a spiritual state of existence;

Resolved, That while we are thankful to our Supreme Grand Master for the many years of social intercourse we have been permitted to enjoy with our brother Eaton, we mourn his departure as a loss to ourselves and our noble craft, no less than to his family and relatives.

Resolved, That we recognize in our departed brother a true type of the noble pioneers who converted the wilds of Michigan into fertile fields, and that we recognize it as our duty to cherish the memory of those departed, and by kindly offices light the pathway of those remaining.

Resolved, That we commend our sister, the widow of our departed brother, to the active sympathy of the craft, and that we extend to our brothers (the sons of the deceased), and to his daughter, the hand of condolence in their sad bereavement; but as a source of comfort in such trying scenes, remind them that his work was fully done, and that he departed full of days, with earth's honors untarnished.

Resolved, That these resolutions be published in the village papers, and that copies be furnished the widow and children of our departed brother.

THE BAKER SETTLEMENT.

The settlement of Francis H. Hagaman and Gershom Bennett in the northwest corner of town eight south, two east (Seneca), in November, 1833, has already been noticed; also the purchase by Cavender of several parcels of land in the fall of the same year.

Besides these, Ebenezer S. Carpenter, John F. Packard, Archibald Brown and Levi Sherman entered land in 1833; but aside from these purchases, the township was Government property in the beginning of 1834. On the first day of February, 1834, Roswell J. Heyward purchased of the United States, land on section thirteen, and settled on it immediately after. Jacob Baker entered land on section thirty, on the tenth day of March, and soon after came with his family and commenced a settlement. Horace Garlick and Arnold H. Coomer accompanied Mr. Baker to the wilderness. Garlick was married, but Coomer was a single man. They proceeded at once to build a log house. Coomer had the bark to peel for the roof, and he pressed the Indians into the service to assist him. The house was the usual log cabin of the early settler —puncheon floor, bark roof and gables, small window holes, and panelless doors. The doors were of the kind called batten doors, but the batten was a piece of timber a little longer than the width of the door and larger at one end than at the other; the large end projected beyond the door, and was bored to serve as a part of the hinge. The boards were fastened to the battens by wooden pins or by nails, as the necessity or convenience of the builder required.

In the early part of May, 1834, Simon D. Wilson, James Wilson, Ephraim Whitman, Ephraim Baldwin and Samuel D. Baldwin came to the township, looking land. They were all young men, and, with the exception of Simon D. Wilson, unmarried. The first two were brothers, and the Baldwins were brothers-in-law of Simon D. Wilson. Charles Baldwin, another brother-in-law, was living in township eight south, three east,—or as then organized, the east end of the township of Fairfield,—and thither this party gathered, preparatory to their contemplated invasion of the wilderness. When the party were ready, Charles Baldwin piloted them to the creek. Simon D. Wilson selected land on section thirty, in town eight south, and on sections six, seven and eight, town nine south. Ephraim Baldwin selected land on section eight, town nine south. The land office at Monroe was their next objective point, which they made, and entered their land on the fifteenth and sixteenth days of May, 1834. Arnold H. Coomer had entered his land on section thirty-one, town eight south, on the eighth day of that month. Simon D. Wilson immediately commenced operations on his land by building the inevitable log cabin, but had not yet got settled when Dennis Wakefield came into the township, prospecting for land; he made his selection—a tract of four hundred and twenty acres—on Bean Creek, which he entered June 14th, and returned to Connecticut. Mr. Wakefield returned to the Valley with his family in the month of August. During his absence several families had purchased homes in the township. On the twenty-ninth day of September Alvah Holt entered his land and commenced to build on it immediately.

During the year 1834, besides those already named, the following persons purchased land in towns eight and nine south, two east: Section 1—G. W. Allen, Jan. 24th; Joseph Griffin, June 2d; David Price, Sept. 24th. Section 4—Ransom J. Crawford, Oct. 6. Section 7—Abner Griffith, Aug. 18th. Sections 8 and 9—William Yerks, June 2d. Section 10—Henry Hayward, Aug. 9th; Ephraim Hollister, Aug. 25th; Isaac N. Powell, Oct. 7th. Section 11—Zeriel Waterman, April 19th; Cornelius S. Randolph, May 27th; Ira Holloway, Sept. 20th; Henry Hayward, Oct. 6th. Section 12—John Camburn, Feb. 1st; William D. Page, March 19th; John Starkweather. Section 13— William Baker, April 4th. Section 14—David Meech, June 2d; John Adams, June 10th; George Packard, June 21st; Manly Smith, July 8th. Section 15—Cornelius Willett, July 15th; James W. Camburn, July 15th; Abel Randolph, Aug. 23d. Section 17—Amos A. Kinney, Sept. 24th. Section 18—Thomas Hawley, Oct. 28th. Section 19—T. Carter, June 10th; Alvah Holt, Sept. 29th; Lucas Atwood, Sept. 29th; George Lee, 2d, Oct. 4th; Samuel Lammon, Oct. 21st. Section 28—Paul Raymond, Franklin W. Walker, Nov. 11th. Section 29—Amos Franklin, July 4th; ———— Barns, Oct. 1st. Section 30—Lydia Noyes, Moses Cole, July 10th. Section 31— Jonathan Saulsbury, June 2d; William Westfield, June 14th; Caleb C. Cooley, Oct. 8th; James H. Sweeney, Nov. 5th. Section 32—Nathan Saulsbury, June 9th; A.

Brown, June 14th; John Franklin, July 4th; Heman Herrington, Oct. 28th; Daniel
Sanborn, Nov. 20th. Section 33—Daniel Reed, June 27th. Town nine south: Sec-
tion 5—Simon Westfield, June 14th. Section 6—Benjamin Hornbeck, June 14th.
Section 7—Ephraim Baldwin, Jr., Joseph L. Royce, J. Calvin. Sections 9 and 10—
Thomas Hawly, Oct. 28th.

The old Indian trail from Jonesville to Maumee lay through this township, and just
below where Morenci now is there was an old Indian burying ground.

THE UPTON SETTLEMENT.

On the 21st day of May, 1834, Dexter Smith, George W. Moore, Nathaniel Upton
and ——— Pierce started from Dean's tavern, Adrian, to locate land in the Bean
Creek Country. Their outfit consisted of an ax, a rifle, ten pounds of crackers and
an Ohio ham. Of this latter article Mr. Moore remarked: "It was as salt as Lot's
wife and as hard as a regulation ball." They traveled on foot, and that day reached
the house of Gershom Bennett, in the northwest corner of town eight south, two east,
now known as Seneca. The next day they viewed land on sections three and four in
town eight south, and on sections thirty-four and thirty-five in town seven south, one
east. The land suited them, and the following day they started on their return to
Adrian by the Indian trail running from Defiance to Detroit. The trail crossed the
Kidder road about three miles west of Adrian. Here they fell in with a man named
Corey, who was also traveling Adrianwards. They learned from his talk that he
intended to locate one hundred and sixty acres of the land their party had selected.
A consultation was held in Dean's barn that night, and Moore and Smith were detailed to go on to Monroe in haste and locate the land before Corey could reach there.
It was raining, but they at once set out and reached Blissfield, 11 miles distant, at one
o'clock A. M. Here they laid themselves down on the bar-room floor and rested until
daylight, then pursued their journey, reached Monroe that afternoon, and entered
their land. Corey arrived the next morning. Smith and Upton returned at once to
commence the new settlement. They arrived at the Creek May 28th. They built a
log cabin,—or three sides of it were logs, the other was open,—and before it they built
their fire. The roof was of elm bark. The bedstead was a fixture of the house. When
the house was laid up, notches were cut in the logs at the proper height and poles laid
in; the outer corners were supported by stakes or posts made of a section of young
trees. Beech withes were woven across in place of cords, and on these elm bark was
laid. It was called a Michigan bedstead, and was probably the first spring bed on
record. In this cabin Smith and Upton lived during the summer, but in the fall they
built themselves a comfortable log house, in which they kept bachelors' hall until the
winter of 1836. The cabin and house occupied by these men was in the township
now called Medina, but as Smith's land was situated in the township now called
Hudson, Mr. Nathaniel W. Upton has been considered the first settler in Medina.

On the 8th day of April, 1834, Cook Hotchkiss and John Knapp purchased the northeast quarter and the east half of the southeast quarter of section two. They brought
their families to Adrian on the second day of June. On the third day of June, William
Walworth purchased the northeast quarter of the southwest quarter of section one,
and on the sixth day of June, John R. Foster purchased the northeast quarter of section six. Knapp, Walworth and Foster each built houses and settled their families
during the month of June, but Foster's family preceded the others a few days, and
Mrs. Foster was therefore the first white woman resident of that township. Mr.
Foster's house was built near the northeast corner of his farm, and was built after the
model of the early log houses, only this had no chamber. The floor was of split and
hewed basswood, the roof of bark, two small windows, and a stick and mud chimney.
John Knapp built a somewhat better house—in fact, it smacked a little of aristocracy.
It was twenty by twenty-six feet, one and a half stories high; the floors were of split
and hewn basswood, and the roof was covered with shakes. Shakes were rived out

of oak timber; they were about thirty inches long, all the way of a thickness, and as wide as could be made out of the quarter of an oak log. The shakes, therefore, varied in width according as they were split out of a large or small tree, or was the first or last riven out of the bolt. The shakes were laid on poles flattened to the rafters and held in place by other poles, the poles, underneath and top, being fastened together with hickory or blue beech withes. But, notwithstanding these aristocratic notions, Mr. Knapp was compelled to have a stick and mud chimney, because there were neither brick or stone to be had. The house stood near where Allen's tavern, in Medina village, now stands. The land bought by William W. Walworth was that on which the Canandaigua mills now are. He built a house a little northwest of where the old saw mill was afterwards built.

Charles A. Prisbey, October 4th, purchased the northeast fractional quarter of the northwest quarter of section two. Samuel Fincher bought the northwest quarter of the northwest quarter of section two, October 5th. Both these men built houses on their lands in the summer and fall of 1834. During that summer the following named persons purchased lands in the township: Section 1—William M. Wadsworth, June 3d; Samuel Sweeney, Jr., Nov. 5th. Section 2—Amos S. Knapp, Nov. 4th. Section 3—Nathaniel Moore, Aug. 25th. Section 5—Andrew McFarland, March 10th. Section 6—James Barns, Nov. 10th. Section 11—William P. Hobbs. Section 12—Hiram Lucas, Oct. 3d. Section 23—Benjamin Rodgers, Sept. 24th. Section 24—Chester Savage, Aug. 4th; Thomas Hawley, Oct. 28th. Section 25—Horace Garlick, March 10th; George Bennett, June 9th; Dennis Wakefield, Aug. 29th; Charles M. Hewitt, Sept. 8th; James Wilson, Nov. 14th. Section 26—Joseph Hagaman, May 27th; James Jackson Hannah, Nov. 8th; William Yerks, Nov. 17th. Section 27—Samuel Chambers, Dec. 30th. Section 34—Justus Coy, Oct. 11th. Section 35—Dennis Wakefield, Oct. 6th; Ira Clark, Oct. 9th; Archibald Purdy, Oct. 9th; Thomas Tadman, Nov. 17th. Section 36—Charles M. Henry, July 5th; Dennis Wakefield, Aug. 24th; Samuel Sweeney, Nov. 5th.

In town nine south, on section 1—Calvin King, June 17th; Dennis Wakefield, Aug. 29th; Albert Davis, Aug. 23d; Horatio Wilson, Aug. 29th; Amos Franklin. Sept. 16th; Section 2—Dennis Wakefield, Aug. 29th; Levi Goss, Sept. 4th; Amos Franklin, Sept. 16th, Dennis Wakefield, Dec. 18th. Section 3—Orville Woodworth, Sept. 3d; Levi Goss, Sept. 3d. Section 4—Orville Woodworth, Sept. 3d; James Farley, Dec. 8th. Sections 6 and 7—William Clark, Nov. 14th. Section 8—David Meech, Dec. 24th. Section 9—Miles Baker, Nov. 1st; Justus Cooley, Nov. 1st; John Farley, Dec. 8th; David Meech, Dec. 24th. Sections 10 and 11—Hiram Farwell, Oct. 25. Section 12—Uriah E. Wright, Oct. 29th. By consulting the map, the reader will see that sections 8, 9, 10, 11 and 12 are now in the State of Ohio, but at that time Ohio had not attempted to exercise jurisdiction over the disputed territory.

Land looking and land locating was the principal business of that year, and guides through the forests and to the most desirable unlocated lands were in great demand. There were also land centers from which land explorations usually started. From Canandaigua the northern part of Medina, southern part of Hudson, and the township of Wright were reached, while Jacob Baker's house in Seneca was the point from which southwestern Seneca, southern Medina, Royalton, Chesterfield and Gorham, now in Ohio, were explored.

A good story is told of Levi Goss and Orville Woodworth. They were strangers to each other, but came to Baker's land-looking at the same time. Arnold H. Coomer was detailed to guide Goss, and Garlick performed that service for Woodworth. They carried on their explorations separately, and pretty thoroughly scoured the country. Coomer and Goss, having finished, came in late one afternoon, and found that Woodworth had preceded them. Mr. Goss was already somewhat advanced in age, and was considerably fatigued. He had written the description of land selected on a slip of paper thus: S. E. half sec. 3, T. 9 S., 1 E., &c., and placed the slip in his hat, which on coming in he sat on the floor. Woodworth sat where he could see into the hat, and was observed to be earnestly looking in that direction. All at once Woodworth started up and inquired, "How far is it to Hagaman's?" "Five miles," was the reply. "Then," said Woodworth, addressing two fellow travelers, "we have time to reach there before dark; let's go." And immediately they started. Their sudden departure was a cause of wonderment to Baker, his household and guests. Goss sat demurely contemplating the movement, when his eyes resting on the slip of paper in his hat, he exclaimed: "He has gone to enter my land." After a moment's further thought, he asked: "Is there no way of reaching Adrian to-night? He will go no further than Hagaman's to-night, and if I can reach Adrian I may save my land yet." Baker told him there was no way, unless he could make some arrangement with Coomer. Said he, "I have two horses in the barn; may-be you can make some arrangement with Coomer to bring them back." The hint was acted on, and without waiting for supper, the horses were mounted, and away went the adventurers towards Hagaman's, through thick woods, with nothing but a bridle path to follow. It was dark early in the forest, but Coomer had provided himself with a tin lantern and candle, which lighted, enabled them to pursue their journey with tolerable speed. When they reached Hagaman's it was dark in the clearing, but beyond the house were some log heaps burning. To prevent discovery the candle in the lantern was put out and the house passed as noiselessly as possible. At the most remote log heap the candle was relighted and the journey pursued. They now had a wagon track to follow and they traveled more expeditiously, and reached Jordan's somewhat past midnight. Mr. Jordan was aroused to get the travelers something to eat. It was here arranged that Coomer should go no farther, but that Jordon should take Goss on as soon as light appeared. Jordan was to remain up to insure an early start, but so great was Goss' anxiety, he could not sleep, so the two were up the entire night. With the appearance of light they were off for Adrian, and from there to Blissfield. It will no doubt occur to the reader that via Adrian was not the shortest route from Jordan's to Blissfield, but on the more direct route there was no road through the wilderness. At Blissfield, Goss hired a man to take him to Monroe in a wagon (the journey had so far been made on horseback), but it was stipulated that the driver was to let no man pass him, and away they went towards Monroe. Coomer, sharing none of Goss' anxiety, slept soundly at the house of Jordan until long after the departure of the others, but at last awakened, and breakfast procured, he set out on his return to Baker's. A little way out he met Woodworth on foot, who recognized him, and at once asked "Where's the old man?" Boy like, Coomer desiring to worry him, sang out, "He's in Monroe by this time." Woodworth probably suspected that that could not be true, but Goss was ahead, and something must be done. He traveled on at as quick a pace as possible until, somewhere eastward of Jordan's, he found a man plowing in his field. Woodworth walked up to the team and commenced unharnessing one of the horses. While unfastening the harness he told his story, and as he sprang upon the horse's back, he said, "I have no intention of stealing this horse. If you want him, follow me." The other horse was stripped and mounted, and away the pair went over the road traveled by the other party in the gray of the morning. At Blissfield the horses were changed, and Woodworth and his new companion proceeded towards Monroe. Expecting to pass Goss on the road, Woodworth attempted a sort of disguise by changing hats and coats with his companion. Towards evening, as Goss and his driver were jogging along near the end of their journey, two men appeared riding along in the distance. One of the men appeared to be better mounted than the other, as he neared the wagon much more rapidly. "Are you afraid of that man?" said the driver. "No," said Goss, "he lives hereabouts I think," and the man rode by. Woodworth, for it was he, rode rapidly forward, while his companion jogged leisurely along, some way behind the wagon, seemingly in no hurry. Riding up to the door of the land office, and thrusting his hand into his pocket, he called out, "I want to enter—" but alas! his memorandum was in the pocket of his own coat, on the other man's back. Giving rein and whip to his horse he dashed away, met and passed the wagon, rushed up to his companion, secured his paper, and turned again towards the land office. The driver of the team seeing the same man coming again, apparently very anxious to pass, said. "There is some deviltry there," and put whip to his horses. Woodworth passed. however, and as he passed, Goss recognized him. Away they went towards the land office, where they arrived almost at the same instant. "I want to enter—" said Woodworth. "I want to enter—" cried Goss, at the same time jumping, but his foot caught on the wheel and he fell heavily to the ground, knocking the breath from his body. When Goss recovered consciousness, Woodworth had entered his land and was quietly chewing his quid, chuckling over the success of his scheme. Goss cared little for his bodily injuries, but mourned pitifully over the loss of his land. The receiver tried to comfort him by suggesting that perhaps some other land in the immediate neighborhood would answer as well. "Let me see your description," said Miller. The paper was produced, when lo! it appeared that Goss' land was not the Woodworth land at all. Woodworth had selected and entered the southwest quarter of section three, and Goss had selected and now was but too glad to enter the southeast quarter of the same section. And thus it came about that after an exciting race. each man had secured his own land, and neither man had any intention of getting the other's land. Looking with suspicious eye at the slip in Goss' hat, Woodworth had confused the southeast with the southwest, and hence the race. The two men settled on their land, where they lived and died, respecting each other, and each enjoying the respect and esteem of their neighbors.

THE LAKE SETTLEMENT.

Early in January, 1834, the little settlement near the south shore of Devil's Lake was reinforced by its fourth family, that of Mr. William Beal. These four families and Ephraim Sloan are believed to have constituted the entire population of the territory now embraced in the township of Rollin in the winter of 1833-34. The spring of 1834 brought many settlers to the Bean Creek Valley, and a large proportion of them concluded to make their home in this township. David Steer settled on land he located in 1833, on section 5. John T. Comstock and James Sloan located land and settled on section 7, Orson Green on section 10, Levi Jennings and Salem Vosburg on section 22, John R. Hawkins on section 20, Matthew Bennett on section 24, James Macon and Joseph Allen on section 27, Jonathan Ball, Warner Ayelsworth and John Upton on section 28, and Roswell Lamb on section 29. Besides those above named, the following persons purchased land in the township during 1834: Cynthia C. Aldrich, Elmer Cole, Elvira Cole, Darius Cole, John Tingley, William Hathaway, Elijah Bennett, Elkenah Bates, Silas Orcutt, Mayhew Steward, Cyrus B. Packard, Joshua Packard, William Godfrey, David Crout, John Crout, Jacob Foster, Asa R. Bacon, James Bacon, Phœbe Foster, John Belcher, Daniel Russ, Sylvester Boody, Justus G. Newcomb, Ira Sly, John Hunt, John Haskins, Barnabas Bonney, Alden Gregory, Luther Evans, Jonathan C. Freeland and James Wescott.

The first marriage in town six south, one east, occurred this year (1834), and it may be that it was the first in the Valley. There was a marriage on the Chicago road this year at the house of Cornelius Millspaw, within the territorial limits of the township now called Woodstock, and another at or near what is now called Gambleville, in the township of Somerset, but the time of year is at present unknown. The only other marriage in the Valley, this year, was that of Mr. and Mrs. Sprague, of Pittsford, on Christmas day. This Rollin marriage took place at the house of Mr. William Beal. Hiram Aldrich and Eliza Titus were the parties, and John Comstock, a justice of the peace of the township of Logan, tied the knot.

The wife of John Upton died in June. 1834, and was buried on the farm of her husband. Mary Vosburg, daughter of Salem and Lydia Vosburg, was born on the 27th day of August, 1834. She was the first white child born in that township, and still lives on the old homestead. Thus there was a birth, marriage and death, within the limits of the township during the first year after the settlement of its first family.

MILLSPAW'S.—In the year 1833, there were two families residents of town five south, one east—Cornelius Millspaw and Jesse Osborn. Quite a number of persons bought land during that year, but the larger part were persons who lived or afterwards lived in the neighboring townships, and it was held for speculative purposes only. In 1834 a large number of other persons purchased lands, and some of them settled on their lands. Among the latter was Nahum Lamb, who arrived in the township on the first day of September, 1834. Mr. Lamb remained an inhabitant of the township until his death. When Woodstock was organized as a separate township in 1836, Mr. Lamb was elected its first Supervisor. During this year, 1834, Mr. Jacob Lair settled in the township. Besides those already mentioned, the following named persons purchased lands in the township: Section 4, Moses N. Davenport, June 23d. Section 8, Bartholomew Johnston, June 19; Matthew Bushberry, Dec. 24th. Section 9, King D. Betts, July 21st. Section 10, Willard Joslin, July 3d. Section 11, Abner Graves, Jr., Elisha Benedict and Charles Benedict, May 27th. Section 12, Theodore J. Van DenBrook, May 22d; Thomas McCourtie and William Powers, June 13th. Section 18, Edward S. Bascom, Oct. 27th; Charles S. Cleveland, Nov. 5th. Section 22, Martin Case, May 20th; Stephen Perkins and Jedediah Raymond, July 14th. Section 25, Charles White, June 7th; Nelson Crittenden, Feb. 4th. Section 33, Isaac Titus and David Binns, March 3d. Section 34, David Steer, Aug. 27; Alexander Ellsworth, July 14th; Samuel Skinner, July 10th. Section 36, Nehemiah Hands, June 24th.

The first wedding occurred this year at the house of Cornelius Millspaw, and the bride was Mary Ann, the daughter of that worthy pioneer. The bridegroom was Thomas Jolls, and the officiating clergyman was the Rev. Mr. George, a Universalist minister of Philadelphia.

GAMBLE'S.—On the ninth day of March, 1834, Thomas Gamble, the senior, bought out James Van Houvenburg and settled in town five south, one west, where he continued to live until his death. Jonathan Haynes settled in the township. He was afterwards for many years a preacher of the Methodist Episcopal Church, and he was a good neighbor and a zealous Christian until his death. The other settlers of 1834, were : Amos Hixson, Lewis Carrier, Samuel Mills, Elias H. Kelley, Hezekiah Griswold, Jeremiah Loucks, Daniel Strong, Samuel O. Clark, Eli Bugbee, George Oncans, Arza Finney, David Binns, William Welch, Rufus Gilford, David Catelle, Benjamin D. Bond, Stephen Darlington, Gideon Harkness, David Harkness, Zachariah Van Duzer, Jabez H. Jackson, William Gallop, Stephen Vail, Welcome Graham and William T. Webster. It is probable that some of these did not become actual settlers of the township.

During the winter of 1833–4, David Herrington died, the first death in the township. On the 8th day of April, 1834, Mrs. Griswold departed this life, a few days after giving birth to a daughter. The child died about two weeks later.

Sophia Pratt was the first school teacher of the township. She was married the following winter to Samuel Clark. It is related, concerning this marriage, that an itinerant Baptist Elder, named Bodley, was expected around about that time, but on account of the lack of roads, the coming of itinerant ministers was so uncertain, they could not be depended on in an important matter like this, so a justice of the peace was brought from Jonesville to perform the ceremony. The Elder was on hand, however, but the majesty of the law triumphed and the 'Squire married the couple.

The first church in the township was organized in the spring of 1834. It was a Baptist church at or near Gambleville. Mrs. Gay tells an amusing story concerning her first attendance at religious meeting in the territory. She had latterly lived in Albany, where people dressed up to go to church, and to her it seemed a necessary concomitant to church going. She had brought her apparel with her, of course, and nothing was more natural than for her to wear it to church. Arrayed in her silk dress, leghorn bonnet and lace shawl, silk stockings and morocco slippers, she entered the extemporized sanctuary. The contrast was so great as to at once carry a pang to her heart. Her sisters of the settlement were there in calico dresses and sun-bonnets, coarse shoes and woolen stockings, and at least two had no stockings at all. The services were not interesting to Mrs. Gay. How earnestly she wished for her calico dress and sun-bonnet, that she might be at ease and unobserved. So true it is that propriety is essential to happiness, that good and harmless, and even the useful and valuable things of earth in unseemly surroundings will give pain to a sensitive and cultivated mind. Silks and furbelows, leghorn and morocco, were out of place among the homelier but more appropriate attire of backwoods life. Mrs. Gay realized all this in an instant, hence the acute misery she endured during the services of that day.

MOORE'S SETTLEMENT.

When the winter of 1833 closed in, there was but one family within the territorial limits of township six south, one west, and that was Silas Moore's. Three other men had purchased land, viz: Mahlon, Jacob and Edmund B. Brown. The next informa-tion of the town we have been able to obtain is of the date of June, 1834. In that month Mr. Stephen Knapp, of Clarkston, Monroe county, N. Y., visited the township and lodged at the house of Edmund B., commonly called Burrows Brown. Brown told Knapp he had some excellent land, which he would show him. The next morning he took Knapp out and showed him two lots on section fourteen. One was what is known as wind-fall, the other was handsome timber. Knapp had intended to pur-chase two lots, and had brought three hundred dollars with him for that purpose, but Brown asked four hundred dollars for these two lots. It was finally agreed that Knapp should buy the land, pay three hundred dollars down, and the other one hundred when he returned to settle on the land. The contract was put in writing by Timothy Gay, of the next township north, now called Somerset. Mr. Knapp after-wards learned that, at the time he made the contract, Brown had no title to one of the lots, but purchased it of the government afterwards. This Brown was a land-shark, and perpetrated his little joke on quite a number of settlers. One of his intended victims was warned by Brown's wife, and escaped his clutches. Some time in the month of September following, Stephen Knapp and family left Clarkston, Monroe county, N. Y., for their new home in Michigan. Their departure had been delayed more than a month by an expected domestic event. Their goods were shipped by canal to Buffalo, from there by steam to Detroit. James Knapp, the eldest son, ac-companied the goods; with his wife and three other children, one of them a month old infant, Stephen Knapp came by wagon through Canada. The trip through Canada consumed eleven days' time, and on their arriving at Detroit they found James there with the goods. The family came on by the Chicago road, which they found very soft, and the traveling was very slow. From Clinton they turned southward, through Tecumseh and Adrian, to the house of Zebulon Williams, then residing in the township of Madison, three miles, or thereabouts, south of Adrian. Here the wife and smaller children were left for a time, until a house could be built, and the household goods could be brought from Detroit. The drawing of the goods, owing to the almost impassable condition of the roads, was a tedious operation; ten miles a day with a load was all the distance the team could make. Perry Knapp says he remem-bers to have heard this yarn spun in a Chicago road hotel while hauling those goods: " A traveler saw a hat lying on the surface of the thin mud; he attempted to pick it up, when he heard in sepulchral tones, ' Let go my hat.' The finder inquired, ' What are you doing there ?' ' Traveling on the Chicago pike.' ' Do you want any help ?' ' No, I have a good horse under me.' "

At length, however, despite the bad roads, the last load of goods was in, and on the 30th day of November, 1834, the family of Stephen Knapp took possession of the house, which had meanwhile been built. This family made the fourth in that township. The others were Silas Moore, Anson Jackson, and Burrows Brown. During the winter Mr. Knapp fenced twenty acres of his wind-fall land.

Eli Eastman entered his land June 16th, 1834, but did not move onto it until the next year. Other persons entered lands during the year, viz: Hiram Hatfield, May 16th; John H. Converse, April 22d; Seaton Hoxie, May 6th; Manly Holmes, May 20th; William Holmes, Dec. 13th; Thos. Farmer, May 5th; Stephen Vail, June 19th; Job A. Moore, Aug. 23d; Hiram Graham, Oct. 8th; Stephen K. Geddings, Oct. 20th; John Jackson, March 27th; Jabez H. Jackson, April 10th; Burton Lamphere, Nov. 20th; Myron McGee, Dec. 9th; Jesse Hill, June 2d; Achsah Eastman, June 16th; Frances Hill; George W. Brearly, May 30th; Israel Pennington, June 7th; Orange Latourette, June 9th; John Bryant, June 11th; Clarinda Cook, June 16th; John Howell, April 18th; Jacob Brown, June 12th; Closinda Cook, Nov. 15th; Jesse Hill, Jan. 2d; Marshal Alvord and Joseph Alvord, June 10th; John O'Brien, June 12th; Robert August, Nov. 21st; Zebulon Williams, Dec. 17th; Amos Hare, May 30th; Robert Cox, June 5th and 13th; John Pennington, June 7th; Lorenzo Church, July 14th; Joseph W. Ashley, Oct. 6th; L. Church, July 14th; Walter Culver and William Culver, Nov. 26th; Burr S. Northup, June 2d. None of these except Farmer settled on their land that year.

Silas Farmer must have settled on his land in the month of December, 1834. Perry Knapp says he was not there when their family came, November 30th, and Eli Eastman says he was there when he came in January, 1835.

In town five south, two west (Moscow), there was quite a large increase of population during 1834. Among those who settled that year were Aaron Spencer, Peter Atwell, and William Benson. Mrs. Brown, mother of Mrs. Daniel Aiken, died this year.

In the summer of 1834 Delilah Blackmar taught a school in a private house. In the winter of 1834-35 Seth Kempton taught the school, the first part of the term in the same private house, and the remainder of the term in the first school house, which was finished during that winter.

1835, AND TO MARCH 1st, 1836.

In the winter of 1834-5 the Legislative Council broke up the Valley into smaller organizations. Town six south, one east, was organized and named Rollin. Towns five, six, seven, eight, nine and fractional ten south, range one west, were organized into a single township and named Wheatland; and towns five, six, seven, eight, nine and fractional ten south, range two west, were organized into a single township and named Moscow. At the close of the session of 1834-35, town seven south, one east (Hudson), remained a part of the township of Lenawee; towns eight, nine and fractional ten south, ranges one and two east (Medina and Seneca in Michigan, and Gorham and Chesterfield in Ohio), remained a part of the township of Fairfield. Townships now named Somerset, Wheatland, Pittsford and Wright constituted the township of Wheatland, and townships now called Moscow, Adams, Jefferson, Ransom and the east part of Amboy constituted the township of Moscow.

ROLLIN.

The first township meeting was held on the sixth day of April, 1835, at the house of Joseph Real, so says the statute; but for Real we should evidently read Beal, for there the meeting was in fact held. Matthew Bennett was elected moderator, and William Beal, clerk. Matthew Bennett was elected supervisor; William Beal, township clerk; David Steer, James Bacon and Joseph Beal, assessors; Elijah C. Bennett, collector; David Steer and John T. Comstock, directors of the poor; Warner Aylesworth, Asa R. Bacon and Joseph C. Beal, commissioners of highways; Elijah A. Bennett, constable; Joseph Gibbon, Orson Green and Joseph Steer, commissioners of common schools; Joseph Gibbons, Orson Green, Joseph Steer, Elijah C. Bennett and James Boodery, "school inspectors of common schools."

It was voted that "our cattle, hogs and sheep, run at large the ensuing year;" and "our pathmasters be fence-viewers." The record does not state the number of votes polled at the township meeting, but at the general election, held on the fifth and sixth days of October, 1835, there were fifteen votes polled for Governor, three votes for Lieutenant Governor, nine votes for Senator, fifteen votes for Representative in Congress; three votes were given for "Representative of Michigan." Of the votes given for Governor, Stevens T. Mason received three, and John Biddle received twelve; Edward Mundy received the three votes for Lieutenant Governor; Olmsted Hough, Edward D. Ellis, and Laurent Durocher, each received three votes for Senator; William Woodbridge received thirteen votes for Representative in Congress, and Isaac E. Crary received three votes; Allen Hutchins, Hiram Dodge, James Wheeler, and Darius Meed, each received three votes for "Representative of Michigan." There were also twelve votes cast against the ratification of the Constitution of Michigan, and one for its ratification. The reader will notice, perhaps, a discrepancy between the statement of the whole number of votes given for the office of Representative in Congress and the aggregate of votes stated to be given to the two candidates. Fifteen is said to be the whole number given for the office, while Woodbridge is said to have received thirteen, and Crary three. From a careful review of the vote it seems plain that Woodbridge only received twelve votes.

The reader will also have noticed, perhaps, that at the township meeting no justices of the peace were elected. That meeting was held under the territorial laws, and by these laws justices were appointed by the Legislative Council. That position was held, no doubt, by Joseph Beal, whose name appears as one of the inspectors of the election.

In May, this year, Dr. Leonard G. Hall settled in this township, and has ever since been a resident of the Bean Creek Valley. For several years his ride extended over a vast extent of territory. He was kind, skillful and attentive, and nearly all the earliest settlers have had occasion to call down blessings on his head. In the same month Daniel Rhodes and his son William came into the township, and in June John Foster located land on section twenty-seven, and immediately commenced operations there. Barnabas Bonney settled on section thirteen, and Samuel Comstock, having purchased an interest in the lands of the Rollin Mill Company, built a house and moved into it in the month of July.

In April of this year, work was commenced on the saw mill in Rollin. Mr. William Beal was made superintendent of the work, and for that purpose left his farm and dwelt on the mill property. The mill frame was raised in the fall of that year, and in November of that year the sawing of lumber commenced and enabled the settlers to make their cabins more comfortable for the approaching winter. The saw mill finished, preparations were at once commenced for the building of a grist mill.

In the fall Bishop Van Wert, Jacob Foster and the three Haskins settled in the township.

Sometime during the summer of this year a postoffice was established at or near the mill property, and William Beal was made postmaster and Porter Beal mail carrier. Before that, the settlers of all the northern part of the Valley had to go to Adrian for their mail matter, which was no small task. From the western part of the Valley a day and a half was required to go to the postoffice, and each letter cost the recipient twenty-five cents,—compulsory prepayment was not then in vogue.

Thompson, who had opened a small trading establishment south of the lake, attempted to sell whisky to settlers and Indians. He was cited to appear at Adrian, which effectually squelched the business in that township for some time.

Among the purchasers of real estate in 1835 were these: Erastus Farnham, July 3d; Elijah Brownell, July 11th; John Talbot, May 11th; Amos Steer, June 25th; Oliver Griswold, Nov. 6th; Darius Cole, Feb. 20th; Leonard G. Hall, June 22; Stephen Vail, Barnabas Bonney, June 1st; William Godfrey, June 3d; James Kenly, June 18th; Harvey Houghton, May 27th; Joseph Webster, Nov. 21st; Abraham P. Vosburgh, William Campbell, Nov. 21st; J. Warner Aylesworth, Ezra Lord, July 10th; John Haskins, Matthew Bennett, Abijah S. Clark, Phebe H. Clark, May 11th; Luther Evans, July 3d; Lydia Howland, June 4th; Calvin Jenks, June 13th; Samuel Comstock, July 7th; Hiram Hitchcock, Jared Comstock, June 19th; Rachael S. Beal, July 18th; Sylvester White, Oct. 20th; John Foster, June 1st; Lorenzo Sheldon, Thomas Kealey, June 9th; Edward Knapp, May 26th; Daniel Peck, May 26th; Rufus Peck, Ira Jones, June 26; Moses T. Bennett, July 16th.

LENAWEE TOWNSHIP.

At the township meeting, held on Monday, the sixth day of April, 1835, William R. Porter was elected Supervisor, Jeremiah D. Thompson, Township Clerk, and Calvin Bradish, Lyman Pease and Stephen Perkins, Assessors. The wolf bounty—three dollars per head—was continued. During the year William Mills received bounties for eleven wolves slain, Bart White for six, Edward Bassett for four, Jacob Jackson for three, David Bixby for four, Joseph Cerow for one, and Robert Johnston for four, —making a total of thirty-three wolves killed.

We are more especially interested in that part of the township of Lenawee lying within the valley of the Bean, and we therefore will turn our attention to town seven south, of range one west.

During the winter, axes had been wielded by busy hands in and around the Lanesville settlement, and in the early spring time preparations for clearing began. The mill dam was repaired and the mill started; the maple was tapped and the year's supply of sugar and vinegar provided. But before sugar could be made kettles suitable for boiling must be provided, and Simeon Van Akin relates that he took Mr. Lane's oxen and drove to Adrian in search of kettles. He found none there, and went thence to Tecumseh and Monroe. In the latter place he procured two—one for himself and one for Mr. Lane.

In the spring of 1835 Michael Dillon came in and commenced chopping on his land entered the year previous. He was accompanied by his brother Dennis. Sometime in the summer Michael returned East for his family.

In the month of April, 1835, Mr. John Rice and Mrs. M. K. Douglass were united in the bands of wedlock by Oliver Purchase, a justice of the peace. Mrs. Douglass was a widow, a sister of Mr. Lane. This was the first marriage in the territory which now constitutes the township of Hudson.

In the month of May, probably the third day, Mr. Lane organized a Sunday school at his house. In a published statement, Mr. Lane said it occurred May seventh; but as the almanac for that year makes the seventh fall on Thursday, there is a strong probability that Mr. Lane is mistaken.

On the 10th day of June, 1835, Noah Cressey and wife settled on section thirty-two, adjoining land of Michael Dillon. Mr. Cressey, as well as the Dillons, came to the Valley by the southern or Canandaigua route, and because the lands of northern Medina were well culled, drifted over into Hudson and commenced a settlement. Between them and the Lanesville settlement there was an unbroken belt of timber, which effectually cut off intercourse, while the Medina settlements were comparatively easy of access. Therefore for many years that neighborhood traded and visited with the Medina people, and were, for all business and social purposes, identified with them.

July 27th, Mrs. Davis, the mother of Reuben and Samuel Davis, died. It was the first death in the township.

On the 28th, same month, George Salisbury opened the first Lanesville store. The stock comprised groceries and notions.

During the spring and summer the Kidder mill was kept in constant motion, sawing out lumber, with which to finish the log houses of settlers in the township and also in the townships of Rollin and Wheatland. These two saw mills possessed great powers of civilization, and through their agency puncheon floors and bark roofs and gables began to disappear, and new houses were now finished with shake roofs and sided gables. It marked a new era in the settlement of the Valley.

On Saturday, the 8th day of August, the citizens of town seven south, one east, met to consider the propriety of petitioning the new State Legislature, which, if the new constitution was adopted at the October election, would convene for its first session on the ninth day of November, to organize town seven south, one east, into a separate township. The question was decided in the affirmative, and on the suggestion of Hiram Kidder it was named Hudson, after Dr. Daniel Hudson, of Geneva, N. Y., who was the senior partner of the company that purchased the first land in the township. The Legislature only continued in session six days, and took no action in reference to organizing townships. The State was not yet admitted into the Union, and the Legislature only took action in reference to a transfer of jurisdiction when the State should be admitted.

Among the items of expenditure mentioned in the appropriation bill of that session were the following: To Mrs. Warren and daughter, for making carpet, the sum of eight dollars; to Levi Skinner, three dollars for polishing stoves for Senate chamber, Representatives' hall and Governor's room; to Wright & Solomon, for two mahogany tables and desks furnished Senate chamber, the sum of eighty dollars; to McArthur & Hurlburt, for candles, two dollars and nineteen cents. No petroleum! No gas! The primitive capitol of our State was lighted with tallow candles.

On Sunday, the ninth day of August, the first religious meeting was held in the township, at the house of Mr. Lane.

About this time William Frazee came and bought out Reuben Davis. The premises now occupied by William Ocobock, on the southwest corner of section nineteen, was a part of his farm. Salmon Trask, wife and daughter, and also a Miss Abigail Dickinson came from Massachusetts and settled on section eighteen.

In November Mr. Lane built a frame house where the Comstock House now stands. It was the first frame house built in the township, and was occupied by Father Nathaniel Lane and wife and their son Erastus.

The same month Mr. Alexander Findley came and cleared a part of the Cobb land, and built a log house in anticipation of the arrival of Harvey Cobb and family.

During this month (November) the settlement in the south part of the township received some recruits. On Monday the second day of November, Father Elisha Brown and family arrived at the house of his son-in-law, Noah Cressey. The Brown party consisted of Father Brown and wife, his son Lorenzo L. and wife, and his other sons, Clement, David, Lewis, George, William and Noah, and Dolly Elwell, a niece of Mr. Noah Cressey. Miss Elwell afterwards married Dr. Stephen Caner, and is now the wife of Mr. Oliver Kelly, of Pittsford. Father Brown had purchased his lands of Robert Huston, and there was the body of a small house, roofed, but otherwise unfinished, on the land.

About two days after, Michael Dillon arrived with his family, and on Sunday evening, November eighth, the Rev. William E. Warner and family arrived at the cabin of Father Brown. He had bought his land of second hands without having seen it, and he was now in search of it. His land proved to be on the north side of section four, in town eight south, about two miles from the Brown domicil. Mr. Warner was invited to make his home among the Browns until he could build a house, and he accepted the invitation. During his stay there were no less than

D

twenty persons fed and lodged at the Cressey and Brown small, one-roomed cabins. It was rather crowded, but then, they were not lonesome.

The Rev. William E. Warner had, in the State of New York, been a local preacher of the Methodist Episcopal church for many years, at times taking temporary work under Presiding Elders. Here he found himself providentially thrown in the midst of a large family of Methodists, and he improved the occasion by preaching at the house of Noah Cressey the next Sunday, November the 15th, and organizing a class, of which he appointed Lorenzo L. Brown leader. The congregation that day was made up from the members of three families, viz., Brown, Cressey and Dillon.

As Mr. Lane remembers the incident, on teh 11th day of December, 1835, Friday, the Rev. William Wolcott preached the first sermon in the Lanesville settlement. He also organized a temperance society. Both the religious and temperance meetings were held at Mr. Lane's house. In the fall of 1835, Miss Abigail Dickinson taught a school in the village of Lanesville. July 8th, Beriah H. Lane sold a one-fourth interest in the saw-mill to William H. H. Van Akin, and December 1st sold a one-fourth interest to Simeon and William H. H. Van Akin.

During the year the following persons purchased land in the west third of Lenawee township, viz.: Edward Knapp, John Johnson, Lester C. Bennett, Ezekiel Yerrington, Ezra Lord, Reuben Snell, Calvin Jenks, Jesse R. Treadwell, Samuel Sager, Dudley Worden, Thomas Keeley, Edward Keeley, James Green, Ami Crosby, Griswold Latham, Edward Edmunds, Silas Palmer, Benjamin Palmer, John Hutchins, Reuben Hutchins, John W. Stockwell, Uriah Daniels, Jeremiah D. Thompson, L. Hotchkiss, John R. Willis, Elias Gage, John Hooper, Prudence Page, Constans Rowley, John Townsend, William Clark, Porter L. Howland, Noah Palmer, Moses Moore, Pardon Davenport, James Van Akin, 2d, Elizabeth Van Akin, Thomas Will, Benjamin Mills, Joseph Mills, Reed Sutton, Joseph R. Reynolds, John Rice, Solomon Seymour, Caleb D. Ferris, John Colwell, Daniel C. Cooper, Augustus W. Childs, Oren C. Nichols, Gideon L. Bebee, James Grannin, Jason Gratton, Peter Bovee, Abram Bovee, Thomas Farroll, Joseph Rickey, Richard Hawkins, William Haley, Matthias H. Bovee, John H. Bovee, Oliver W. Alverson, John Drew, Dennis Dwyer, William Carson, Noah Cressey, Hiram Van Akin, Alexander D. Anderson, John Beal, Henry Barton, Thomas J. Huntington, Artemas Allen, Edward H. Miller, Gordon H. Leeds, Jacob LeRoy, Timothy Sabin and Nathan Elliott.

On the twenty-fourth day of February, 1836, several persons assembled at the house of Alpheus Pratt in Wheatland (now Pittsford), to consider the propriety of organizing a church. The Rev. William Wolcott presided as moderator. Twenty-four persons presented letters of church membership, viz.: Salmon Trask, John L. Taylor, Elijah B. Seeley, Nelson R. Rowley, Daniel Loomis, Ozen Keith, John Perrin, Simeon Van Akin, Jesse Smith, Stephen W. Perrin, Beriah H, Lane, Cecil Keith, Orinda Seeley, Phœbe Lane, Sarah Nye, Emily Perrin, Bethesda Perrin, Huldah Caldwell, Sarah Frazee, Clarinda Taylor, Minerva Rice, Margaret Van Akin, Zeruiah Trask and Martha Keith. These persons adopted a resolution agreeing to unite themselves together in a church of Christ, to be called the "First Presbyterian Church of Bean Creek," and on their request thus expressed, the Rev. Mr. Wolcott constituted them a church by such designation. William Frazee and Caroline Loomis, upon profession of their faith, were baptized and received into the new church. Salmon Trask, Elijah B. Seeley, Nelson R. Rowley, and John L. Taylor were elected Elders, and the three first were immediately ordained. Beriah H. Lane was elected church clerk. The reader will have noticed that the meeting for organization convened in the township of Wheatland, now Pittsford, and it is equally true that seventeen out of the twenty-four persons participating in its organization, lived in the township of Wheatland as then organized; but as the church afterwards became the Congregational church of Hudson, it is grouped with the historical incidents of western Lenawee.

The same day there was a wedding at the house of Beriah H. Lane, in Lanesville.

The bride was Miss Abigail Dickinson, and the groom Mr. George Salisbury. The Rev. William Wolcott performed the ceremony.

WESTERN FAIRFIELD.

William Cavender settled on his land in the month of March, 1835, and his brother-in-law, Samuel Gregg, built a house on the land Cavender purchased in town eight south, one east, and commenced keeping tavern. That original tavern stood on the site of the present hotel in Canandaigua. Of this enterprise Mr. Gregg says: Mr. Cavender moved on his premises, and in March, 1835, I went there and built me a log house twenty by thirty feet, took my lumber from Adrian, and moved my family April 16th. Soon after I made an addition of twelve feet to one side, for a cook-room and dining-room, and came to Adrian to purchase some groceries—whisky and brandy—and told them I was going to keep tavern. They thought that was a novel idea, and laughed at me, and had their own fun about it. I told them all I wanted of them was to send on the land-lookers; and in June and July I had more customers than I could attend to, frequently from twelve to twenty at a time, and one night thirty-five land-lookers.

Francis H. Hagaman, Burns Cavender and Orrin Pixley stood ready at all times, with compass and chart, to pilot the land-lookers to where they could find government land, at a charge of two dollars per day. In less than six months most of the land in the township was purchased, and a large portion by actual settlers.

Among the persons who purchased land in town eight south, range one east, in the year 1835, were these, viz: William M. Woodworth, Feb. 2d; Joseph Pixley, March 12th; Henry Barton, Jan. 29th; Thomas Williams, May 11th; W. V. J. Mercer and H. Handy, June 15th; Dan B. Miller, July 30th; Moses S. Beach, June 2d; William T. Pratt, June 18th; William H. Manning, June 20th; Joseph Fellows, June 16th; Calista Budlong and Alfred W. Budlong, Jan. 18th; Thomas Dewey, Aug. 14th; Benjamin C. Durfey, May 25th; Lorenzo G. Budlong, Jan. 18th; Salem T. King, Jan. 22d; Alexander Duncan, July 6th and 22d; Paul Raymond, July 10th; Luther Bradish, June 23d; Bartlett R. Bradish, Seth W. Bradish and Charles W. Bradish, June 23d; Jacob Le Roy, Dec. 5th; Samuel Warren, July 30th; John D. Sutton and Levi Salisbury, May 29th; H. Edmunds, June 10th; S. Johnson, June 4th; Joseph B. Marry, June 13th; John Martin, Dec. 12th; John L. Bean, May 29th; Samuel Ranger, Jan. 29th; Joseph Hagaman, Feb. 10th; Morris Boughton, April 18th; Henry McCumisky, April 22d; Jonathan N. Pickard, May 7th; Peter Countryman, May 7th; John L. Hall, May 20th; Robert Craven, June 8th; Russell Forsyth, June 29th; Suffrenas Dewey, Jan. 21st; Alexander D. Anderson, Aug. 17th; John Starkweather, March 16th; Simon D. Wilson, June 2d; Richard P. Hunt, July 27th; Alanson Munger, Sept. 18th; John Powers, May 21st, Cornelius DeMott, Oct. 13th; Mary P. Todd, May 27th; Gabriel H. Todd, June 12th; Orphelia B. Hopkins, Jan. 13th; Ruel Thayer, July 11th; John O'Brien, Sept. 8th; George Bennett, July 21st; Joseph Bailey, Oct. 30th; William B. Waldron, June 3d; William Walworth, May 22d; James A. Rogers, June 1st; John B. Skinner, July 23d; Willard Stevens, Sept. 18th; Seba Murphy, Oct. 3d; John Countryman, May 7th; Amasa P. Converse, May 16th; Christopher H. Stillwell, June 1st; Russell Forsyth, Jan. 29th; James S. Dawes, Sept. 26th; James Murray, Jan. 13th; Martin Millett, Jan. 13th; Chester Savage, Feb. 25th; Rollin R. Hill, May 7th; George Lee, May 22d; Theodore Coburn, June 29th; Lewis Shepardson, May 15th; Noah K. Green, June 1st; Thomas Denny, Aug. 14th; Calvin L. Rogers, June 6th; Ephraim Baldwin, June 6th; Cornelius Bayless, Oct. 5th; Hannah Camburn, April 18th; Paul Raymond, June 1st; John McVicar, June 1st; Alexander Seeley, Oct. 6th; James W. Morris, Dec. 22d; Almon Palmer, Sept. 9th; George W. Brower, Dec. 3d; David Countryman, Dec. 9th; James Hornbeck, July 20th; Elkanah Parker, May 19th; Cornelius G. Palmer, May 22d; Lorenzo D. Perkins, June 10th; Justus Cooley, Oct. 20th; E. J. Baldwin, June 2d.

In town nine south, one east, Calvin King, March 30th; Juba S. Palmer, March 31st; Tibbals Baldwin, June 2d; Dennis Wakefield, Aug. 29th; Levi B. Wilder, March 13th; Cornelius G. Palmer, May 22d; Levi Goss, July 11th; E. Barnes, July 7th; Lewis M Gates, July 14th; Isaiah Townsend and Jabin Townsend, June 29th; William Jones and John Jones, July 14th; David Cross, Jan. 26th; Cornelius G. Palmer, May 22d; Azaph R. Porter, May 22d; Marquis Baldwin, June 2d; Christopher Bush, Jan. 15th; John Gould, Feb. 19th; Jacob TenEyck and Moses C. Baker, Jan. 19th; Uriah E. Wright, May 8th; Peter Burns and Patrick Burns, May 19th; W. Lee, May 22d; Joseph W. Turner, June 8th; Adam S. Sebring, Jan. 9th.

In the month of September, 1835, the first sermon was preached by the Rev. William Wolcott, then of Adrian, now a resident of the village of Hudson. The sermon was preached in Gregg's bar-room, on the invitation of Mr. Gregg.

In October, 1835, Dr. Increase S. Hamilton settled in Canandaigua. The same fall the first school house was built, on the farm of William Cavender. Dr. Hamilton taught the first school in the winter of 1835-6.

In the fall of 1835, William Cavender bought the land owned by William Walworth —the site of the Canandaigua mills—and commenced building a saw-mill. It sawed its first lumber April 12th, 1836.

In the month of November, 1835, the Rev. William E. Warner settled on section four in town eight south, one east. He had formerly resided in the State of New York; was there a member of the Methodist Episcopal Church and a local preacher. His large and still increasing family rendered it impossible for him to enter the itinerancy permanently, but for several years he had traveled circuits under the direction of the Presiding Elders thereof. In 1835, feeling the importance of finding a home for his large family, he traded what property he had for Michigan land, never having seen the land or even been in the territory. He came by wagon to Adrian, and there inquiring for the Bean Creek country, was directed to go out on the Territorial road. After several days' travel, he found himself on the Chicago road, north of Devil's Lake. He then turned southward through the forests, and made his way as well as he could towards where he supposed his land to be. After a tedious journey he arrived at the abode of Noah Cressy, on section thirty-two, in town seven south, two miles from his land, on the evening of Sunday, the eighth day of November, 1835. There he found brethren of his own church, for the Brown families had arrived only the Monday previous. A few weeks later he moved into a cabin on his own land. Mr. Warner was one of the most eloquent men this country was ever blessed with. Always ready, he obeyed every call for ministerial services, whether to break the bread of life on a Sunday, or to speak words of consolation to mourning friends on a week day. He had no regular work; he went everywhere, among all classes of people—fearless always, reposing with confidence on the promise, "Lo, I am with you always." His name was a household word among the settlers, from the Chicago road to the Maumee river, from the Raisin eastward to the utmost bounds of the west, as applied to the Bean Creek Valley. As without regular work, so he was without salary. However hard the labor endured in answering the demands for ministerial labor, he always accepted the proffered remuneration, whether it was a silver dollar or a peck of potatoes, with a pleasant smile and a hearty "God bless you." He lived in Medina township for several years, and then removed, about 1852, to the township of Ransom, Hillsdale county, where he lived until his death, which occurred about the year 1871.

After his removal to Hillsdale county, Mr. Warner united with the Wesleyan Methodist Church. He was a strong Abolitionist, and believed the Methodist Episcopal Church would go to pieces on that question, and that he only preceded by a few years the transfer of the entire body of anti-slavery Methodists to the Wesleyan fold. But, whether Episcopal or Wesleyan Methodist, he always had a word for the Master's cause, which he never failed to deliver with impassioned eloquence. And yet Mr. Warner was not a backwoods preacher; he was possessed of considerable culture, and would have made his mark in polished society. The old man always wrestled with poverty. His responsibilities increased year by year, and with so much time given to others, it was impossible for him to meet them and accumulate property. Some years after he had removed to Ransom, and while his fame as an orator still lingered in the memories of his brother pioneers, he was invited to Hudson to deliver a Fourth of July oration. The messenger found him boiling potash, but he promised to come. He never could say no, when the interests of others required sacrifices on his part. When he appeared on the streets on the morning of the Fourth, his wardrobe was in a sad plight. The Hon. William Baker, a man of large heart and generous impulses, took the matter in hand, and when the order to march was given, the Elder appeared in procession dressed from top to toe in a new suit of clothes. Well were the donors repaid by the fervent eloquence that fell from the old man's lips that day. He always spoke extemporaneously, and as he warmed with his subject, his spirit was lifted to the regions of prophecy, and he portrayed the certain retribution awaiting the nation's sins in words enchanting, yet appalling. The old man lived to see the beginning of the end.

After the Rev. Mr. Wolcott's sermon in Gregg's bar-room in September, 1835, Mr. Wolcott continued to preach there once in four weeks during the fall, and a Congregational society was organized, but it soon became extinct. The religious element of the Upton and Gregg settlements was largely of the Baptist order, and on the 29th day of January, 1836, a church was organized under the name and style of "The Baptist Church of Canandaigua." Mr. Cook Hochkiss was Deacon, and Superintendent of the Sunday School. Religious services were held in the school house at Canandaigua.

SOUTHERN FAIRFIELD.

Comparatively but little land was sold in towns eight and nine south, two east (Seneca), in 1834, but in 1835 many purchases were made, among which were the following : Joseph Griffeth, July 22d ; Jacob LeRoy, Sept. 26th and Dec. 5th ; Washington Perry, July 25th ; Jonathan Marsh, jr., Sept. 12th ; Leeds & Miller, Dec. 5th ; Almon Palmer, June 9th ; Lucy R. Haywood, Aug. 10th ; Edgar Webb, Dec. 12th ; Samuel Bean, May 29th ; Alexander Duncan, July 6th ; Orrin Pixley, Jan. 19th ; Ira White, July 6th ; James D. Manchester, May 30th ; Joseph Hagaman, Edgar Webb and Samuel Skinner, July 10th ; Theron White, Sept. 25th ; James S. Kinney, May 26th ; David Dunlap, June 13th ; Elias Kinney, July 2d ; John B. Allen, July 8th ; Hiram B. Reed, July 22d ; Philemon Newman, June 17th ; Cornelius S. Randolph, Nov. 13th ; Horatio L. Forbes, June 6th ; Thomas Gerrish, Nov. 3d ; Robert P. Thompson, Sept. 23d ; Joseph Ferguson, May 22d ; Thomas C. Aldrich, May 25th ; James Rogers, June 1st: Hiram Flager, Oct. 15th ; Asa Farley, Peter Flughler and Zachariah Flager, Feb. 25th ; Benjamin F. Archer, June 29th, Alexander B. Callison, July 16th ; Wilmarth Graham, July 18th ; Samuel Lammon, Oct. 21st ; John Coddington, Nov. 11th ; Joel Shapley, Jan. 15th ; Oliver Welch, June 24th ; James R. Westcott, June 24th ; Lucius Atwood, Aug. 14th ; Lyman Wilcox, Nov. 26th ; Reuben G. Field and Jesse W. Thayer, Sept. 23d ; John W. Eaton, Oct. 20th ; Richard H. Whitney, Oct. 24th ; Cyrus Whiting, Oct. 24th ; Erastus C. Woodworth, James Dalton and John Osborn, May 19th ; George W. Sparks and George Brown, Sept. 23d ; John Halstead, Sept. 30th ; Norman H. Thurber, Nov. 3d ; Oliver Phelps, Nov. 3d ; David Price, Russel Forsyth and Mary Lammon, July 3d ; Paul Raymond, Nov. 2d ; Jeptha Whitman, Oct 6th ; Benjamin Hornbeck, May 27th ; David Burgess, Dec. 7th ; Ezra Cole, Dec. 8th. Town nine south, two east, Joseph R. Williams, Nov. 10th ; Howland Hagaman, Nov. 14th ; Nehemiah Crane and T. Coburn.

Mrs. Brower is said to have been the first white woman settler within the present limits of Seneca township. The first child born, which must have been early in 1835, was named Alma Brower. In January, 1835, Judith P. Hayward died. In May, the second day, the first school house in town eight south, two east, was finished. Miss Parson, now Mrs. Miller, still residing in the township of Medina, taught the school that summer, and Simon D. Wilson taught it the next winter. The school house was a log structure, and was situated in the grove just north of Charles B. Wilson's residence. The first saw-mill was built in 1835.

WHEATLAND.

In the month of January, 1835, Eli Eastman moved into town six south, one west, and built a log house on the land he had entered the year previous. He left the State of New York in 1833, coming to Fairfield, Lenawee county, in November, 1833. Here he spent the winter of 1833–4, and in January, 1835, moved to Wheatland. Before he had the body of his house up, Harvey McGee came in and commenced a settlement on his land. Mr. Eastman names, as living in that township, the following families: Moore, Brown, Knapp, Jackson and Farmer.

On the 17th day of March, 1835, the Legislative Council organized towns five, six, seven, eight, nine and fractional ten south, one west, into a township and named it Wheatland. The first township meeting was held at the house of Thomas Gamble, on the Chicago road. The records of that township meeting are lost, and it is uncertain who were elected to office, but it is believed that Heman Pratt was the supervisor.

A large number of persons settled within the territorial limits of the township during the year 1835. In town five south, one west (Somerset), the following were among the settlers: Robert T. Brown, C. M. McLouth, Robert Bilby, Abraham West, Alonzo Olds, Elijah Slayton, Albert Woods, Leonard Bailey, Elisha Smith, Aaron Van Vleet, Simon H. Baker, Isaac Derby, Alpheus Hill, Albert Parmelee, William Weaver, S. Mercer. Mr. Mercer came in the month of October. He bought a yoke of oxen near Detroit, and his two sons—William, a young man, and Andrew, a lad— drove them in. Mr. William Mercer says there were plenty of taverns on the road then; there were fourteen or fifteen between Clinton and Gambleville.

All the old settlers agree that during this year there was an immense travel on the Chicago road. There was no time during daylight that there were not some teams in sight, and usually there was a continual and close procession throughout the whole day. The Chicago road had become pretty well settled, the LaPlaisance Bay road had been completed, and the Adrian Territorial road had been so far completed as to be used to some extent. Mr. Geddes, speaking of the scenes on the LaPlaisance Bay turnpike in 1835, says: "One living on the turnpike to-day can scarcely realize the wonderful changes that have taken place upon that thoroughfare since its construction. From 1835 to 1840 there was one continuous procession of movers' wagons. Six four-horse coaches each day ran over the road, loaded with passengers, and all was life and activity." This immense travel of the La Plaisance Bay road united with the travel from Detroit at Walker's Junction, in the township of Cambridge, and thence westward it was a mighty procession.

Among those who purchased lands in town six south, one west (Wheatland), were the following: John L. Johnson, Amos White, Sylvester White, Bartlett Bump, Benjamin Johnson, Stephen L. Gage, Henry S. McQuig, Elijah Gillett, Jr., Albert Vreedenburg, John L. Edmonds, Jonathan Robbins, Lyman Crothers, Samuel Clement, Edwin L. Way, Calvin Carr, Van Rensalaer Conover, Stephen Hoeg, John Bradish, Edson Witherell, Isaiah Straw, Gamaliel Burbank, Darius Douglas, Almon Goff, Zachariah Paddleford, Samuel D. Douglas, Joseph W. Ashley, George Miller, George Whitney, Abel S. Bailey, Nathan P. Colwell, Nathan Whitney, Adam Lull, John McKnight, Joseph Paddleford, Charles Carmichael, Bradford Carmichael, Silas Carmichael, Zebulen Williams, John Bailey, Isaac Lamb, A. N. Martin, James McGee, Simeon P. Gillett, David Currier, Charles H. Tucker, George Nokes, John Penoyer, Lyman P. Gillett, Edward Lumley, James A. Bissell, Samuel Brown, Hiram Ferguson, William Bigelow, Charles Mitchell, Ebenezer Trumbull, Jeremiah Ferguson, Lyman

"He bought a yoke of oxen near Detroit, and his two sons - William, a young man, and Andrew, a lad - drove them in." (p. 54)

Pease, Ambrose Allen, Levi W. Harrington, Griffin Sweet, Joseph R. Briscoe, Simon Jacobus, Henry Walker, Anthony Ten Eycke, Abram Viel, Fred Van Patten, Charles Osgood, George D. Bradford, Isaiah Talmadge, James Wescott, Fifield H. Richardson, Barnard Gregory, Willis Kelley, David Strong, Seymour Van Alstine, Abram Van Alstine, Leonard Bilby, Jesse Elsworth, Cromwell McLouth, Alonzo Olds.

Charles Carmichael moved into the township in the month of October, 1835. He left his old home in 1834, and came to Michigan. He tarried about one year a little south of Adrian, and then in October, 1835, came to this township. He came alone and commenced building a house. He boarded with Eli Eastman, who lived in a small, one-roomed log house. There was a large emigration that year, and many land-lookers, and the house was full of people day and night. Mr. Carmichael says Mrs. Eastman kept the table spread all the time, and all were welcome: at night they lodged on the floor, and the floor was covered nightly.

Henry Carmichael came December 24th, 1835. He was an unmarried man, and had stopped in Ohio the year previous, when the family were coming through that State on their way to Michigan, and taught school for several months. He entered his land in 1836.

During the winter of 1834–35 Stephen Knapp and his boys fenced a part of their wind-fall lands, and in the spring planted eight acres to corn. There were only two log heaps on the eight acres, and it plowed as easily as sward land.

Going to mill was no easy task in those days, although they went no farther than Adrian or Tecumseh. From four to five days was the usual time, but Mr. Knapp went to mill once when it took eleven days to make the round trip. While outward bound and waiting for the grinding it rained so hard that bridges were carried off and the causeways submerged; the bridges had to be rebuilt and the causeways repaired before the return trip could be accomplished.

Sometime in the summer of 1835 Edmund B. Brown—or Burrows Brown, as he was called—sold out his property in this township and traveled westward. In 1852 he owned a pleasant and valuable farm on the shore of Sand Lake, in St. Joseph county. In the fall of that year, while grinding cider apples, he was bitten by a horse; his arm was so badly mangled that amputation was necessary, but this he refused to have done, and he died.

Seaton Hoxie was a justice of the peace, whether appointed by Territorial authority or elected by the people at their first township meeting does not appear. He was not very highly educated, and it was difficult for him to follow the forms of the law, or to understand the necessity or utility of so doing. Being called upon to swear a party to an affidavit in attachment, he put it in these terms: "You swear by G—d that you are afraid of your pay." But this is no more amusing than the performance of that other man, who, seventeen years later, desiring to be sworn to an affidavit, the officer having administered the usual oath,—"You do solemnly swear that the statements set forth in the affidavit by you subscribed are true,"—pulled off his hat and assuming a grave aspect answered, "Yes, by G—d, I do."

Among those who purchased land in town seven south, range one west, during the year 1835, were the following: Samuel Van Fleet, Joseph Webster, John L. Edmonds, George W. Merrick, George Williams, Henry Rose, Stephen Clapp, Peter W. Dean, Joel Alexander, Bowen Whitney, William Edmonds, William Donaldson, Olive Howard, Asa Worden, Warren Day, Charles Howard, Lewis Nickerson, David Strunk, John Williams, Samuel Starkweather, Harvey A. Anderson, Henry Lindenbower, John Osborn, Lewis Woodruff, James Grant, John Perrin, John Berger, Reuben Davis, Samuel Lawrence, Stephen B. Johnson, Elijah K. Blythe, Ira Rose, John B. Broklebank, Elijah B. Seeley, James B. Marry, Joseph Maxson, Reuben Mallory, William H. Davis, Sidney S. Ford, Charles Boyle, Julia Seeley, Michael Stuck, Jr., Theron B. Seeley, Archibald Dunn, Stephen W. Perrin, Israel Smith, Theron Skeel, James Wheeler, Charles Helm, Nathan G. Elliott, Charles Converse, Henry W. Seymour, Charles Spear, Henry Barton, Archibald Mercer.

In the spring of 1835 Theodore, son of Charles Ames, died. He obtained access to the medicine chest and drank from a vial of wintergreen oil. Rufus Estes was immediately dispatched to Adrian for a doctor, but before the doctor arrived he was dead, having died within twenty-six hours after drinking the oil.

On the fourth day of September, 1835, the wife of Henry Ames died at the house of Charles Ames. During her illness she had been removed for convenience of nursing from the house on the Clark Ames farm to the residence of Charles Ames.

In the spring of 1835 Mr. Alpheus Pratt set out an orchard of thirty-two trees. These he purchased of Jesse Maxson, who had brought them from the State of New York, and he carried all of them on his back at one time from Jesse Maxson's farm to his own house, a distance of two and one-half miles. He paid eight dollars for the trees, and he says it was all the money he could raise.

In the fall of 1835 the citizens of town seven south, one west, met at the house of Alpheus Pratt to consider the propriety of asking the Legislature, at its next session soon to be held, to organize the township. They determined that it would be proper to do so, and decided to call the township Dover. The petition was signed by Charles Ames, Jonathan French, John L. Taylor, William B. Ames, Ozen Keith, Daniel Loomis, Elijah B. Seeley, Jesse Kimball, James Sprague, Samuel Day, Robert Worden, Robinson H. Whitehorn, Lewis Gillett and Jesse Smith.

In the fall of 1835 Isaac A. Colvin bought a stock of merchandise, a large part of which was whisky and tobacco, and opened a store on the Charles Ames farm. He occupied a small building nearly opposite the large building used as a cheese factory by the late Charles Ames. In 1834 William Ames and Pennock engaged in the shoe business in Adrian, but now William, having closed his business there, was installed chief salesman in "Colvin's grocery." The grocery was the center of attraction of the settlement. The settlers were working very hard felling timber. In all directions the sound of falling timber could be heard—in some directions almost continually; and the grocery was the only place at which to procure the little delicacies of life, such as pipes and tobacco, and the more substantial comforts in the grocery line, and it became the center of traffic. Here the Indians brought their furs and game and exchanged for tobacco and the much used "fire water." Their encampment was at what was then known as the Squawfield, on the little St. Joseph, in the township of Pittsford. This St. Joseph river rises in Hillsdale county, flows southerly, and unites with the Maumee river, and is called on the maps the "St. Joseph of the Maumee," and must not be mistaken by the reader for that other St. Joseph which takes its rise in the vicinity of the head waters of the first and flows westward into Lake Michigan.

Their chief, Meteau, his son John (Indian John the settlers called him) acting as interpreter, was their principal trafficker. He carried the purse of the tribe. They would have nothing to do with paper currency—their medium of exchange was silver only, which they called *shuniah*. Having disposed of their articles they would purchase their bags full of corn and turnips, and such other articles as they needed, not for once forgetting the indispensable whisky, and then return to camp.

William kept a bottle standing on the shelf, from which he dealt out the whisky by the drink to those who only wanted that quantity at a time. One day Meteau came alone to make the purchases of the tribe, and having learned William's ways, walked up to where the bottle stood and waited for his drink. The bottle and tumbler were set down; he turned out a tumbler full, paid his six cents, and drank his whisky. He sat down and smoked for a long time, and then walking up, repeated the operation, again taking a tumbler full, and retiring to enjoy his pipe. William was alone and he began to fear that the Indian meant mischief, for becoming intoxicated he might also become quarrelsome. In such an event the Indian would have much the advantage, for he was armed with two large knives and a large cavalry pistol. Meteau came up for a third drink. William tried to make him understand that it would take him down. The Indian, evidently understanding William's fears, and determined on getting his drink, said, "Give whisky, marche quick," thereby meaning if William would give him another drink he would go away. William gave him the drink, but the Indian did not seem disposed to go home. William stepped up to him and told him to go away home. Meteau, saying "I shoot you," drew his pistol and pointed it at William, who quickly struck it with his hand, and throwing the muzzle upward the ball passed over his head; then fearing that he would draw his knife, William closed in, and after a severe struggle succeeded in throwing him on the floor, where he held him until he became so drunk he could not help but lie still. William then disarmed him and drew him forth to rest upon the snow without. Henry Ames in the meantime coming in, as soon as Meteau could stand they filled his bag with corn and turnips and started him home; but he only went a little way, built a fire on Pennock's place, the Finney farm, and sat down in the snow all night. In the morning he returned to the grocery and asked for his pistol. Ames told him he must "marche quick"—he tried to shoot William, and he could not have it. In about a week he returned and laid upon the counter a nicely dressed twenty-four pound wild turkey. William walked up and laid down a twenty-five cent piece and said, "Swap?" Meteau, smiling, said, "Very good." William sat the bottle down, they drank and smoked together, the feud was healed and they were friends; and William was duly installed the Indian trader for Squawfield, which arrangement continued until the Indians were removed west.

Soon after this settlement with Meteau, Bawbeese and some other Indians came to Colvin's grocery for more whisky. William told them if he sold them whisky and they did any damage he was liable to be fined twenty-five dollars. They plead so hard, and so faithfully promised to do no harm, William gave them some to drink. Then they wanted some to carry to a sick squaw. A half pint was given them for that purpose, but it has always been supposed that the squaw got well without it. The next morning a man came in and reported that the Indians, passing Mr. Barrett's house just as his supper was ready, gathered round the table and ate every bit of it, and as they evidently had been drinking they were supposed to have obtained their liquor at Colvin's grocery. But William, with that innocence of expression and apparently honest appearance which have not yet forsaken him, professed entire ignorance of any such transaction, and the matter passed off without investigation.

An Indian died near the present residence of Bishop Ames, and the Indians buried him near by in a sitting posture. They prepared a grave of such a depth that in a sitting position his head would be one foot below the surface of the ground. After placing him in the grave they repaired to Colvin's grocery to obtain a bottle of whisky for the dead Indian to carry with him to the hunting grounds of the Great Spirit. William's theological training being at that day rather deficient, he told them the Indian did not need it; but they insisting, William filled a half pint bottle and repaired with them to the grave. They placed the bottle in the dead Indian's hand and covered him to the chin with earth, and covered the grave over with bark. They then commenced a mournful howl, which continued for some time, and then saying "Hawkebe,"—gone to sleep,—they left him to pursue his journey alone.

Whisky was sold for thirty-eight cents a gallon at the Colvin grocery, but if we may judge from the following story told of Father Alpheus Pratt, it contained quite as much spring water as corn juice. The story, for the truth of which we will not vouch, runs as follows: In mid-winter Alpheus Pratt and Samuel Day prepared to go to mill. Alpheus having some knowledge of the effect of frost upon human bodies, provided himself with a pint of Colvin's whisky, which he hid in one of his bags. When two-thirds, perhaps, of the journey had been accomplished and they had wearied themselves whipping arms and stamping feet, Pratt slapped Day upon the shoulder, saying, "Well, neighbor Day, let's take something to warm us up." "Have you anything?" asked Mr. Day. "Certainly," said Mr. Pratt; "I have some of Colvin's best whisky, and it will send the blood tingling through our benumbed limbs and give us courage for the journey." While talking, he had undone the bag and produced the bottle. His changed looks told the story—the whisky had frozen solid.

A Dutchman named Johnson occupied the house on William Ames' farm. He had been having the ague so long he had been shaken nearly to death, without being able to seriously disturb it by all the means known to the early settlers. One night a bear that would weigh between two and three hundred pounds thrust his paw through the glass of the window, with a savage growl that scared the Dutchman gray and effectually cured him of the ague. To use his expression, "scared it out of him."

A laughable, yet serious, incident occurred among a party of hunters during the fall or early part of the winter. Jesse Smith and his son William Smith were hunting in company, and Thomas Lewin was out by himself. While Jesse was sitting beside a log he was espied by Thomas, peering through the brush, and mistaken for a turkey. Thomas blazed away, putting a bullet through Mr. Smith's arm just below the shoulder. The old man's cries discovered to Thomas his mistake; he assisted him home and then went for Dr. Hall, who lived near Devil's Lake, to dress the wound. When everything had been done to make the patient comfortable, Thomas returned home. His father had heard of the adventure, told Thomas he should hunt no more, and demanded a surrender of the gun. Thomas did not surrender unconditionally. A struggle for the possession of the rifle ensued, during which it was discharged. the ball inflicting a flesh wound in the old man's arm, passed through the chamber floor. Thomas succeeded in keeping possession of the gun and made good his escape to the woods.

On the second day of January, 1836, Mr. John Griswold and family, then late of Ontario county, New York, arrived at the house of William Frazee, on the southwest corner of section nineteen, Hudson, where William Ocobock now lives. They had made the journey by team and wagon, at first coming to Adrian, thence to Canandaigua, west on the town line (as near as roads then ran on lines) to the county line, and thence northerly to Mr. Frazee's residence. Mr. Griswold found only the following houses on his route from Canandaigua, viz: That of Mr. J. R. Foster, near the present Tiffin mills, Elder Warner, near the northwest corner of section four, Medina, and Whitbeck, on town line, half mile east of the west line of the towns. The family stayed with Mr. Frazee until Monday morning,—the day of their arrival being Saturday,—when they removed to the house of Ira Rose, where they remained until a log house could be built. Before coming, Mr. Griswold had purchased the northeast quarter of the southeast quarter of section twenty-four, town seven south, one west, of John B. Brocklebank, who had entered it the year previous. Here, now, Mr. Griswold built a log house, into which he moved his family a few weeks later. On this place, just beyond the southwest corner of the village of Hudson, he lived more than thirty-five years. He died April 17th, 1874, aged eighty-seven years. Mrs. Griswold preceded him about two years, having died April 8th, 1872.

January eighth the village of Keene was platted by Charles Ames. The village was all on the farm lately owned by him in the township of Pittsford.

As has before been remarked in these pages, persons desiring to find homes, and land speculators as well, were very active during the year 1835. In this one year nearly all the land in the present townships of Seneca, Medina and Wright was purchased of the Government. Among the persons who purchased land in town eight south, one west, were these, viz: On section 4—Gates, Lothrop & Olney, Lewis M. Gates and Charles Converse, Feb. 15th; N. Bryant, Nov. 4th; David Short, Nov. 16th. Section 5—Lewis Gates, July 15th; Mary Marshal and Royal Raymond, Nov. 3d; John M. Lickley, Nov. 7th; David Short, Nov. 16th. Section 6—Christopher Clement, Oct. 17th; Royal Raymond, Nov. 3d; Wilber Ames, Nov. 7th. Section 7—Jonathan Howland, Oct. 24th; Samuel Miller, Nov. 2d; Stephen Thorn and S. D. Daken, Nov. 9th. Section 8—Michael Lickley, Nov. 7th; Moses Moore, Nov. 9th; Stephen Thorn, James Sager and James Thorn, Nov. 10th. Section 9—Lewis M. Gates, July 15th; John B. Skinner, July 31st; David Short, Nov. 16th. Section 10—Lewis M. Gates, July 15th;

John B. Skinner, July 23d; A. S. Berry, Nov. 12th. Section 11—Alexander Duncan, July 6th. Section 12—Job S. Littlefield, June 26th; Alexander Duncan, July 6th; Asa D. Reed, July 18th; Thomas C. Sawyer, Sept. 30th; William Cavender and Arthur Lucas, Oct. 7th. Section 13—Alexander Duncan, July 6th; Thomas C. Sawyer, Sept. 29th. Section 14—Alexander Duncan, July 4th; Hiram Lucas, Oct. 7th; A. J. Comstock, Dec. 26th. Section 15—Nathaniel Silsbee, July 30th; Samuel Coman, Oct. 7th. Section 17—Isaac M. Sturgis, Nov. 9th; Stephen Thorn, J. Sawyer, Nov. 10th; Nathan Birdsall, Dec. 12th. Section 18—David Short, Nov. 16th. Section 20—Joseph R. Williams, Nov. 10th; Jane Shute, Nov. 26th. Section 21—Joseph R. Williams. Section 22—Alexander Duncan, July 6th; Joshua Tompkins, July 18th; Samuel Coman, Oct. 7th. Section 23—Alexander Duncan, July 6th; William Tappenden, July 9th; William Raleigh, Oct. 27th. Section 24—William Tappenden, July 7th; Alexander Duncan, July 21st. Section 25—Thomas Smith, July 9th; Benjamin F. Bown, Dec. 10th. Section 26—Thomas Smith, July 9th; Henry P. Gardener, Oct. 27th. Section 27—Langford G. Berry, Nov. 12th. Section 29—Charles H. Conall, Oct. 20th; Jane Shute, Nov. 26th. Section 31—Charles H. Conall entered entire section Oct. 20th.

In the spring and summer of 1835 Mrs. Hiram Lucas, then a resident of the village of Adrian, wrote her father, Samuel Coman, then residing at or near Rome, in the State of New York, such glowing descriptions of the emigrants' Eldorado—the Bean Creek Country—that he resolved to move Westward. He wrote his son Russell, then residing in Dearborn county, Indiana, to meet him at Adrian on such a day in the month of September, for the purpose of assisting in the location of homes for his large family of boys. They met in Adrian according to appointment, and accompanied by Hiram Lucas, they proceeded to Canandaigua. There they obtained the services of Arthur Lucas and Calvin Pixley as guides through the wilderness. They at once proceeded to town eight south, one west, and selected lands on sections fifteen and twenty-two; and on his way home Samuel Coman stopped at Monroe and entered the land on the 7th day of October, 1835. The entire party, guides and all, must have been captivated by the beauty of the country, for on the same day Hiram Lucas, Calvin Pixley and Arthur Lucas all entered land in the township. Indeed, it was just the time of year when men would be captivated by a primeval American forest. The gigantic trees newly dressed in their autumn costumes of red, yellow, and purple leaves; large bunches of fox grapes pendant from clinging vine, the continual falling of mast loosened by the early frosts; the woods filled with the more valuable species of game, bounding, running, or flying away at the approach of the strange visitor, man, formed a scene likely to enamor more obdurate hearts.

The two Comans, father and son, returned to their respective homes to prepare for emigration. Russell, immediately on reaching home, packed his goods, which he loaded in a Hoosier wagon with his wife and three children, the wagon drawn by two yoke of oxen, and started for Michigan. Mr. Russell Coman had left the parental home, in the State of New York, in the year 1825. He purchased a small boat, which he loaded onto a wagon, the boat serving as a box, and, accompanied by a young man, he conveyed to, and launched it upon, the head waters of the Ohio river. In this boat they dropped down the Ohio to the mouth of the Miami river. There he disembarked and found a home in Dearborn county, Indiana, where he lived until 1835. March 12th, 1829, he inter-married with Miss Ann McMath, and their union was blessed with three Indiana-born children, one of which was an infant at the breast when the journey to Michigan began. After their arrival at Adrian the youngest child died. Mr. Coman employed Hiram and Arthur Lucas to help him build a house, and meanwhile the family was left at Hiram's house, in Adrian. The house was so far completed that the family moved into it sometime between Christmas, 1835, and New Year's day, 1836. Russell Coman's family was the first, and until February the only family in town eight south, one west. The house thus built and occupied was built on section fifteen, where Samuel Coman, the elder, afterwards resided for many years, on the farm now owned by Jacob Shanour.

THE TOLEDO WAR.

The story of the settlement of the Valley of the Bean would be incomplete without some mention of an event which divided it between two States and robbed our Valley of the townships of Gorham and Chesterfield, and Lenawee of those, and also the townships of Royalton, Amboy and Richfield. On the sixth day of July, 1834, Governor Porter, who had succeeded Mr. Cass as Governor of the Territory, died, by which event Stevens T. Mason, of Virginia, Secretary of the Territory, became the acting Governor. January 26th, 1835, the Legislative Council passed an act for the election of delegates to a constitutional convention, and the convention convened on the 11th day of May following. This movement toward the organization of a State government for Michigan invested the territorial dispute with new interest. The territory in dispute was a strip along the line between the States, from the Indiana line to Lake Erie, five miles wide at the west end and eight miles wide at the east end. The southern line, claimed by Michigan to be the boundary, was known as the "Fulton line," and the northern line, claimed by Ohio to be the boundary, was called the "Harris line." This belt of territory contained some very valuable farming land, but its chief value in the eyes of the contestants was the port at the mouth of the Maumee river, known successively as Swan Creek, Port Lawrence, Vistula, and Toledo. Outside of Toledo the disputed country was a wilderness. The early settlers of the territory acknowledged their allegiance to the government of Michigan, asked for and received appropriations for the building of roads leading to their village, and some of them became corporators of the Erie and Kalamazoo railroad, under a charter from the Legislative Council of the Territory of Michigan. But when the Wabash and Erie canal became a possibility, and its eastern terminus at Toledo probable, if that place should be found to be within the limits of Ohio, many of her citizens at once discovered that they were citizens of Ohio, whereas they had heretofore acted as citizens of Michigan. Some, however, still acknowledged the sovereignty of Michigan. Governor Mason, having been apprised of the proposed action of the authorities of Ohio, sent a special message to the Legislative Council, recommending immediate action to forestall that of the Ohio Legislature.

On the 12th day of February the Legislative Council enacted "That if any person residing within the limits of this territory shall accept of any office of trust from any State or authority other than the Government of the United States or Territory of Michigan, every person so offending shall be fined not exceeding one thousand dollars, or be imprisoned five years, at the discretion of the court before which any conviction may be had."

In the same month the Legislature of Ohio passed an act extending the jurisdiction of that State over the disputed territory, established townships and directed that township elections should be held in the April following, and also directed the re-marking of the Harris line.

March ninth, Gov. Mason wrote Gen. Brown, then in command of the Michigan militia, to hold himself in readiness to repel by force any attempt to carry out the provisions of the Ohio law; and later in the month Gov. Mason, and Gen. Brown and staff, with from eight hundred to twelve hundred men, encamped in and around Toledo.

On the thirty-first day of March, Gov. Lucas and his commissioners arrived at Perrysburgh to find the enemy in possession of the bone of contention. Under his direction Gen. Bell, of the Ohio militia, mustered a force of about six hundred men and went in camp at Fort Miami. The delay was for the purpose of allowing the partisans of Ohio to hold their township elections.

While the two armies were watching each other's movements, two commissioners appointed by the President arrived from Washington. President Jackson had taken the opinion of his Attorney General, who had advised him that the act of the Legislature of Ohio extending jurisdiction over a part of the territory of Michigan was "repugnant to the act of Congress of the 11th of January, 1805," and that the act of the Michigan Legislative Council was a valid law and could properly be enforced. The commissioners proposed:

First—That the Harris line should be re-marked without hindrance.

Second—As elections had then been held under the laws of Ohio, the people should be left to obey the laws of the one jurisdiction or the other without molestation until the close of the next session of Congress.

Gov. Lucas affected to consider Gov. Mason as a minion of the President, and that the arrangement was to be made between himself and the President, and would be complete as soon as his acceptance should be signified; he therefore at once accepted the propositions and commenced disbanding his forces. On the other hand, Gov. Mason, considering himself at the head of a restricted sovereignty, refused to compromise the rights of his people by a surrender of possession and jurisdiction, and, therefore, while he allowed his forces to return home, held himself in readiness to repel by force any invasion of the territorial rights of Michigan.

Notwithstanding the determined attitude of Gov. Mason, Gov. Lucas directed the commissioners to proceed to run the Harris line, commencing at the western end. Gen. Brown kept a line of scouts in the woods along the line to report the progress of the surveying party. As soon as the party came within the limits of Lenawee county the under-sheriff, armed with a warrant from a justice of the peace, and accompanied by a *posse comitatus*, went to arrest them. The force started on Sunday morning. The infantry, about one-half the force, were carried in wagons about ten miles out; from that point they had to march, about ten miles. They arrived a little after noon, the mounted men considerably in advance. The surveying party were occupying two cabins. As soon as the mounted men arrived, Gen. Brown, who accompanied the expedition, assumed command and ordered the surveyors to surrender, which they promptly refused to do. But when the infantry arrived, the occupants of one of the cabins, including the commissioners, became alarmed and broke for the woods, hastened by a volley of musketry. They dashed into Maumee nearly disrobed by the briars and thorns that beset their path through the wilderness. The occupants of the other cabin, including the engineer corps, were arrested by the officer and taken in triumph to the Lenawee county jail at Tecumseh. The civil authorities concluded to hold Col. Fletcher, the chief of the engineer corps, in nominal imprisonment to test by law the validity of the arrest. The others were permitted to return to their homes in Ohio. Col. Fletcher was allowed to be his own jailor. When he desired exercise he would carefully lock the door, and putting the key in his pocket, stroll through the village or drive out with the village belles. This first clash of arms in this singular affair occurred within the Valley of the Bean.

The Ohio commissioners reported to Gov. Lucas that they had been attacked by an overwhelming force under command of Gen. Brown, and forced to retreat. The President, to whom the matter was referred, asked Gov. Mason for a statement of facts "by the officers engaged in the transactions complained of." The under sheriff reported that a civil force made the arrest of nine persons upon a warrant issued by a justice of the peace, and that there was no blood shed. Gov. Lucas immediately convened the Legislature in extra session. It met on the 8th day of June, and at once proceeded to enact a law "to prevent the forcible abduction of citizens of Ohio." Another act was passed to create the county of Lucas, making Toledo the county seat. A session of court was directed to be held on Monday, the seventh day of September, then next ensuing, at any convenient house in Toledo. Still another act was passed appropriating $600,000 to carry these laws into effect over the disputed territory.

The authorities of Michigan were not idle. Prosecutions for holding office under he laws of Ohio were pressed with the greatest vigor. The people of Monroe county were kept busy assisting the sheriff in executing processes of the Monroe county courts in the disputed territory. Every inhabitant of the district was a spy for one or the other of the contestants, as inclination dictated, and was busily employed in reporting the movements of Monroe county or Wood county officials, as the case might be. The Ohio parties, when arrested, were incarcerated in the Monroe county jail. Major Stickney was arrested after a violent resistance by himself and family. He refused to mount a horse. He was put on by force, but would not sit there. For a long distance two men, one each side, held him on. At last, wearied by his resistance, they tied his feet under the horse, in which way they at last reached Monroe.

Gov. Lucas sent commissioners to Washington to confer with the President. After a lengthy correspondence between these commissioners and the Secretary of State, the President consented to cause an earnest recommendation to be made to Gov. Mason that no obstruction be made to the re-marking of the "Harris" line; that all prosecutions under the territorial act of February, 1835, be discontinued, and no further prosecutions be commenced until the next session of Congress. This "recommendation" was conveyed to Gov. Mason on the third day of July, but it had no effect on his action. Prosecutions went on as before. On the 15th of that month an attempt was made to arrest Two Stickney, a son of Major Stickney. In the scuffle the officer was stabbed with a knife; Stickney escaped and fled to Ohio. The wound was slight, although the blood flowed freely. Two was indicted by the grand jury of Monroe county, and a requisition made on Gov. Lucas for his surrender. The Governor refused to surrender the fugitive, and a report of the affair was sent to the President, with a sworn statement that Gov. Lucas was protecting him. This aroused the President to action; he at once removed Gov. Mason, and appointed Charles Shaler, of Pennsylvania, his successor. He also advised Gov. Lucas to refrain from any act of jurisdiction over the disputed territory pending the action of Congress. Mr. Shaler never entered upon the duties of the office, and soon after, John S. Horner, of Virginia, was appointed Secretary and acting Governor; but he did not enter upon the duties of his office until the twenty-first day of September. In the meanwhile Mason continued acting Governor.

Gov. Lucas now felt sure that Old Hickory was aroused, and that he would tolerate no more show of force on his part; but he also felt it necessary to perform some act of jurisdiction, so it would not be said he had backed down. The Legislature had ordered a session of court to be held on the seventh day of September, in the village of Toledo. Gov. Mason was aware of the fact, and was on hand with Gen. Brown and the militia to prevent the consummation of the order. To actually hold this court in defiance of Gov. Mason and his military force, and also in defiance of the President's recommendation, looked to Gov. Lucas like a grand achievement; one that would burnish his tarnished honor, and maintain the dignity of the gubernatorial office of the great State of Ohio. He, through his Adjutant General, ordered out a regiment of troops to escort the judges to Toledo, and protect them in the performance of their duty. They were to march from Maumee on the morning of the seventh, but the evening previous a report was circulated that Gen. Brown was in Toledo with twelve hundred men, ready for any emergency. The report was untrue, but it served to test the valor of the judges; they hesitated and trembled at the prospect. The Colonel in command provided a forlorn hope, and taking the judges in charge, marched them into Toledo at three o'clock Monday morning, September 7th, 1835, proceeded to a school house, held court less than five minutes, and then hastily returned to Maumee. How easily was Ohio honor vindicated. Not a soul over whom they came to assert jurisdiction knew of their coming, doings, or retreat.

September 21st, acting Governor Horner assumed the duties of that office, and Gov. Mason retired to private life.

While these events were transpiring the convention had been elected, met, formed a constitution, and adjourned. The constitution was submitted to the people on the fifth and sixth days of October, and was duly ratified. At the same election a full set of State officers were elected, Stevens T. Mason being elected Governor. Gov. Mason was at once inaugurated, the Legislature met on the ninth day of November, and the machinery of a State government set in motion. Michigan was not yet admitted as a State; the machinery of a Territorial government remained, which was recognized by the general government and the several State governments as the lawful government of Michigan; but it was totally ignored by the people, who yielded obedience to the new State government. This state of things made it very unpleasant for Mr. Horner, and in May, 1836, he left the Territory to assume the duties of Secretary of the Territory of Wisconsin, created at that session of Congress.

On the fifteenth day of June, 1836, Congress passed an act accepting the constitution and State government of Michigan, and admitting her into the Union, provided she should, by a convention of delegates chosen for that purpose, consent to the boundary line claimed by Ohio, and take in lieu thereof the territory now known as the Upper Peninsula. Gov. Mason called a special session of the Legislature, to meet on the eleventh day of July, 1836. On the twentieth day of that month, an act was passed providing for the election of delegates and the assembling of the convention on the 26th day of September, at Ann Arbor.

The convention met, and after a four days session, rejected the proposition of Congress relating to the boundary. The people were unanimous in reference to the merits of the controversy, but a large party thought deferred admission would work greater injury than loss of territory. They were therefore dissatisfied with the rejection of the proposition, and they determined that another convention should be called without waiting for the assembling of the Legislature. Two large meetings of the dissatisfied citizens were held, one in Detroit, the other in Ann Arbor. These assemblies united in a request to the Governor to call a convention by proclamation. The Governor approved of a second convention, but as it was wholly unauthorized by law, he declined to issue the proclamation. On the fourteenth day of November, a circular was issued by the leaders of the assenting party, which recommended the qualified voters in the several townships to meet on the fifth and sixth days of December and elect delegates to attend a State convention to be held at Ann Arbor on the fourteenth day of that month. It further recommended that the number of delegates be twice the number elected to the popular branch of the Legislature, and that the election should be held at the proper places for holding elections, and should be conducted by the same officers and according to the forms of law governing other elections. The opposition to the second convention refrained from voting, deeming the whole proceeding void. As but one party voted, all the delegates were in favor of accepting the proposition of Congress. Therefore, on the fifteenth day of the month—the second day of its session—the convention unanimously resolved to accept the condition imposed by Congress, protesting, however, against the constitutional right of Congress to require this preliminary assent as a condition of admission into the Union. The action of this convention was submitted to Congress. A lengthy and spirited debate ensued, but on the 26th day of January, 1837, Congress passed an act which, reciting by way of preamble that the people of Michigan had consented to the proposed boundaries, admitted the State into the Union of American States.

Since the ninth day of November, 1835, the people of Michigan had lived under a dual government. For all internal purposes the State government was supreme, but for the purpose of communion with the General and State governments, they had the machinery of a Territorial government.

ORGANIZATION OF TOWNSHIPS.

The State Legislature, by an act approved March 23d, 1836, organized several townships in the Bean Creek Valley. Town five south, one east, was named Woodstock, and the first township meeting was ordered to be held at the house of Jesse Osborn. The reader will notice that the spelling of the surname here differs from its spelling in the first sections of this book, which is explained by the statement that when the family first came to Michigan they spelled their name Osburn, but in after years they changed it to Osborn.

Town seven south, one east, was named Hudson, the first township meeting to be held at the dwelling house of Beriah H. Lane.

Towns eight and nine and fractional ten south, ranges one and two east, were organized into a township, the first township meeting to be held at the house of Jacob Baker, in town eight south, two east, and was named Seneca. Seneca then included the present townships of Medina and Seneca in Michigan, and Gorham and Chesterfield in Ohio.

The township of Wheatland was divided. Towns seven, eight and nine, and fractional ten south were organized into a township named Pittsford, and the first township meeting was directed to be held at the dwelling house of Alpheus Pratt. The people had petitioned to have it called Dover, but the committee on townships having already named town seven south two east, Dover, they named this Pittsford upon the suggestion of a man who had known Mr. Pratt in Pittsford, Monroe couty, N. Y. The township as then organized comprised the present townships of Pittsford and Wright in Michigan, and Mill Creek in Ohio.

Towns five and six south, one east, retained the name of Wheatland.

Towns six, seven, eight, nine and fractional ten south, two west, were organized into a township named Adams, and the first township meeting was directed to be held at the southeast corner of section sixteen in said town six south. The township of Adams then included the present townships of Adams, Jefferson and Ransom, the east half of Amboy in Michigan, and Madison, in Ohio.

4. HUDSON.

On the fourth day of April, 1836, the first township meeting of the township of Hudson was held at the house of Beriah H. Lane. Officers were elected as follows: Simeon VanAkin, supervisor; George Saulsbury, township clerk; Beriah H. Lane and Henry Ames, justices of the peace; Thomas Kealey, John Davenport and John Colwell, commissioners of highways; John Carleton, assessor; and Noah Cressey, treasurer. It was voted to raise fifty dollars for contingent expenses.

On the 28th day of April, Beriah H. Lane, esq., was called upon to perform a part of the duties of his office. Word was brought to the newly elected justice that Dexter Smith and Mrs. Elvira Stearns desired to unite their destinies; therefore, following an Indian trail, he wended his way to the farm of Smith, near where the village of Tiffin now is, and performed the marriage ceremony.

In May a postoffice was established and named Lanesville. Mr. Lane was postmaster. His commission bore date May 19th, and was signed by Amos Kendall, postmaster general.

In June the Rev. David Pratt came, and for two years was pastor of the Presbyterian church. He bought the piece of land known as Pratt's block, and built a house, where his widow, the sole survivor of that family, still resides.

During the summer, H. P. Oakley came and bought out George Salisbury's grocery and notion trade, and David Stuck commenced blacksmithing. In the fall Harvey Cobb came and occupied the house prepared for him by Alexander Findley. Augustus Finney came some time during the season, but did not purchase property until the next year.

Miss Adelia Champlin taught the Lanesville school in the summer of 1836. A log school house was built during the autumn. It stood on a piece of ground a little way south of the highway, on the section line, near the brow of a hill. Its position is now marked by the low, long building on east side of Church street, owned by J. K. Boies & Co., it being the second south of their store building. There then were no other buildings south of Main street between Church and Market streets. The long, low building spoken of, or rather the west end of it, was the school house of 1841, of which much has been said. It was formerly adorned with a cupola or steeple, and was used for the double purpose of a school house and church.

In the fall of 1836, the Messrs. VanAkin harvested about one hundred and fifty bushels of wheat. It grew on the square of ground bounded west by High street, north by Main street, east by Wood street, and south by the hill on which Dr. J. C. Dickinson, Mr. Webster and Thomas Bate live. It was nice wheat land, except the lots afterwards owned by Dr. R. A. Beach, which were mostly frog pond.

It was in this summer that several men associated themselves together in what was called the Great Bend Company. The project was to create a vast water power by digging a race across the neck of the bend. Immediately after crossing the section line, between sections nineteen and thirty, the creek bends to the westward, crosses into Hillsdale county about forty rods south of the north line of section thirty, bends again to the eastward on section twenty-five in Pittsford, leaves that township at the corner of section thirty-six, crosses the east line of section thirty-one, Hudson, about forty rods north of its south line; turning northward, it crosses the north line of section thirty-two, not more than forty rods east of the northwest corner of that section; it then runs northeasterly across the southeast corner of section twenty-nine, and southeasterly across the southwest corner of section twenty-eight, and thence in nearly a direct southeasterly course to the village of Medina. By constructing a race from the point near where the creek crosses the south line of section nineteen, to the

E

point on the east line of section twenty-nine, where the creek takes its southeasterly course, a distance of less than two miles, a large fall would be obtained; sufficient, indeed, to propel all the machinery it were possible to build on the route. In order to accomplish the project, it was necessary to procure the right to turn the water of the Bean from its natural channel, and the right to do so must be purchased, the company buying water rights where they could, and where they could not buying the land right out. The first purchases made in the furtherance of the project were made by Isaac French on the 18th day of July, 1836. On that day he bought the Samuel Davis farm, and about the same time purchased the farm of Horace Hitchcock. The two farms here spoken of are now owned, the first by Joseph Fletcher, and the second by Henry Carmichael.

In September following, David Tucker came on, as the purchasing agent of the company. The first purchase he made was the undivided one-half of the Lanesville mill and mill property. It was deeded to him September second by Beriah H. Lane. There must have been some private arrangement between Simeon and William H. H. VanAkin and Mr. Lane, for at that time Mr. Lane had no title to the property, as shown by the record. In July of 1835 he had deeded a one-fourth interest to William H. H. VanAkin, and in December of the same year had sold the remainder of his interest—one-fourth part—to Simeon VanAkin. The other one-half interest was owned by Erastus Lane until February 16th, 1837, when he deeded it to Augustus Finney. On the 20th day of July, 1837, William H. H. VanAkin re-deeded a one-half interest in the mill to Beriah H. Lane, but he does not appear to have taken any possessory right, as that half of the property continued to be owned by various members of the Great Bend Company until it was abandoned in 1842.

Tucker bought the following lands: Of John Davenport, the south half of the middle subdivision of the southwest fractional quarter of section nineteen; of Joseph Reynolds, the west half of the southwest quarter of section twenty; of William Woods, the south half of the northeast quarter of section twenty-nine; of Elisha Brown, the southeast quarter of the southwest quarter and the northeast quarter of the southwest quarter of section twenty-nine; of Harmon Whitbeck, jr., the east half of the southwest fractional quarter of section thirty; of William Chapman, the northwest quarter of the southwest quarter of section thirty-four; of Frederick Corey, the east half of the southwest quarter and the southwest quarter of the southwest quarter of section thirty-four: of Nicholas Fratts, the east half of the southeast quarter of section eighteen; and of Harvey Cobb, the southwest quarter of the southeast quarter of section eighteen.

He also bargained for the land of Simeon VanAkin, for which he was to pay $4,750. He paid $1,500 down, and took a contract for a deed on the payment of the remainder of the purchase money, which was to be paid within ninety days from the date of the contract. The remainder never was paid, but Tucker assigned his interest in the contract to Joel McCollum, of Rochester, N. Y., and subsequent to the expiration of the contract McCollum came to Lanesville and offered to pay $400 on the contract. McCollum says VanAkin accepted it, and it was indorsed on the contract, and that, McCollum says, renewed it for all time. Such was the foundation of the McCollum claim, which our older readers will remember to have heard so much about.

Tucker also purchased of Sylvester Kenyon and William Frazee the right to divert the water from its channel. The description in Kenyon's deed reads as follows: "The full and free privilege, right and authority to alter or change the course of the waters of Bean creek, so as entirely forever to direct and control its waters, or any part or portion thereof, from its present channel or bed, where it now runs (except so much as is necessary for farming purposes)." The description in Frazee's deed is the same, except that the exception in regard to water for farm purposes is omitted.

Tucker bought other lands in this township, and also some in the township of Pittsford. These lands, rights and privileges Tucker deeded over to the members of the Great Bend Company, the larger part of them to Benjamin F. Southworth, of

Monroe county. Thus the lands purchased during the months of September and October he deeded to Benjamin F. Southworth on the 29th day of October, except the land purchased of Elisha Brown. This land he deeded, part to Elisha Brown, and the remainder to Lorenzo L. Brown.

This Great Bend project was much talked of during this and the following year, but the financial panic of 1837 bankrupted its projectors, and put an end to the venture. Before this, however, Tucker had to leave the country. He had left a wife and family at the east when he came to Michigan, but at Adrian, which was his headquarters, he passed as an unmarried man. At length, however, yielding to the fascinations of an Adrian lady, he put his head into the matrimonial noose. Mrs. Tucker No. 1, having been apprised of his doings, threatened to make it warm for him, and he left the country. A son of the first Mrs. Tucker has twice visited the country and threatened to press his mother's claim for dower, but beyond scaring a few men into settlement, he has done nothing.

As a great deal has been said about the ancient saw mill of Lanesville, it may be well to stop here and give the history of that pioneer institution. The land—the middle subdivision of the southwest fractional quarter of section eighteen—was purchased of the government by Reuben Davis in March, 1834. On the twenty-third day of July, 1834, Reuben Davis deeded the land to Erastus and Beriah H. Lane, except one-half acre on the brow of the hill east of the creek. Davis afterwards sold this half acre to John Davenport, but it was, later still, absorbed by the railroad. Erastus and Beriah H. Lane built the mill in the summer and fall of 1834. On the eighth day of July, 1835, Beriah H. Lane deeded an undivided one-fourth interest to William H. H. VanAkin, and on the first day of December he sold an undivided one-fourth interest to Simeon VanAkin. September 2d, 1836, Beriah H. Lane deeded a one-half interest in the mill land and fixtures to David Tucker, and October 29th Tucker deeded the same interest to Benj. F. Southworth. February 16th Erastus Lane deeded the other undivided one-half interest in the mill, land and flowage to Augustus Finney. On the 20th day of July William H. H. VanAkin deeded an undivided one-half of the mill property to Beriah H. Lane. This transfer perfected the title of Tucker and his assigns in a one-half interest in the mill property. February 28th, 1838, Benjamin F. Southworth conveyed an undivided one-half of the mill property to William L. Riggs. April 18th William L. Riggs conveyed it to Philo C. Fuller, and by another deed, made the same day, deeded it to Isaac French. January 27th, 1840, Isaac French deeded it to William V. Studdeford, and July 11th William V. Studdeford deeded it to Augustus Finney, who then became the owner of the entire mill property. On the 12th day of September, 1842, Augustus Finney deeded the mill property to Ed H. Winans. Soon afterward Winans deeded the land to Isaac French, but in that deed no mention was made of the mill or race. The old mill race took the water from the creek a little way above the railway embankment, west side, and discharged it between the railroad and Main street bridges. The depression in which Bean's pump factory, Benjamin Wright's, Nathaniel Lane's and George W. Carter's shops are built is the old tail race. The mill was situated on the hill beside the race, a little south of the railroad ground, perhaps just in rear of the house occupied by Mr. Homer Rawson.

But to return to the incidents of 1836. On the 24th day of December Harvey Anderson purchased a half interest in the Kidder mill.

In January, 1837, the Legislature of the State passed the Internal Improvement Act, providing for three lines of railroad across the State, the southern to span the State from Monroe to New Buffalo; and in pursuance of that act commissioners were appointed to locate the routes. Of course the people of this part of the Valley were excited. Upon the location of the Southern road depended, in a great measure, their future welfare. The commissioners at once determined the principal points on the route, viz: Adrian, Hillsdale Center, as it was then called, Coldwater, Constantine, etc. As we shall not have occasion to refer to this matter again, it may as well be remarked in passing that Constantine was not finally made a point on the road, in consequence of the road being turned into Northern Indiana. The causes of its deflection do not come within the purview of this work. The direct route between Adrian and Hillsdale Center lay through or near the village of Rollin. The inhabitants of the twin villages, Lenawee and Keene, desired to deflect the road two miles from a straight line to accommodate them, and the Lanesvillans desired to deflect it three miles to accommodate them. Of the three proposed routes the Lanesville route was the most unlikely to be adopted. The Lenawee and Keene folks had a better route to offer in place of the shorter Rollin route, but the Lanesville route was the longest and most difficult of the three, and if a company had been locating the road it would have taken a mint of eagles to buy it from its proper course. The result proved the correctness of the old saw, "Where there is a will there is a way." In the person of Augustus Finney, Lanesville possessed a valuable agent for the accomplishment of her purposes. Gentlemanly in appearance and pleasant in address, and having an eloquent and persuasive tongue, he was just the man to make "the worse appear the better reason." Added to the above qualifications were these: He had a perfect knowledge of human nature, could read character like an open book, and was not over scrupulous in the use of means. He was put together for a diplomat, but the times being out of joint, he never graced the station for which he was intended.

Mr. Finney also possessed a personal interest in the location of the road. He had purchased a half interest in the saw mill, and five acres of land with a frontage extending from Market to Church street. In the spring of 1837, a few weeks after the appointment of the commissioners—Levi S. Humphrey, of Monroe, being one—Mr. Finney appeared at Monroe to advocate the claims of the Lanesville route. A public meeting was convened in the Court House to listen to the statements and arguments of the Lanesville orator. It did not take much to arouse the enthusiasm of Monroe city people then. The Toledo war was but just closed, and the State but three months admitted under the hated compromise that robbed them of a harbor. The State had just borrowed five millions of dollars, and was going to build them a railroad across the State. Monroe was to become the metropolis of Michigan, while the ague-shaken denizens of Toledo would hover over the swamps that environ the place, until their bloodless bodies should find a sepulcher in her miry soil. Under such a state of feeling the Court House was easily filled with the business men of Monroe. Mr. John C. Hogaboam, then a citizen of Monroe, was present and heard the address of Mr. Finney. He spoke of the beautiful country around Lanesville, and of the fertility of the soil; but principally of the mammoth water power about to be created near by, by the famous Great Bend race; the power would be estimated by the thousand horse power, and the machinery driven would not only equal, but would surpass the greatest manufacturing cities of the world. Then he recounted the names of the members of the Great Bend Company, emphasizing the names of their own townsmen interested in the venture, and dwelt on each branch of the subject, until the audience fancied they saw a great manufacturing town on the Bean, only fifty miles away, furnishing the food, the furniture, and the clothing for the hundred thousand inhabitants of the city of Monroe.

Satisfying the people paved the way for labor with the commissioners. However well satisfied they might be of the growing importance of Lanesville, still they must be governed in a great measure by the reports of the surveyors who should run the preliminary lines, and these would not be run until the autumn. When the reports were in, the fullest consideration would be given each of the proposed routes, so said the commissioners. It was, therefore, necessary to attend to the surveyors from whom the report was expected. The preliminary surveys were made in the autumn of 1837, but the road was not established until the fall of 1838. During all that time the question was open, and argument, persuasion, and more substantial inducements were the order of the day.

July 24th Levi N. Bowlsby, one of the surveyors, became the owner of six and eighty-three one-hundredths acres of land in Lanesville. The tract now known as the Bowlsby plat is a part of that purchase. The consideration mentioned in the deed is four hundred and twenty dollars. A member of the engineer corps, within a few years, speaking of the location of the road at Lanesville, said "there were visions of corner lots never realized." Whether he meant the citizens did not fulfill their promises, or that Bowlsby did not divide, is unknown.

Whether the inhabitants of the other routes offered any substantial inducements is unknown, but the probability is they relied upon their superior route, and deemed it impossible that the road would be laid on the longest and hardest route, until its location was fixed, and then offers were useless. The inducements operating on the minds of surveyors and commissioners will probably never be known, but that they did locate the Michigan Southern Railroad between Adrian and Hillsdale on the most ineligible route is a fact that can never be obliterated. The State commenced to take conveyances of right of way between Adrian and Hudson in November, 1838. The release of Stephen Allen bears date November 28th.

In the spring of 1838 Mr. Finney brought his wife to Lanesville, and lived in a house that then stood near where the Friend bakery now is. Here he kept tavern—the original Hudson tavern.

HARD TIMES—CAUSES, Etc.

It becomes necessary here to notice another series of events that had an important bearing upon the development of the Valley, as well as Michigan in general. At the beginning of 1837 there were sixteen chartered banks in the State; nine of them were chartered by the Territorial Legislative Council, and seven by the State Legislature of 1836. The following is a list of the banks, in the order of their organization: Michigan, Detroit; Monroe, Monroe; Pontiac, Pontiac; River Raisin, Monroe; Washtenaw, Ann Arbor; Erie and Kalamazoo, Adrian; Farmers' and Mechanics', Detroit; Michigan State, Detroit; Merchants' and Mechanics', Detroit; St. Clair, St. Clair; Clinton, Clinton; Calhoun, Marshall; Oakland County, Pontiac; Constantine, Constantine; Ypsilanti, Ypsilanti; and Manhattan at Manhattan, Monroe county.

It would seem as though these sixteen banks ought to do the business of this then new State, but on the 15th day of March, 1837, the Legislature enacted a law providing for the incorporation of moneyed institutions. This law provided that any number of men might associate together, subscribe fifty thousand dollars for a capital stock, and by filing articles of association with the county clerk, become incorporate. One-third of the capital must be owned in the county, ten per cent. be paid in before election of directors, and thirty per cent. before bank notes should be issued. The law also contained this *restrictive* clause: "It shall not be lawful for any such banking association to issue, or have outstanding or in circulation at any time, an amount of notes or bills loaned or put in circulation as money exceeding *twice and a half* the amount of its stock then paid in and actually possessed; nor shall its loans and discounts at any time exceed *twice and a half* the amount of its capital stock so paid in and possessed."

This was bad enough, but a subsequent statute allowed them to deposit, instead of specie, a bond secured on real estate. Under the operation of this law hundreds of banks sprang into existence. Nearly every cross road had its bank, and it is indeed a wonder that the inhabitants of the Bean Creek Country could forego the luxury of a banking association. Every kind of property was quoted at inflated prices and wild land, valued at three or four times its actual value, became the security for the bank circulation of Michigan. These banks, on account of the character of their securities, were called wild cat banks, and the old banks were known as chartered banks. Banks of the wild cat species existed in Adrian, in Tecumseh, and in Palmyra, in Lenawee county.

About the time these wild cats had got to work, the country experienced one of

those financial panics which so frequently shake commercial communities to their
very center. In order that the reader may understand the subject, it will be necessary briefly to trace the causes which produced this disaster. In December, 1816, a
new United States bank was chartered for a term of twenty years. This institution,
located at Philadelphia, became in the course of years the center of business interest.
It was the custodian of the moneys of the government, and the government was the
owner of a considerable amount of its stock; it could and did control the rates of discount; it could make or break private or State banks by a bestowal or withdrawal of
its confidence, and as it controlled the pockets of the nation, so it began to also control
its opinions and political action. President Jackson attacked the bank in his first
annual message, 1829, and returned to the attack in the annual messages of 1830 and
1831. Notwithstanding the hostility of the President, Congress, in July, 1832, passed
an act granting the bank a new charter. This act the President promptly vetoed, but
its failure produced no immediate effect, as the old charter did not expire until December, 1836.

The Presidential campaign of 1832 was then in progress. Jackson was nominated
for re-election, and the re-chartering of the bank was one of the issues between parties at that election. Jackson was re-elected, and with him a House of Representatives sympathizing with his financial views. In his message of that year the President
recommended the removal of the deposits and the sale of the bank stock belonging to
the United States. So thoroughly entrenched was the bank in the business
interests of the country that Congress dare not make the attack. But so soon as Congress had adjourned, the President directed the Secretary of the Treasury to remove
the deposits. The Secretary, Mr. William J. Duane, hesitated. There were about
$10,000,000 of government funds in the bank; the bank loans amounted to $60,000,000,
and were so distributed as to effect almost every hamlet in the nation, and the Secretary had not sufficient courage to jostle the monster that might easily crush whole
parties, and whose destruction, if accomplished, would bring ruin on almost every
business house, and whose dying throes would be felt in every household in the land.
The President at length made a peremptory order to remove the money, and to deposit
it in certain State banks. The Secretary promptly refused, and the President as
promptly removed him and appointed Roger B. Taney, of Maryland, to the Secretary's
office. The business community were startled, and prophecies of wide-spread disaster freely made, but an iron hand was at the helm of State, and nothing would stay
its work or change its purpose. The new Secretary commenced the removal in October, 1833; the greater part was removed within four months, and the entire work was
completed within nine months. The designated State banks received the deposits,
and to relieve the threatened financial disaster discounted freely. Indeed, the deposit
of the national funds among several rival banks stimulated reckless speculation.
Each bank was anxious to do more business than its neighbor, and therefore in every
possible way made money easily obtainable. They believed the money would remain
until needed by the government for ordinary governmental purposes, and therefore
treated it as so much capital, and increased their circulation in proportion to the deposit. Money was plenty, and business was unduly stimulated. The importation of
foreign goods was largely increased, leaving large balances on the debtor side of the
ledger. These balances had to be paid in gold, which was at a considerable premium.
Internal improvements and all the industrial pursuits were inordinately stimulated,
and reckless speculation, especially in real estate, was largely indulged in, which in
1836 amounted to a mania. Says Lossing, "A hundred cities and a thousand villages
were laid out on broad sheets of paper, and made the basis of vast moneyed transactions." In December, 1835, the great New York conflagration occurred, by which
five hundred and twenty-nine buildings and twenty millions of dollars worth of
property were destroyed.

If Jackson was an enemy of extravagance and its parent and promoter—a paper
currency—he also was a firm believer in the doctrine of State rights, and during his

administration the doctrine was strictly and severely enforced. He was not prepared, like Calhoun, to carry it to the length of nullification and secession; but so far as he believed in it, he unrelentingly applied it to the affairs of the general government. By that code all the receipts of the government, in excess of its expenditures on the narrowest basis, belonged to the States, and to them it should go. Accordingly, in January, 1836, Congress directed the Secretary of the Treasury to divide the money in excess of five millions among the several States, on the basis of their representa- tion in the House of Representatives. Notwithstanding this portent of the gathering storm, it was unheeded, and reckless speculation continued and increased into mad- ness. In the midst of this wide-spread financial dissipation, (July 11th, 1836,) the President caused a treasury order to be issued, directing that all duties should be paid in gold and silver coin. A deputation of New York merchants waited on him to se- cure its rescission. But he was inexorable. He told them hard times were produced by reckless expenditure and speculation, and any measure that would stop the flood- tide of extravagance, although productive of present distress, would eventually be of service to the country.

At length the time fixed by Congress for the distribution of the money arrived. More than a year had elapsed since the passage of the act gave notice to the banks and the business community to prepare for the effects of shortened capital, but no preparation had been made. On the contrary, recklessness had increased in pro- portion as the time for preparation shortened. In proportion as the currency was converted into coin for payment to the Government, the amount available for busi- ness purposes was decreased. Discounts could not be obtained, and therefore business could not be continued. In the months of March and April, 1837, there were failures in the city of New York aggregating more than a hundred million of dollars. A deputation of merchants waited on Mr. Van Buren, then just seated (May, 1837,) in the Presidential chair, and asked him to defer the collection of duties on imports, to rescind the treasury order of July 11th, 1836, and to call an extra session of Congress. He refused, and May 10th all the banks of New York suspended payment, and the banks of the entire country followed their example. On the 16th day of May the Legislature of the State of New York authorized the suspension of specie payments for one year.

It was in times such as these that Michigan launched her system of wildcat banks. They were but just organized when the crash came, and well would it have been for the State if they had been swept out of existence. But they were legal banking houses, and were entitled to any measure provided for the relief of honest bankers. On the 22d day of June the Legislature of Michigan passed an act to suspend specie payments until the 16th day of June, 1838. An act was also passed curtailing the bank circulation. Before that, chartered banks were authorized to issue their notes or bills for an amount not to exceed three times the amount of capital actually paid in, and the wildcat banks were authorized to issue their notes to the amount of two and one-half times the amount of paid in capital. By the act of June, 1837, the circu- lation was limited to once and a half the amount of paid in capital. Banks that had vested interests to protect, were careful in the extreme, discounted sparingly, and then only on undoubted paper. But the wildcats had no vested interests. Their capital existed largely in imagination, and the requirement of the law that thirty-hun- dredths of the capital should be coin in the vaults was almost wholly disregarded. As their own securities were to a great extent a myth, they ran no risk in accepting almost any security for their nearly worthless promises to pay. Therefore their notes were in everybody's hands, while those of the chartered banks were almost as scarce as gold. With two illustrations of the financial state of the times, we will dis- miss this part of our subject.

The bank commissioners were required to visit every bank once in three months to inquire into its condition. After visiting several of these banks the commissioner, Judge Felch, had his curiosity aroused by the seeming similarity in their piles of coin deposit. At each place the coin was counted, and although the amount varied so little, the pieces had a familiar look, and he was almost sure he had handled those pieces daily for a week or more. At last he determined to solve the mystery. On coming out of a bank vault the cashier was surprised to see the commissioner lock it and put the key in his pocket. He immediately retraced his steps and re-examined every bank, and found their vaults destitute of coin. So much illustrative of banking; the other will illustrate business interests.

Mr. John C. Hogaboam at that time resided in Monroe. In the spring and summer of 1838 he built the Monroe City Mills for Frost & Burch. The proprietors had an abundance of money, but it was of the wildcat variety, and they were in no way particular about advancing any amount of it to their workmen. Each Saturday afternoon the contractor would ascertain just how much each man would take, and how much he needed for his own marketing, and then draw that amount and no more. One Saturday night, by some error of calculation, he had four dollars left over. Monday morning it was dead. When the mill was ready for raising, the contractor went to Detroit to procure the tackle. He was furnished chartered bank notes enough for that purpose, but Frost & Burch, who were merchants, had a lot of wildcat money they could not use. This they requested him to take along and buy exchange if possible, but at all events to trade it off for something. He tried to work it off for tackle or sell it for exchange at any rate of discount, all to no purpose. At last he wandered into a lumber yard. He told the proprietor he wanted to buy about eight hundred dollars worth of lumber if his money would pay for it. "From what bank is your money?" asked the proprietor. "The bank of Brest," was the reply. "Well," said he, "if I can use it to pay my debts we can trade." In half an hour he returned with the intelligence that he could use it. The lumber was measured and loaded on a vessel that day. It would not do to leave it in the yard over night. If the bank should fail to open its doors next morning the lumber would be reclaimed. Therefore no rest was taken until the lumber was on the lake.

The railroad having been established through Lanesville, some of the inhabitants of Keene and Lenawee villages commenced preparations for moving their effects to the fortunate ville. January 1st, 1839, Anderson & Colvin purchased of William H. H. Van Akin one acre of land south of the railroad track. On the twenty-second day of July they purchased land of Beriah H. Lane on the west side of High street, and on the fifth day of August, 1839, they purchased the old Franklin lot, where Mrs. Hazlett's house now is.

Dr. L. G. Hall came to Hudson in the spring, and Dr. S. M. Wirts in the fall. Franklin Smith opened a store on the west side of the creek, and William Baker came in, but was employed in railroad surveying. May the twenty-third, Mrs. Phebe P. Lane, wife of Beriah H. Lane, Esq., died. The railroad was partly graded, and the job of building the Hudson bridges was let to William Winans, of Adrian.

In the winter of 1839–40, Anderson & Colvin removed a partly finished building from Keene, and incorporated it into the Franklin Hotel, then building.

On the seventh day of February, 1840, Silas Eaton purchased his old residence lot, on the west side of High street, of Simeon Van Akin. It is said he moved his house from Keene, but Charles E. Ames is as sure he sold his house there to his father, Charles Ames. But be that as it may, he came to Hudson immediately after his purchase, and before mid-summer was living in his own house on his lot.

Early in the spring of 1840, C. H. & H. M. Boies came to Hudson and opened a general store in a long, one story frame building which then stood on the site of the store now occupied by C. R. Beach. Augustus Finney had moved into his new house, which stood just in the rear of the block known as the Exchange Block; indeed, it afterwards formed a part of the old Exchange Hotel. At the time now under consideration, save the store occupied by Messrs. Boies, just alluded to, and the old hotel building, there was no other building north of Main street, between Market and Church streets.

In the spring of 1840, the old hotel was kept by D. P. Hannahs. It was a miserable building and was abandoned as a hotel in the summer or fall of 1840.

In July, Mr. John C. Hogaboam and family moved into Lanesville from Monroe. Mr. Hogaboam came to the Bean Creek Country in March of that year, but he did not remove his family until July. They arrived on the second day, and that summer occupied a little frame building which stood about where Mrs. Loomis' house now is, but the house faced the north. It was a balloon frame upright, with a lean-to of the same sort along the south side. It was a pretty good house in dry weather, and a fair strainer in wet weather. The family remained here until the latter part of October, when they moved onto their farm in Pittsford. The family consisted of the parents and three children, John S. Brownell (an apprentice,) and a maiden lady named Mudge. During the latter part of July and the months of August and September Miss Mudge was the only well person in the house. Mr. Hogaboam had the ague every day, Mrs. Hogaboam the chill fever, Brownell the billious fever, and the children the ague.

Mr. Winans, the contractor for the Lanesville bridges, sub-let the contracts to Eaton, Lane and Childs. They built the bridge over Bean Creek in the summer of 1840, and that over the swamp west of the village in 1841. The bridge over Bean Creek was trestle or bent work from Tiffin street to the bank in front of James Cosgrove's house. There was a long string of bents, and when, several years afterwards, the embankment was made, the dirt was filled in around the timber, leaving the bents standing. The bridge over the swamp was likewise a series of bents, and were filled around in the same manner.

In the summer, Drs. Baldwin and Romyne settled in Hudson. Baldwin remained several years, but Romyne the next season went west and settled in the village of Colon, St. Joseph county, Michigan.

William H. Johnson came to Hudson in 1839 or '40 and engaged in trade. For the next twenty years he was one of Hudson's busiest men. During the war he was quartermaster in the United States service, and made the march with Sherman to the sea.

John M. Osborn came to Hudson in the fall of 1840. He taught the east side school that winter in the back room of W. H. Johnson's store.

This was a year of great political excitement. The Whigs had been out of power for twelve years, and extraordinary efforts were made to regain it. Contrary to expectation, the times had not improved since 1837, but were constantly growing worse. By this time the wildcat banks had run their course and died, and there was indeed no currency. In 1838, and even in 1839, men had been kept at work, and although paid in wildcat money, they were busy, and consequently had no time to grumble. But now nearly the whole working class were out of employment, discontented and complaining.

The Whigs believed the hard times were all chargeable to the destruction of the United States bank, and seemed to believe that with such an institution in the country, extravagance and patent violation of the laws of trade would go unpunished. They had nominated Gen. Harrison for the Presidency, and adopting coon skins, hard cider and log cabins as their insignia, crying "Corruption" at every breath, they made the campaign. On their banners was the inscription, "$2.00 a day and roast beef under Harrison; $0.06¼ a day and sheep's pluck under Van Buren." The idle, the dissolute, and the unthinking rushed after the banner that promised so much, and joined in the hue and cry against the administration. The material for large processions was at hand, for mechanics and laborers had little else to do. Those who could sing were employed in vociferating log cabin songs, and those who could not sing hallooed themselves hoarse in the praise of hard cider, Tippecanoe and Tyler too. The Van Buren administration was literally swept out of existence, and the Whig partisans retired to winter quarters to dream of the two dollars a day and the roast beef that awaited them under Harrison's administration.

The year 1841 opened gloomily enough. The excitement of the previous year had died with the coming of the winter frosts, and now even the most unthinking began to doubt the ability of the incoming administration to grant relief from the hard and still hardening times which oppressed them. The Whig State administration went into power on the first of January, and the Legislature convened. They literally did nothing—indeed, they could do nothing—for the relief of the people. Having cried corruption and promised reform, they found themselves in straightened circumstances. To abandon the public works would be to throw hundreds more out of employment; to continue them required money, for which they dared not resort to taxation, for that would seem to add to rather than lighten the burthens of the people. In this dilemma they resorted to the issue of State script, and with this they paid the laborers on the public works.

The railroad appropriation bill was passed on the 12th day of March, 1841. It appropriated $200,000 for the construction of the Southern from Adrian to Hillsdale, but it had this restriction: "That the commissioners of internal improvement be directed in making contracts on the several works of internal improvement, to make them payable in *drafts* upon the several installments of the five million loan yet due from the United States bank, as they may become due, or from such funds as may come into the treasury to the credit of the internal improvement fund derivable from the five million loan, the sinking fund, or the five per cent. fund; so that the State *shall in no way be responsible* for their payment, and so that no claim for damages *shall be made against the State* in consequence of the delay or failure of the payment of said drafts; and if contracts at a reasonable price cannot be made under the above restriction, *the commissioners are hereby directed to make no contracts.*" These drafts were issued in small denominations and were called script, and this was the kind of money laborers were paid with. Much of the time it was worth forty-seven cents on a dollar.

The east side school district, No. 5, had been organized in the fall of 1840, and this spring (1841) both districts commenced new school houses. That on the east side was built by Mr. J. C. Hogaboam, and finished in time for the summer school. The building still exists, and is now used as a cooper shop, near the residence of Mr. Samuel C. Perkins, on north High street. When first built it was situated near the present residence of Dr. Thomas B. Minchin; it was afterwards removed to Hill street, just west of High street, and after its abandonment for school purposes it was removed to its present location.

The west side school house was built by Messrs. Wade and Lane. The west part of the long building owned by J. K. Boies & Co., on the east side of South Church street, was that school house, except the porch and tower, which have been removed. These latter—the porch and tower—were added by a subscription taken among Congregationalists, to give the building something of a churchly appearance, for they contemplated holding their services there. The building was finished in time for the winter term.

The Messrs. Boies were ardent Whigs, and seemed to believe all the campaign promises of better times. They projected the erection of a new store building, and commenced it early in the spring of 1841. The original Lanesville house was used as a shop for the preparation of the finish for the store. When well advanced, the shop and contents were destroyed by fire. Mr. H. M. Boies withdrew from the firm in May, but the building was raised and covered, and there work on it stopped for want of means. The building was finished in the winter of 1842-3. It occupied the site of the present Beardsell & Plympton store, and was destroyed by fire about 1852.

Some time during this year William Baker opened a store in Hudson, east side, and for thirty years he was one of Hudson's foremost business men. Although he did not always make money in his ventures and sometimes was "hard up," yet the producers loved him for his open, frank ways and evident desire to pay them all their

products were worth. In the first paper printed in Hudson was one of Baker's mani-
festoes. It hás the Baker ring:

In the first paper published in this place I avail myself of the opportunity of tender-
ing thanks to my friends for their liberal patronage for the last twelve years. If we
refer back to our first settlement in this place, we will discover that the change has
been wonderful,—truly astonishing. Then we had only half a dozen houses and a population equally as sparse. One of those pioneers used to invite the few to his house for
public worship on the Sabbath. The scenes of those days are familiar to those only
who passed through them and still survive. Peace to the ashes and honor to the
memory of Goodrich, Lane, Pratt, Cobb, and Wells. These men labored not only for
themselves, but for others; they were the worthiest of the worthy. Now we have
three churches which will compare in size and finish with eastern houses, and a population sufficient to fill them on the Sabbath. Our business has increased, we are
still acting as agents for the people, and the following gentlemen will exhibit a part
of the articles which we have for sale: Mr. S. A. Eaton, O. S. Ames, and R. Knapp.
We will wait upon you with pleasure, and of our gratitude to you for your kindness,
patronage and forbearance we will leave it with Him whose prerogative it is to judge.
Hudson, July 4, 1853.   WILLIAM BAKER, JR.

The year 1842 was still more gloomy than the preceding, and yet the people had
learned to accommodate themselves to the times, and were more contented. By the
inexorable law of necessity, the country was being cleared up. In order to support
any kind of existence something must be produced, and as crops could not be grown
in the woods those woods must be cut down. There was no market for wood, but
there was a market for ashes, and therefore the timber must be converted into ashes.
The products to be disposed of brought merely nothing, for want of market facilities.
From Adrian to Toledo and Monroe there was a sort of railway communication, but
eastward to Buffalo there was none save by lake, and that was frozen up half of the
year. Mr. Eldad Trumbull, of Pittsford, tells of selling pork for one dollar twelve
and a half cents per hundred pounds, and paying one dollar and fifty cents a pound
for tea,—about one hundred and thirty pounds of pork for a pound of tea,—and poor
tea at that. But amongst farmers and mechanics an exchange trade had grown up.
If a farmer wanted a barn built he would seek some person who wanted land cleared,
or a yoke of oxen, or a cow, or something to eat, and an exchange of labor or com-
modities was effected. In this way the country was being cleared up, and substantial
barns and some frame houses built. The greatest drawback on the prosperity of the
country was the fact that it was bankrupt. Michigan merchants owed wholesale
dealers more thon the entire real and personal estate would sell for under the hammer,
and in turn the people owed the Michigan merchants sufficient sums to make that
ruinous aggregate. Under then existing laws every cent's worth of the debtor's
property could be sold on execution. The Legislature of 1842 passed an act exempt-
ing personal property, to certain specified amounts, from sale on execution. They
also passed an act forbidding the sale of real estate on execution. If personal property could not be found sufficient to satisfy the execution, and real estate was levied
on, it was to be appraised by three disinterested persons at its fair cash value, and if
more than enough, at two-thirds of its appraised value, to satisfy the debt, then the
appraisers set off by metes and bounds enough of it to satisfy the debt, estimating it
at two-thirds its appraised value. If the creditor signified his acceptance within ten
days and the land was not redeemed within six months, then the recording of the execution, levy, appraisal and acceptance operated as a deed to the creditor. If the
creditor did not accept within ten days, the officer discharged the levy.

Before the enactment of these laws the knowledge that property accumulated might
be sacrificed by forced sale operated to discourage accumulation, but these enact-
ments encouraged farmers and others to strive to better their condition, and within a
year or two their beneficial influence became apparent.

The Legislature also, on the 17th day of February, 1842, by joint resolution, authorized the commissioners of internal improvement to pledge the net proceeds of the
Southern road for a term not to exceed five years, to purchase iron to iron it, and for
its completion from Adrian to Hillsdale.

At the election held in the fall the Democrats were successful. The Whig administration having failed to perform its "two dollars a day and roast beef" promise, stepped down and out, quietly remarking that Gov. Barry would find only a bogus dollar and a ten-penny nail in the State treasury. And yet the country was gradually improving its condition and clearing the way for the dawn of a prosperous era.

In the month of May, 1843, the locomotive Comet ran into the village of Hudson, and before the close of the season cars were running regularly to Hillsdale.

*It will be impossible from this point onward to give the history of Hudson in detail. It would require a volume to note every arrival and the business career of all her business men. We shall have to content ourselves, therefore, with a brief mention of the more important events in her history. Soon after the opening of the railroad to Hudson the two old warehouses were built,—one by W. L. and E. D. Larned (now the Rodney House), the other by H. M. Boies, who returned to Hudson in the winter of 1842-3. At first the railroad depot was on the west side of the creek, just west of Church street; but when the road was sold to the Michigan Southern Railroad Company, in 1846, they were dissatisfied with its location and surroundings, and the people of the east side offering better accommodations, the water-tub—there was little else to the station then—was removed to the vicinity of the Wood street crossing. The company was not satisfied yet; they had better water, but no ground for yard or buildings. The west side people felt the disgrace and inconvenience of losing the station, and resolved to regain it if possible. With this in view they bargained for the ground which is now included in the depot grounds, and offered to donate it to the company for depot purposes. The offer was accepted, and the depot found a resting place.

Among the men who came to Hudson in 1843 were two who for years afterwards were identified with the business interests of the place,—Lorenzo Palmer and Joseph M. Johnson. Lorenzo Palmer came from Chautauqua county, New York. He was a middle-aged man, and brought with him a large family, two of whom were then young men. He at first engaged in teaching school, then in mercantile pursuits, and for many years held offices of trust in the township. He died in October, 1874.

Joseph M. Johnson was a young man when he came to Hudson. He was born in Yorkshire, Eng., May 12th, 1819, and emigrated to the United States and settled in Wayne county, Mich., in 1831. He became a resident of Hudson in July, 1843, and engaged in the manufacture of furniture. On the 22d day of February, 1844, he was married to Harriet Newell, only daughter of Silas Eaton. From 1848 to 1852 he was engaged in mercantile business. He was burned out in the spring of 1852. In later years Mr. Johnson built one-half of the Arcade Block, and established the manufacturing establishment on the flats between Fayette and Mechanic streets. In 1876 he traded his Hudson property for property in Toledo, and removed thither about the first of June.

FIRES.

Hudson has had her full share of fires, but we can only notice here her three great conflagrations. The first occurred in 1852, and although it burned only two buildings, was a considerable loss for the Hudson of that period. The second occurred in 1858, and by it all the buildings on the north side of Main street, from about where Beardsell & Plympton's store now stands to Market street, were destroyed. The third occurred on the night of Sunday, the third day of January, 1864, and destroyed the buildings on the south side of Main street from Eaton Bros. store to Market street. The buildings were all wood, but they were in good condition and afforded much needed business places. The loss was estimated at about $8,000. Temporary loss has been eventual gain, however, for in each instance a better class of buildings replaced those destroyed.

THE WAR.

During the war of the great rebellion Hudson did her whole duty, both as to men and money, to carry on the war. She gave her DeGolyer, her Preston, her Carleton, her Piper, her Edwards, and a score or more of others, as sacrifices on the altar of a common country. An attempt was made to procure a list of Hudson soldiers, but the difficulties to be overcome were so great it could not be accomplished in time for this work.

BUSINESS FIRMS AND VENTURES.

THE OLD CORNER STORE.—The business conducted by J. K. Boies & Co.—general store—was established in early times, and with the exception of a single year, perhaps, has been continuous. The Hon. Henry M. Boies came to Lanesville in 1840, or thereabouts, and in the summer of 1840 was in trade with Curtis H. Boies. He sold out his interest in May, 1841, purchased a stock of goods, and opened trade in Troy, N. Y. He could do nothing there on account of the crushing times, and thinking he could do better in Jackson, Michigan, with the consent of his creditors he removed his stock thither. Hard times were there also, and in the winter of 1842-3 he again removed his stock, this time to Hudson, and again went in trade with Curtis H. Boies. The partners divided their business about 1845, and Henry M. started business for himself. He built the building on the northeast corner of Main and Market streets, lately used as a bowling alley, in the winter of 1846. About 1846 John K. Boies came to Hudson and commenced work for his brother. In the course of time the business took the name of H. M. Boies & Brother, under which style it was conducted many years. About 1854 they built the brick store at the corner of Main and Church streets, and about 1855 sold out their business to the stock-store people, but that institution going under soon after, sold in turn to the Boieses, and under their management it has continued ever since. Some years later, Henry M. withdrew to engage in the wholesale trade in New York, and then John K. took the helm. Its style has varied —once J. K. Boies, once James, Mosher & Co., and again J. K. Boies & Co.—but it has ever been under the same management. No one knows except the founder how many discouragements were met in the early years of this business house. In 1847 it was really bankrupt, but, thanks to the pluck of the proprietor, the community never knew it, and subsequent prosperous years enabled the house to pay all its liabilities, and to-day its founders count their wealth by tens of thousands. About 1871 the Hon. Henry M. Boies closed up his business in New York and opened a business house in Chicago. So much for pluck, industry and skill, in the management of a business house.

EXCHANGE BANK.—This institution was founded in 1855, by Henry M. Boies and Nathan Rude, but the entire control and management of it has been in the hands of our townsman, Mr. Nathan Rude. That the management has been successful, every business man knows. Several years later, John K. Boies became interested in the bank, since which time the firm has been known as Boies, Rude & Co. Several months since Mr. Rude was compelled, by failing health, to give up the management of the bank, since which time its management has devolved upon the Hon. John K. Boies.

ANOTHER GREAT MILL PROJECT.—In 1847 or '48 Hudson had her second mill excitement. About that time one Rollin, or Rolland, came to Hudson and proposed to put up a mammoth flouring mill. Immediately after the abandonment of the original saw mill, the new race was dug and a new saw mill built on the site of the present grist mill of Tucker & Wiggins. This mill property Rollin bought, or bargained for, and gave out a bill of timber for the new mill. His pretence was that he had just drawn a large prize in a lottery—$50,000 he said—and would realize his money in a short time, but it was important to push the mill right along, and he proposed to make a temporary loan, to be repaid as soon as his money was received. He loaned considerable money of Dr. S. M. Wirts, and W. H. Johnson, who was then in trade, honored his orders for the payment of his workmen. The timber was hauled on to the ground and the work of framing went busily on. The proprietor was a great stickler for nice work. A pattern was made for each sized mortise, and the mortise must be beaten so that the pattern would fit it perfectly, and the timber when finished looked as if planed. Thus matters progressed until the frame was nearly ready for the raising, and then Rollin discovered he had no prize, but he took himself out of the way before his friends found it out. Dr. Wirts and William H. Johnson found themselves short of a large sum of money, with only a lot of timber to show for it. To prevent an entire loss, it was resolved to build the mill on a reduced scale, and run it by steam alone. It had been intended to use both water and steam power. Accordingly the mill was raised on the railroad ground directly east of Wood street. It was finished and run several years, generally, it is thought, at a loss to the operators. At last the frame was sold to Edwin M. Hulburd, who took it down and piled the timber by his mill, with the intention of building a large addition thereto, but the project was abandoned.

THE HULBURD MILL.—In the meantime old uncle Simeon Van Akin became the owner of the water power, and converted the saw mill into a grist mill, but before it had been operated long, Brearley and Hulburd became the owners. They made several additions to it to increase its capacity, and were opening a good business, when the war began. Brearley about that time sold his interest in the mill to Mr. Hulburd, who proposed, as above stated, to enlarge it, but before the work was begun he accepted a Captain's commission in the 18th regiment of Michigan infantry, and was absent from his business until the close of the war. When he returned he found himself unable to make the enlargement. The old building needed repairing, and there was a new dam to be built. These necessary repairs added to his embarrassment, and finally in the spring of 1875 he deeded the property to the mortgagees, who sold it to its present proprietors, Tucker and Wiggins.

THE STOCK STORE.—About the year 1853 the farmers became dissatisfied with the course of trade, and thought they could manage their own business without the aid of middle-men. So a company was organized for mercantile and forwarding purposes. The project was to start a store, in charge of an agent, at which store the stockholders were to purchase goods at ten per cent. advance on New York cost, and others should pay a larger, but at the same time a reasonable profit. Their produce was to be forwarded to New York, sold by a commission house, and the farmer was to receive the whole price, less the cost of transportation and sale. The stock was subscribed, Mr. Edwin F. Wells employed as agent, and a store opened. Prices did come down, of course, and the merchants found their best customers leaving them. They tried to brave the storm by furnishing goods at reduced rates, but they found that a ruinous business, and H. M. Boies & Brother offered to sell their stock to the association. The offer was accepted, and the stock store moved into the corner store building. Here they carried on business for a while, until it became evident that there was fault in the management, for applications for payment of bills began to be made directly to stockholders. An investigation was had, and it was found that the institution was bankrupt. The stockholders must now put their hands in their own pockets to make up the losses, but they resolved to stop that leak, and sold the institution out.

THE SPOKE FACTORY.—In 1852 or '53, Mr. Alexander M. Ocobock built a two-story wood building, on the site of the present spoke factory, for the purpose of manufacturing wagons. From manufacturing his own spokes, hubs and felloes, he got to manufacturing for shipment, and afterwards a Mr. Munson became associated with him. Soon afterwards the building burned down. Mr. Ocobock retired from the business, but Munson undertook to rebuild on a more extensive scale. Samuel

"In the meantime old Uncle Simeon Van Akin became the owner of the water power, and converted the sawmill into a grist mill, but before it had been operated long, Brearley and Hulburd became the owners." (p. 78)

DeGolyer came here and joined Munson in the enterprise. Munson became involved, and through some management he retired, and Samuel DeGolyer managed the business as agent, his New York brother ostensibly owning the business. DeGolyer was a patriotic man; the first tap of the recruiting drum fired him for action. He went into the army in command of company F, 4th Michigan infantry, and James DeGolyer took his place. Soon afterwards the business name was James DeGolyer & Co., Samuel's widow (for he had died of a wound received at Vicksburg), being the company. In the spring of 1876, Mr. William A. Whitney (who had married the widow DeGolyer and had been managing her interest), bought out James DeGolyer, and now the business firm was Whitney & Co. Until the financial panic of 1873 the factory was doing a good business. Since then it has sympathized with the general depression in manufacturing interests.

THE TANNERY was for several years one of the business institutions of the town. It was owned and operated by Samuel Eddy, but it is believed never was a paying institution.

The business ventures originating since 1860 do not properly belong to our theme, and, with one or two exceptions, will not at this time be noticed.

NEWSPAPERS.

The first attempt at journalism in the township and village of Hudson was made by William H. Bolsby, on the 9th day of July, 1853. The paper was called the Hudson *Sentinel,* and Mr. Montgomery was both editor and proprietor. About the beginning of the next year, Canniff & Montgomery became the proprietors of the *Sentinel,* and Andrew C. Mercer editor. In November Mr. Canniff appeared as editor and proprietor, Joseph G. Davenport publisher, and in December, Davenport became editor and proprietor. The paper was soon after consolidated with the *Michigan Republican,* and was published for a short time at Adrian by one Hobart, proprietor.

On the 13th day of September 1855, a new paper appeared. It was called the Hudson *Courier,* and was published by a company, as follows: H. M. Boies, W. H. Johnson, Enos Canniff, Benjamin Turner, A. C. Mercer, L. G. Hall and Alonzo Palmer. A. C. Mercer was editor.

August 15th, 1857, still another new paper appeared, the *Saturday Evening News,* E. Wolverton editor and proprietor. This paper was succeeded, March 26th, 1858, by the Hudson *Gazette,* W. T. B. Schermerhorn editor and proprietor. The *Gazette* has continued for eighteen years under one management, and has been an able village paper. It was printed first as a neutral sheet, then as an independent. Although for several years it was thought its independency leaned, it adhered to that motto until the summer of 1876, when it came out squarely for the Democracy. It has always been an able paper, and for many years it was the pet of all Hudson households, no matter what the shade of their political opinion was.

Late in 1862 Titus Babcock started a Republican newspaper in the village of Hudson, which he named the *Herald.* He continued to run the paper until in 1865 he was succeeded by Russel D. Babcock and Daniel Russell; they were in turn succeeded by A. H. Pattee, who changed the name to *Transcript,* and he, in the spring of 1868, by Laird & Penfield, who again changed the name to *Post.* Chauncey W. Stevens succeeded to the management of the paper sometime in the year 1869, A. H. Pattee in 1870, and James M. Scarritt in the spring of 1872. During the latter part of the ownership of Pattee, Dr. Andrews was editor and manager.

When Mr. Scarritt assumed the management, in the spring of 1872, he found less than two hundred paying subscribers, and that the office had no reputation for job work and but little material to do job work with. The only press that could be used was a Washington. Scarcely any one would subscribe for the paper,—its several changes had invariably been to the pecuniary loss of its subscribers, and they would trust it no more. A few would trust it for three months, and a few reckless persons for six months, but none longer. It was harder business than starting a new paper that would have a reputation to make; this had one reputation to obliterate and another to make. The first year's business showed a loss of about eight hundred dollars; the second scarcely paid, but a reputation had been made, and thenceforward the progress has been steady and constant. Instead of less than two hundred subscribers it has (Sept. 15, 1876,) one thousand five hundred and sixty. In place of the one Washington press, the office has a power newspaper press and a power jobber, driven by steam, and a better supply of material than is found in many inland city offices. As a business manager, Mr. Scarritt has but few equals.

Although Hudson now has but two papers, the time was that it had three as neat papers as are published anywhere. Immediately after the Rev. Jesse T. Webster assumed the duties of rector of Trinity church, Hudson, he commenced the publication of the *Record*, a monthly parish newspaper, as an aid in parish work. This paper he enlarged and improved until, under a change of name, it became the organ, first of one, then of two dioceses. It was a beautiful and able religious journal, and was printed at the office of the Hudson *Post* until some time after the editor's removal to Detroit, when it was removed thither.

CRIME.

Although, perhaps, Hudson has had her full share of petty crime, she has had but one murder (an infant), and but one suicide, and of the other crimes that shock communities it has had only one,—the robbery of the People's Bank, in 1864.

William W. Treadwell was the son of Urias Treadwell, and was born and brought up on a farm in the township of Pittsford. He attended such schools as Hudson and Pittsford then enjoyed, and afterwards graduated in a business course in an Ohio institution. After his return to Hudson he clerked it for a while in a dry goods store, and then for a short time was in the dry goods trade with William W. Palmer. After leaving Palmer he asked and obtained permission to assist in the People's Bank, then owned by the Hon John M. Osborn, without salary, just to learn the business. He was apt, punctual and faithful, and mastered the business rapidly. At length he became a partner in the bank, and finally, in 1859, Osborn sold his interest in the bank to Urias and William W. Treadwell. In 1862, he married Mary E. Hester, of Huron county, Ohio, and a little while before the robbery, became sole proprietor of the bank, his father allowing the use of his name to assist his son. In stature William was considerable below the average height, slender in form, and had a very dark complexion. He had by his pleasant ways and obliging disposition made himself very popular among the farmers and business men, and his safe contained large sums of money deposited on account of such friendship. In December, 1863, the treasurers of the townships of Pittsford, Rollin and Hudson commenced to deposit their collections, which, increasing day by day, would be allowed to remain there until February 1st, when the larger part would be withdrawn to pay State and county taxes. It now seems that he had matured a deep scheme of dark villainy, for on the 16th day of January, 1864, he sent letters to all the bankers of Detroit, Toledo, Cleveland and Chicago, enclosing drafts on the Continental Bank, New York, asking for discount, or in plain words, a loan. The bodies of the letters were alike, except as to amount; the address and postscript varied. Here is a sample:

PEOPLE'S BANK.

URIAS TREADWELL, Pres.
W. W. TREADWELL, Cash.
                                        Hudson, Mich., Jan. 16th, 1864.

Dear Sir:—Herewith I enclose my draft on Continental Bank, New York, for $1,000. Please send me proceeds in treasury notes per United States Express.
                              Yours respectfully.
                                        W. W. TREADWELL, Cashier.
P. S.—Do you keep 5-20 bonds for sale.   T.

These letters and drafts were dispatched by the mails Saturday, Jan. 16th, and he evidently expected to get returns by Tuesday night.

Tuesday morning he went to Adrian and procured of the banks there $4,500. On his return from Adrian he carried in his hand a small black sachel. He went immediately to Mr. Galusha, the express agent, and inquired for money packages, and received seven packages from as many banks. Mr. Galusha remarked, "You are receiving considerable money." "O," said Treadwell, "that is not all I have got," throwing aside the lapel of his overcoat and exhibiting the Adrian packages in the inside pockets thereof. These packages he put into the sachel, and going to the bank threw it under the counter, giving it a careless kick, as though of but little consequence. On Wednesday he received several more packages, but yet the banks had not all responded. He evidently feared to wait longer, and the sequel shows that his fears were well founded.

That (Wednesday) night the clerk of the bank (Mr. Webb) and Chester C. Pease spent the evening with some lady friends in the south part of the village, and instead of returning to his boarding place that night, Mr. Webb went out to his father's house, a little south of Lowe's mill. He came into town next morning and proceeded to the bank. The bank building had been burned in the fire of the 3d of January, and temporary quarters had been provided for it in the hardware store near by. Pease saw Webb go towards the bank and started to go in that direction, but he met Webb, ashy pale. "Chet," said he, "there is something wrong; I can't open the safe." "Perhaps," said Pease, "Billy has changed the combination." "No," replied Webb, "he never does that without telling me." So saying, they reached the store. Again and again was trial made without success. At this juncture a New York "runner" came in and said, "Let me try it." He took hold of the knob, and in a few minutes the door swung out on its hinges. But what a discovery! The well-filled safe of the night before was empty—every dollar in currency had flown. "Where is Treadwell?" was the next inquiry; but he could nowhere be found, and then the fact became patent that he had robbed the bank and run away. Then Galusha told of the little black sachel, but it, too, was gone. An examination of the books showed he had taken forty-two thousand dollars in round numbers from the safe, but the money he obtained of the banks did not go into the safe nor onto the books. He said nothing to his clerk of those transactions. To say there was intense excitement conveys but a faint idea of the situation. Money deposited to await investment, the soldiers' earnings, and the widow's mite all were gone. So intense was the excitement that it was almost unsafe for the grief-stricken father to appear upon the streets. A partner of his guilty son,—only in name, yet so far as the people knew, a real partner,—he was supposed to be, as he really was in law, answerable for the sums entrusted to the bank. The powers of the law were invoked, and before night a score of suits had been commenced, and the bailiff's voice became familiar as household words to his ears.

From all the information afterwards obtained, it appears that after the clerk left the bank Tuesday night, Treadwell returned and transferred the money packages from the safe to his black sachel. About two weeks previous he had sent his wife to her father's house on a visit, and he was for the time being boarding at the Exchange Hotel. About ten o'clock he sauntered into the office, sachel in hand, and, requesting the clerk to call him for the morning train, went to his room.

At three o'clock Thursday morning, January 21st, 1864, William W. Treadwell, sachel in hand, wended his way to the depot. He carried with him his father's wealth, the savings of the widow and the fatherless, as well as the thousands of the rich men, but he left behind a crushed and heart-broken father, home and home associations, but above all, and more than all, his honor and his integrity. He carried thousands of dollars, but the hand that grasped it was a felon's hand.

The reader shall not be wearied with a recital of the means resorted to for his capture. Suffice it to say that the telegraph was put in requisition, and the various points informed of the robbery and flight. The discounted drafts commenced arriving at the Continental Bank on the 20th, and, so great was the confidence in the People's Bank, although its account was already overdrawn, the bank officers paid the drafts presented to the amount of $7,000 before a dispatch sent the 21st apprised them of the condition of affairs. Five thousand dollars arrived after his departure, but the express agent at once returned it to the banks from which it came.

February 11th, 1864, the following dispatch was received at Hudson:

MANSFIELD, O., Feb. 11, 1864.

Thos. Bate, Hudson:
I have arrested William Treadwell. What shall I do? Answer immediately.
C. C. KEECH.

Mr. Keech was on the police force at Mansfield, had formerly known Treadwell, and seeing him in a carriage at Mansfield depot, he at once arrested him. The officers at Adrian were at once notified, and in a little time Sheriff Hough, W. H. Walby, J. M. Osborn, J. J. Hogaboam and some others were on their way to Mansfield. Before leaving Adrian, however, they learned that Treadwell had procured a writ of *habeas corpus* returnable before the Probate Judge immediately. Keech was instructed to procure counsel and prolong the matter until the arrival of the party. They have a peculiar law in Ohio which provides that if while a person is before a court on a writ of *habeas corpus*, a sheriff of another State, with a proper warrant, demands the prisoner, the court shall make an order for his removal without waiting for a requisition. Keech, as directed, employed counsel, and they (there were two of them) raised and argued objections until ten o'clock at night. One of them was on the floor speaking when the party arrived, and, looking over his shoulder at the party, he continued, "But I see, your Honor, the sheriff of Lenawee county has arrived with a proper warrant for the prisoner's arrest, and he now demands an order for his removal." The Michigan papers were immediately examined and an order made for Treadwell's removal.

As soon as Keech could be got aside the question was asked "Where's the sachel?" As soon as Keech could collect his thoughts he answered: "When I arrested Treadwell there was a man and a woman in the carriage with him. There was a little black sachel on the seat, but as Treadwell did not claim it I left it, supposing it to belong to the woman." A little more inquiry revealed the fact that the man and woman were Treadwell's father-in-law and wife, and that the man took the sachel into the cars with him. Hester was seen, but he denied any knowledge of sachel or money. Treadwell was brought to Adrian and lodged in jail.

After he had been in jail a few days, Treadwell offered to make an assignment for the benefit of his creditors, but claimed to have only $32,000. In consideration of his assignment he wanted all prosecutions dropped, his creditors to sign a paper to that effect. This they unanimously declined to do.

On the 30th day of March, Treadwell made an assignment to Charles M. Croswell, the assignment to become operative when the creditors should sign the desired agreement. He made a detailed statement of his affairs, from which it appeared his total assets were $31,489.17; his father-in-law was to put in $30,000 more, making in all $61,489.17. He also stated his liabilities to be $66,190.61. Believing it to be the best that could be done, many of the creditors signed the agreement; but so many refused the offer went for nothing.

On the seventh day of May Hester came to Hudson to talk up Treadwell's matters. It was generally believed he had the money. The boys held an impromptu meeting in front of the hotel and discussed the matter. Warming up, some of the boys expressed their belief in the efficacy of mob-law in such cases. It happened his room was so located he could hear every word that passed. He became so frightened that he dressed himself, went down the back stairs, and walked to Clayton, where he took the morning train home.

Treadwell was tried and convicted Friday, July 1st, and remanded for sentence.

About five o'clock the same afternoon he escaped from jail in company with John Cowell, a convicted horse thief.

On the 14th day of July the body of a man was found in the woods in Wood county, Ohio, one mile from any road, and about thirty-six miles from Adrian. The body was badly decomposed, but the unfortunate victim had received a series of severe blows on the head, for there was a large fracture of the skull on the right side. A club lay near the body, also a part of a lunch tied up in a calico rag. A Mrs. Eastman, living about two miles from the place where the body was found, testified that on the fourth day of July two men called at her house for dinner. The smaller of the two men paid for the dinner and also for a lunch which she gave them tied up in a piece of calico. The larger of the men carried a sort of club. She identified the calico and string found by the body as being those she gave the two men, and the club as that carried by one of the men. A lady living in Hester's neighborhood, being at Napoleon at the time the body was found, related the matter on her return home. Hester at once suspected the truth, went to Sandusky and caused Cowell's arrest on suspicion. When arrested he had $200 in his possession. It was also said he had had larger amounts and a gold watch. This he denied, but he said Treadwell gave him $110 and his gold watch when they parted, at two o'clock on the morning of the fifth of July, Treadwell saying he was going to Omaha.

Hester and Mrs. Treadwell went to Napoleon. The remains were so decomposed as to render identification impossible, but they identified some fifteen articles found on the body as Treadwell's property.

At the trial of Cowell, which took place in May, 1865, Mrs. Treadwell testified that before Treadwell left the Adrian jail she managed to give him $900 in $100 bills. A portion of them were on the Union Bank, of Rochester, N. Y., and one such bill was found with Cowell at the time of his arrest. Dr. Horace Welch, of Hudson, identified the body by peculiar workmanship on the teeth. Cowell was convicted, and was executed July 7th, 1865.

As soon as it was found that Treadwell was dead, the creditors petitioned for probate of his estate, and letters of administration were granted to Chauncey L. Treadwell, of Wheatland. Suits were brought against Hester to recover the money, and after considerable delay a large sum was recovered. The creditors had paid two assessments to carry on the prosecution, and hoped to realize at least a portion of their claims out of the proceeds of the judgment; but so great were the expenses of the trial, and the amount claimed by attorneys so large, that, aside from the return of the amounts paid on assessments, they realized nothing.

ORGANIZATIONS.—CHURCHES.

CONGREGATIONALIST.—In a former section it was stated that early in 1836 a Presbyterian church was organized at the house of Alpheus Pratt, in Pittsford. The Rev. David Pratt became pastor of that church in June following, which relation existed two years. The Rev. D. R. Dixon succeeded to the pastorate soon after. During Mr. Pratt's pastorate the name of the church had been changed from the "Presbyterian Church of Bean Creek" to the "Presbyterian Church of Hudson and Pittsford," and now, on the seventh day of May, 1839, it was resolved that the First Presbyterian Church of Hudson and Pittsford be organized into a Congregational church, to be called the Congregational Church of Hudson and Pittsford. Salmon Trask, Elijah B. Seeley and Nelson R. Rowley were elected deacons. At a church meeting held on the first day of May, 1841, it was ordered that the church of Hudson and Pittsford should thereafter be known as the First Congregational Church of Hudson.

Some time in 1841 the Rev. J. W. Pierce became pastor of the church, and that relation existed until the summer of 1844. During that year large accessions were made to the church membership from the arrival of Presbyterians and Congregationalists in the community. Samuel Van Fleet, Abram, Mary L., William R. and Ruloff

Leonard, Edmund and Eunice Childs, Barbara, Jacob and Mary Robbins, Noble, Susannah, Harriet N. and Sarah B. Squier, Benjamin and Sarah Bevier, and Ezekiel and Sarah Lowe were received by letter.

The spring of 1842 was a season of revival influence, and on the 10th day of April Andrew Wade and wife, Oren Whitmore, Warren M. Colgrove, Mrs. A. W. Childs, Miss Mary O. Loomis and Miss Jane Keith were admitted to church membership on profession of faith, and Lemuel Squier and Julia Bovee were received by letter. On the 28th day of April Messrs. Trask, Seeley and Rowley were re-elected deacons.

At a church meeting held at the school house in Keene, Christopher, Elizabeth and Jane Clement, Barbara and Mary Robbins, Tamar F. Douglas, Louisa Colwell, Margaret Wilcox and Nelson R. Rowley were dismissed and recommended to the church in Wheatland.

On the 20th day of June, 1843, the church dissolved its connection with the Presbytery, and soon after united with the Jackson Association of Congregational churches.

Early in the spring of 1844 the Rev. Isaac Crabb, a Presbyterian clergyman, became the pastor of the church. At a church meeting held June 22d, a distinguished member was presented for gathering sap on Sunday. The church took no action in that particular case, but adopted the following resolutions: "1. In the opinion of this church it is a violation of the fourth commandment to travel on the Sabbath, and we caution our brethren and sisters against starting on a journey, or arriving at their place of destination, or returning home on the Sabbath. 2. It is a violation of the fourth commandment to work in harvest or haying on the Sabbath, and we caution our members to beware of any temptation that may arise to gather grain or hay on that day. 3. That it is not a work of necessity to gather sap on the Sabbath in any case whatever."

The pastorate of the Rev. Mr. Crabb terminated on the first day of April, 1845, and he was succeeded by the Rev. Robert Laird. During the winter several members of the Congregational church, without taking letters of dismissal from it, had proceeded to organize a Presbyterian church. On the sixth day of April the Congregational brethren, in church meeting assembled, appointed a committee to labor with the offending members, and if they did not return to report them to the Presbytery.

At some point of time the church had dissolved its connection with the Jackson Association and united with the Monroe Presbytery, and June 1st, 1845, Jesse Smith was elected a delegate to the Presbytery to be held at Clinton on the third day of that month.

In February, 1846, Messrs. Seeley, Trask and Avery were elected deacons.

The winter of 1845-6 was a great revival season in Hudson. The Rev. Mr. Laird conducted the meetings on the part of this church. As a result of the winter's campaign against sin, Samuel and Lucy Day, Myndert Bovee, Bradley Loomis, William and Julia Ann Smith, Julia Ann Kelley, Lorenzo Smith, Henry Goodrich, Susan A. Trask, Mary Sample, James Bevier, and Anna Maria Lane were admitted to membership on probation.

In the spring of 1847 a church building was commenced, and it was completed and dedicated early in the spring of 1848. In September, 1848, the labors of the Rev. Mr. Laird terminated, and the pastorate remained vacant until the following May, except occasional services by visiting clergymen, yet the church maintained its services by prayer and conference. The church sent a delegate this year to the Jackson Association and also one to the Presbytery. Mr. Jesse Smith represented the church at the first, and Abiel Coburn at the other.

May 21st, 1849, the Rev. John W. Baynes, a Presbyterian clergyman, became pastor of the church. The call was in these words: "That this church and society will give the Rev. J. W. Baynes a call to become our pastor, for the sum of four hundred dollars a year so long as said connection shall exist between him and us, in hopes ere long to afford him a more ample support." Modern clergymen would consider themselves on short allowance with such a salary, but Mr. Baynes preached as often, and

In labors was as abundant as any who receive ample salaries. He remained in the pastorate of the church until 1854, and was in all respects a model pastor. At a church meeting held this summer, (1849), the following resolution was adopted:

Resolved, That for the purpose of meeting the views of those fellow-christians of the Presbyterian order who may hereafter unite with this church, should any case of discipline arise in which they may be personally concerned, the book of discipline in use by the Presbyterian church in the United States may be taken as the rule and guide, if a majority of the persons interested shall prefer it, the standing committee of this church being in lieu of the session of a Presbyterian church, it being clearly understood, however, that this resolution shall never be construed as affecting, in the least degree, the general order and discipline of this church in its organization as a Congregational church.

On the 16th day of October, 1850, the Rev. J. W. Baynes was installed pastor of the First Congregational church, by the Monroe Presbytery. The Rev. J. B. Taylor, Moderator, presided. Rev. W. Cockran read the Scriptures. Rev. W. Watson offered prayer. Rev. H. H. Northup preached from Acts xx: 31. The Moderator proposed the constitutional questions. Rev. G. C. Curtis offered the installation prayer. Rev. J. Monteith addressed the pastor, and Rev. J. B. Taylor the congregation. Benediction by the pastor.

At the meeting for the election of officers, in 1852, pending the election of deacons, the question of the eligibility of females to vote was raised, and the pastor, says the record, took occasion to state his views on the subject, showing that such a course would be contrary, not only to the usual manner of doing such business in this church heretofore, but also at variance with the usage of Congregational churches in both Old England and New England, that it would be subversive of order, and might lead to other disorders; and especially that it was directly contrary to the teachings of the Word of God as contained in 1 Cor. xiv:34, 35. and 1 Tim. ii:11, 12. Notwithstanding the expressed views of the pastor, the church decided, by a vote of eight to five, to allow females to vote,—against which decision the pastor and Mr. Jesse Smith protested.

At a meeting of the church held on the 16th day of March, 1853, they voted "that this church withdraw from the Monroe Presbytery, and that our pastor be instructed to ask for a letter of dismission at the next regular meeting of the Presbytery."

At a church meeting held March 15th, 1854,—the last at which Rev. Mr. Baynes presided,—delegates were elected to the Southern Michigan Association, with instructions to ask the admission of this church into said association. Since the commencement of Mr. Baynes' pastorate, thirty-seven persons had united with the church on profession of faith, and nineteen by letter; seven had been dismissed by letter, and two excommunicated. One of the oldest members had died—Deacon Salmon Trask. Among those who united with the church during that period, we discover the names of many of the most prominent and active members of the church at the present time, viz: Augustus Kent, Hon. J. K. Boies, L. P. Whitney, and Deacon S. B. Pease. The church was temporarily supplied until November, 1854, when the Rev. Atwater became its pastor.

At a church meeting held February 20th, 1856, a committee was appointed to ascertain what articles of faith have been adopted by this church for their use; also to prepare and recommend for adoption by the church a set of articles and covenant; also a set of rules and declaration for the regulation of the church, and to prepare a history of the church, all of which, together with a catalogue of the members, to be printed in a manual for the use of the church. Moses Hume, Samuel B. Pease and A. L. Hill were such committee. The committee reported March 19th articles of faith, a covenant, and rules of discipline. The covenant was adopted, it "being the one adopted by the Monroe Presbytery." The articles of faith reported "were those which were adopted by the Monroe Presbytery in 1856," but action on them, as well as on the rules of discipline, was deferred. At an adjourned meeting, held March 26th, the rules of discipline were adopted. Pending the consideration of the articles of faith, it was moved to "amend article eighth so as it shall read after the Lord's

Supper, 'and that it is the privilege of believers to dedicate their children to God in baptism,' which was passed." But on the adoption of the articles as amended, the vote being taken by ballot, the vote was averse. A vote was then taken by ballot on the motion to rescind the vote by which the eighth article was amended, and it was rescinded. The articles as reported (those of the Monroe Presbytery) were adopted by a vote of twelve to two. "The committee were continued, after Messrs. E. B. Seeley, Jesse Smith and B. H. Lane had been added, with instructions to prepare a list of members and some historical facts for the new manual, and have it printed.

At the meeting of May 21st, A. L. Hill was appointed a delegate to the General Association of Michigan; also to a council to convene at Jackson to install the Rev. Mr. Mahan pastor of that church. Mrs. Hannah Van Akin was granted a letter of dismission, for the purpose of uniting with the First Presbyterian Church of Hudson. June 18th, E. B. Seeley was elected a delegate to a council at Adrian for installation services. September 17th, D. H. Spencer and Augustus Kent were elected delegates to the Southern Michigan Association.

The annual church meeting for 1857 was not held; but at a monthly meeting, convened April 3d, after preparatory lecture, the manual committee reported that document prepared, and Messrs. Hume, Pease and Hill were appointed to see it properly printed. April 15th, Deacon Seeley and D. H. Spencer were chosen delegates to the Southern Michigan Association, and May 20th J. L. Taylor was elected delegate to the General Association of Michigan. July 5th Mrs. Deline, and Ed. M. Hulburd and his wife Helen were admitted to membership by letter. September 10th the Rev. W. W. Atwater and wife were dismissed by letter, and January 3d, 1858, Mrs. Maggie Adams was received by letter.

At the annual meeting of the church, held January 20th, 1858, D. H. Spencer was chosen clerk.

This brings the history of the church down to comparatively modern times. The history of the church during the succeeding eighteen years ought not yet be written in detail, nor can its doings yet be criticised impartially. Suffice it to say that during that period the church has experienced some of her greatest triumphs and deepest sorrows. During that period the old church property has been sold and a splendid new edifice erected and dedicated to the service of Almighty God, and scores of souls have professed saving faith and been admitted through her doors into the church militant. During the same period many of its most useful members have been dismissed to the church triumphant, some of whom participated in the organization of the first church in Hudson. We recall the names of A. L. Hill, Mrs. Simeon Van Akin, Mrs. John K. Boies, Deacon John L. Taylor, Phillip Beasom, Elijah B. Seeley, Francis B. Beasom and wife.

METHODIST EPISCOPAL.—On Sunday, the 8th day of November, 1835, the Rev. William E. Warner, from Lewiston, New York, arrived and settled with his family on the farm on the Medina side of the township line, directly opposite the residence of James Gahagan. On the next Sunday, November 15th, he preached in Noah Cressey's log house, and organized a class of sixteen members, with Lorenzo L. Brown for leader, to whom he preached regularly, and also traveled largely through the surrounding country. But as Mr. Warner was only a local preacher, and as yet in no way connected with the work in this State, his action was only temporary and preliminary to a regular organization of the work. Tecumseh circuit was the nearest organized work, and the Adrian appointment was the nearest approach to the Bean Creek Country. Mr. William Rhodes (afterwards the Rev. William Rhodes) then lived on the Stubly farm in Rollin. He and his wife, both Methodists, attended a quarterly meeting somewhere on the Tecumseh circuit, and invited the preachers of that circuit to visit the Bean Creek Country. The Rev. Washington Jackson, then the junior preacher on that circuit, and the Rev. Allen Staples, a local preacher of the Adrian appointment, made such visitation in August, 1836, on their way to the conference at Maumee. They held a two days meeting in Ames' barn in Keene. Mr. Eldad Trumbull, of Pittsford, has on his diary a memorandum of attending quarterly meeting in Ames' barn, August 14th and 15th, 1836. He neglected to mention the preachers' names, but no doubt it was the occasion of the visit of Jackson and Staples. They proceeded down the valley of the Bean, preaching at Brown's, at Foster's (Tiffin), at Alvah Holt's, Seneca, and so on down the valley to Maumee.

At that conference the Bean Creek mission was formed, and Lorenzo Davis appointed missionary. Its boundaries are not defined, but something of an idea of the field may be formed by looking at its surroundings. Tecumseh was the nearest appointment on the east, Coldwater on the west, Spring Arbor on the north, and on the south it had no boundary—the missionary traveled through Medina to Morenci, and across the border into Ohio. It was a pretty extensive territory for one man to travel over, and that almost an unbroken wilderness.

It does not appear where the mission headquarters was, but no doubt it was in the saddle. There was no appointment in the village of Lanesville. It had scarcely began to be. He had one appointment at Keene and another in the Brown settlement. At the latter place the preaching was alternately at the houses of Father Elisha Brown, Noah Cressey and Michael Dillon. Mr. Dillon was then a communicant of the church of Rome, but his wife was a Methodist, and he opened his house for Methodist preaching.

The first quarterly meeting of the mission was appointed to be held in the Brown neighborhood, on New Year's day, 1837. The presiding elder of the district, the Rev. Henry Colclazer, was unable to be present, and as the missionary was in his second year, and consequently unordained, the Rev. Father Foote, a local elder, preached on Sunday and administered the sacrament of the church. The next quarterly meeting was held in the Keene neighborhood July 15th and 16th, and the Sunday services were held in Mr. Ames' barn. Capt. Brown tells of going with his class to attend the meeting, in a lumber wagon drawn by an ox team, and being quartered at the farm of Father Alpheus Pratt.

Mr. Davis served his large mission as well as its extent permitted, and at the conference of 1837 was succeeded by John Scotford and Allen Staples. Mr. Staples had been received the year previous from the Adrian appointment of the Tecumseh circuit, and appointed to Salem. Mr. Scotford was received on trial at this conference (1837), and although a year the junior of Mr. Staples, was placed in charge of the mission. Mr. Scotford moved into a house situated, as near as can be remembered, on the farm now owned by Clark Ames. At the time of Mr. Scotford's arrival, Mr. and Mrs. Carleton, John and Sabra Griswold, Mrs. Champlin and Mrs. Ann Cobb, all Methodists, were living in and around Lanesville.

In the winter following, Mr. Augustus Finney brought his wife from Vermont, and soon after her arrival it was determined to organize a class in Lanesville. Mr. Finney, then keeping the pioneer hotel of the future Hudson, near where the Friend bakery now stands, threw open his house for the services, and on the night appointed, the boys, with flaming torches of hickory bark, proceeded to the house of Mr. Scotford and escorted him to the village, where he preached and organized the above mentioned persons—viz: Mr. and Mrs. Carleton, Mr. and Mrs. Griswold, Mrs. Champlin, Mrs. Cobb and Mrs. Finney,—and Sabra Ann, daughter of Mr. Griswold, (now Mrs. N. O. Cady,) who had been baptized and admitted to the church at Keene, and perhaps a few others, into a class, with John H. Carleton for leader. The only surviving members of this nucleus of Hudson village Methodism are Mrs. Carleton and Mrs. Cady.

At the conference of 1838, held at Tiffin, O., Bean Creek mission was erected into Jonesville circuit, and attached to the Marshall district, E. H. Pilcher, presiding elder; Peter Sabin and Zebulon C. Brown, circuit preachers. So far as any information can be obtained from the published minutes of that year, the boundaries of the Jonesville circuit were co-extensive with the boundaries of the old Bean Creek mission. We have been unable to learn of any incidents occurring that year in the history of the Lanesville class, illustrative of the times.

At the conference of 1838 Bean Creek mission was reported to have five hundred and twenty-seven members, and at the Conference of 1839, held at Ann Arbor, Jonesville circuit was reported to have four hundred and fifty-six members. This year John Scotford and Peter Sabin were appointed to Jonesville circuit. These preachers, like their predecessors on circuit and mission, saw pretty hard times, both for bodily comfort and the facilities for inaugurating denominational work. The settlement was new; the people lived in small, incommodious log tenements. Where school houses existed at all they were of the same material, but in the village of Lanesville there was not even a school house in 1839 and 1840, the old log school house having been burned. But these Methodist preachers, on their monthly rounds, preached in a log house standing in the vicinity of the gothic house occupied by Mr. Rawson, on North Market street. The house had been used as a dwelling. It was the pioneer house of the town, the foundations of which were laid by Reuben Davis in 1834. It was about twenty feet square, and had a hole about ten feet square underneath for a cellar. The floor was made of plank split out of basswood logs, sized on the under side where they rested on the sleepers. This split flooring was about ten feet long, and met in a continuous joint on the middle sleeper. One Sunday in mid-summer, in 1840, the people had gathered here for divine service, and were calmly listening to the word from the lips of the Rev. Mr. Sabin, when all at once the floor gave way in the middle, letting the central portion of the audience into the cellar. The preacher, leaning on the back of the chair which served him for a pulpit, waited patiently until the people had scrambled out, and then proceeded as though nothing had happened.

At the conference of 1840, held at Marshall, Mr. Scotford was returned to Jonesville circuit, now attached to Monroe district, with the Rev. Jonathan Jones for a colleague. This year there was a dividing up of religious influence and support, and denominationalism established. The religious condition of the people was somewhat peculiar. The country had recently been settled by people from the East, every one of whom had brought with them early religious impressions, and in this sparsely settled country, among the part that are religious at all, were to be found adherents of all the prominent religious bodies of the East.

Religious privileges were so rare that all who cared about them at all had hitherto united in sustaining them. In the village of Lanesville and vicinity the Congregationalists and Presbyterians were the more numerous; in the social meetings, in the Sunday school and in society they carried the sway, and were the ruling power. Indeed, so late as 1840 the Methodists of the Lanesville class were completely subject to their neighbors, and denominationally without influence.

About that time some Methodists moved into the community who had not been used to wearing the yoke of ecclesiastical inferiority, and by earnest effort induced the Methodists to move independently, and very soon, with the help of the Brown class, they had a Sunday school of their own started, and general independence followed.

No remarkable event marked the last year of the pastorate of the Rev. Scotford, and at the Conference of 1841 Hillsdale circuit was organized, to which Hudson was attached, and Revs. Charles Babcock and Gideon J. Shurtliff were assigned to it as preachers.

In the spring of 1842 Babcock and Shurtliff held a protracted meeting, which resulted in the conversion of a large number of quite prominent personages. The Rev. Babcock was a fine appearing man, and an impressive preacher. He was energetic, and fearless in the performance of duty. At one of the inquiry meetings, during his protracted meeting. a prominent man, but a backsliding Methodist, was present, and when spoken to in reference to his soul's interest, replied that the church was so full of hypocrites he couldn't live a christian life; and at some length berated the members of the church for their ungodly ways. "Brother," said Mr. Babcock in reply, "you remind me of the squaw who, reeling through the streets of Boston, filled.

with people, exclaimed, 'See, all these people are drunk!' The fact was, she was the only drunken person there." His usefulness was somewhat impaired, however, by his performances as a phrenologist. Phrenological teachings were then quite novel, and it was the subject most talked about in mixed gatherings. Mr. Babcock believed in the theories of phrenology, and believing it, gave it a prominent place in his thoughts, and discoursed it everywhere. Standing of an evening in a village store and talking phrenology and examining heads, is not the most effective way to preach the gospel. But he was an enthusiast in all his convictions, and for him to conceal them, or refrain from discussing them with unbelievers, was impossible, and so his influence became impaired. The following incident shows the fearlessness of the man, and his honesty of expression when it became necessary for him to say anything. Discussing phrenology in the village store one day, a man named DeForest—suspected of dishonesty, but a stranger to Babcock—said: "Feel of my head." Babcock passed his hand carelessly over his head, and kept on talking to the others with whom he had been conversing. Pretty soon DeForest said, "What do you think of my head!" Babcock said nothing in reply, appearing not to have heard the question. Waiting a little while, DeForest again said, "What do you think of my head?" "I think," said Babcock, "you can hide as well as you can steal." DeForest never became an enthusiastic believer in phrenology.

Mr. Shurtliff, on the other hand, was a man of abundant sympathy—kind in manner, eloquent in expression, and apparently absorbed in the ministry, making it the one business of his life, and, to all appearance, possessing great piety; he was beloved by all, and almost idolized by the young people of the community.

The annual distribution of work made by the Conference of 1842, returned Mr. Shurtliff to Hillsdale Circuit, with the Rev. Washington Jackson in charge. The arrangement of the work brought Mr. Shurtliff to Hudson first. After the sermon, he, of course, remarked on the fact of his having been returned to this circuit, and proceeded to introduce his colleague. Said he, "You must not form a hasty opinion of him at first sight, for you will find him as the old Dutchman found his horse—like a singed cat, better than he looks!" The magnates of the class were disposed to find fault with what they thought an undignified and un-minister-like style of introduction; but when the senior came here, they revised their opinion of the improbability of his portraiture being correct, if it was undignified. The Rev. Washington Jackson was, probably, the homeliest man that ever graced the pulpit of the Michigan Conference. Externally, he presented an uncouth appearance in, as well as out of, the pulpit: and, to add to his misfortunes, he had no roof to his mouth, which rendered articulation difficult. He was a christian, however, and a faithful christian minister. His piety was of the substantial rather than the showy kind, and he commanded the respect of all with whom he became well acquainted. He located in 1845, and long since fell asleep, no doubt with a rational and blessed expectation of awaking in the likeness of his Divine Master.

It has been stated in a former part of this work that the west side school house had been embellished with a porch and tower, at the expense of the Congregational people. Soon after it was done, the Rev. Mr. Babcock, then in charge of the Methodist work, asserted his right to use it half the time, and during his stay had held it by a display of cheek; but in the fall of 1842 the right of the Methodists to its use was disputed by the Congregationalists, and a series of adjourned school meetings were held to determine the matter, but the district voted that the two denominations should divide the time.

In a few weeks they were occupying it on alternate Sundays, and since then but little has occurred to disturb the good feeling between those large and influential churches. During the next summer, however, a little incident occurred which created a little ill-feeling for a short time. The incident was trivial in itself, and only shows how much strife a very little fire kindleth, especially when persons are on the watch for offenses. Mr. Shurtliff was as kind-hearted a man as ever lived—a true christian gentleman, who generally was careful of the feelings of others, and scarce ever injured them by any words of his. He was preaching one day to a mixed congregation, and while elucidating a point of his subject, he said he was reminded of the prayer of an old Presbyterian elder: "Oh, Lord, bless me and my wife, my son John and his wife—us four and no more; amen." No sooner were the words out of his mouth, than some of the Presbyterian portion of the congregation, deeply offended, started for the door, and left the preacher to get along without their presence. One old lady said she had often heard the story told of an old man, but no one had ever before intimated that he was a Presbyterian elder.

When, a year and a half later, Mr. Shurtliff became insane, these inopportune speeches were attributed to an insane predisposition, rather than to a desire to wound the feelings of others.

At the Conference of 1843 Mr. Jackson was returned, with Adam Minnis for junior. The Rev. Mr. Minnis became a resident of Hudson. Although junior preacher, he had had considerable experience in the ministry. He was first "admitted on trial" at the Conference held at Tiffin, Ohio, in the fall of 1838, and stationed at Defiance, in the Maumee District. In subsequent years he had preached at Plymouth, Dexter, Dearbornville, and Brooklyn. At the Conference of 1842 he was ordained Elder, and stationed on the newly-made Medina Circuit, in charge. As a preacher, Mr. Minnis was exegetical rather than declamatory. His sermons were a series of premises traced to their logical conclusions; or known effects traced to their logical and inevitable causes, rather than a declamation brilliantly studded with sparkling ideas, startling phrases, and impassioned appeals. Mr. Minnis was a very quiet man, never in any manner lowering the dignity which became his ministerial position; yet he immensely loved, and could quite easily lend himself to aid the perpretration of an innocent joke.

To illustrate this point, also to show how bigotry will sometimes over-reach itself, the following story is given as it was related to the author several years since: The minister appointed to the Morenci Circuit in 1855, early in 1856 vacated his pastorate, and the Presiding Elder of the District directed the Rev. John Crabbs, a local deacon living at Morenci, and another local preacher, to fill the appointments for the remainder of the year. The Rev. Crabbs is a Free Mason, and quite a large faction of the church at Morenci refused to hear him preach. During that summer Mr. Minnis, who had become a photograph artist, stopped at Morenci, and there prosecuted his business. The malcontents had known him as the preacher in charge of Medina Circuit, and immediately they solicited him to preach for them at the Wilson Grove school house, just out of Morenci, the day and hour Crabbs was to preach at the church in Morenci, which, after conference with Mr. Crabbs, he consented to do. Regularly on Crabbs' preaching day these devoted Methodists wended their way to the Wilson school house and listened to the ministration of the word, prepared especially for them by the Rev. Minnis. In preaching ability there was not much difference between the two men, but there was a difference, of which his hearers were ignorant, but which the ministers could fully appreciate; Crabbs was a *Master*, but Minnis was a *Royal Arch* Mason. The Rev. Minnis remained on the Hillsdale Circuit two years—the last year in charge, with Robert Dubois as junior.

In the fall of 1845, William P. Judd and Thomas Seeley were appointed to Hillsdale Circuit. They only remained one year, but it was a year of revival influence in Hudson.

At the Annual Conference of 1846, the townships of Adams, Wheatland, Rollin, Hudson and Pittsford were set off from the Hillsdale Circuit and called Hudson Circuit, and Revs. Henry Worthington and Robert Bird were appointed to the new work. The first Quarterly Meeting was held in the North Wheatland church on the 5th day of December, 1846—present, Josiah Brakeman, presiding elder; Henry Worthington and Robert Bird, circuit preachers; Barber M. Sheldon, local preacher; L. D. Welton and Hiram Haynes, exhorters; Lorenzo Dobson, Harley Bump, Nathan Whitney and

A. S. Wells, leaders. W. H. H. VanAkin, William B. Foote, Charles Carmichael, David B. Tuttle, Gaylord G. Tabor, Wm. Brooks and David Strunk were appointed stewards; W. B. Foote was elected recording steward, and W. H. H. VanAkin district steward; Augustus Thomas and the two circuit preachers were appointed a camp meeting committee.

There was little of interest transpired under the pastorate of Worthington and Bird, or their successors, Joseph Jennings and Hiram Roberts. The year these last were in charge of the circuit, 1847, the church in Hudson was almost rent asunder by a controversy which arose in consequence of Mr. Roberts joining the Odd Fellows. John H. Carleton led the anti-secret society raid, and the preacher in charge sympathized with it, and altogether poor Roberts had a hard time. Jennings was a fair preacher, but his wife sickened and died that year, the affliction taking him from his work much of the time. The persecution of Roberts rendered him powerless for good, and altogether the church not only made no advancement, but rather retrograded.

The next year, 1848, Worthington was returned to Hudson, but he was unable to arouse the church to action.

In the fall of 1849 Ebenezer Steele and Isaac Taylor were appointed to the Hudson circuit. They were men of earnest piety, and although neither of them were great preachers, they succeeded in arousing the church, and there was considerable revival spirit manifested. They agitated the question of church building, and got the frame up and covered.

At the Conference of 1850 Mr. Steele was returned alone. He pressed the church building along, and succeeded in having it dedicated during his pastorate.

During 1851-2 William Mothersill was in charge of the work, and made it but little progress.

The Rev. Henry Penfield came in 1853. He was by odds the most intellectual preacher that up to that time had been sent to the church, and if he had no revival, those already attendants had the pleasure of listening to sound sermons, intellectually and theologically.

The Rev. Harrison Morgan succeeded Penfield in 1854. During the first part of his pastorate the Rev. Mr. Adams, an evangelist, came here and held a series of meetings, and large accessions were made to the church. In the latter part of the year another attempt was made at anti-secret society persecution, again led by Mr. Carleton. Mr. Morgan deemed it his privilege to join the Masonic lodge, and Carleton at once declared war. But Morgan was not as easily persecuted as Roberts had been. He assumed the offensive, and pressed the anti-secret society men to the wall. Quite a large party secretly sympathized with Mr. Carleton, but seeing the determined attitude of their preacher, they quietly left the more valiant Carleton to fight it out alone. Carleton left the church, and the Conference sent Morgan to Coldwater the next year, but this was the last attempt at anti-Masonic persecution in the Methodist church of Hudson. For nearly half the time since 1854 their pulpit has been filled by Masons; some of them have been popular, and all have been useful.

In the fall of 1855 the Rev. Fred W. Warren came to the Hudson church, and remained two years. They were prosperous years spiritually, but in the month of January, 1857, the church building was burned. It was on Sunday; the morning service was ended and the Sunday school commenced when the cry of fire was raised. In one short hour the sanctuary was destroyed—" burned with fire." The remainder of that year was consumed in getting material for a new house.

The next year, 1857, the Rev. C. M. Anderson came, and the house was commenced; but like the Samaritan of old, he hindered the work, so at the Conference of 1858 he was sent elsewhere, and the Rev. A. R. Bartlett came to the church at Hudson. He remained two years. Under his pastorate the new house was finished and dedicated. In the fall of 1860 he was succeeded by the Rev. John A. Baughman.

We shall leave the history of the Methodist Episcopal church for the succeeding sixteen years unwritten, save to give a list of pastors, and to state that during the first year of the pastorate of the Rev. Thomas Stalker the church was enlarged and improved.

Pastors.—John H, Burnham, William G. Stonex, E. R. Haskill, Thomas Stalker, William E. Bigelow, Richard R. Richards, Daniel C. Jacokes, and Joseph Frazer.

THE BAPTISTS.—On the eighth day of July, 1843, the following named persons met and organized themselves into a church, viz: Samuel R. Close, Charles Coats, Ansel Coats, M. S. Lathrop, Daniel Saulsbury, John C. Lewis, Abiathar Powers, Melinda Close, Harriet Lewis and Emily Lathrop. Their action was recorded in the following form; "We, the undersigned, having letters of dismission and recommendation from sister churches of our faith and order, do hereby resolve to hand in our letters, and unite ourselves together for the purpose of forming a Baptist church of Christ in Hudson, to be known as the Baptist Church of Christ in Hudson, to receive members, either by baptism or by letter, and to do and transact any business, in obedience to the Gospel and according to law, in such case made and provided.

"*Resolved*, That we adopt the declaration of faith and church covenant, recommended by the Baptist State Convention of Michigan, October 6th, A. D. 1842."

On Wednesday, the 27th day of September, 1843, a council, composed of delegates from the churches of Wheatland, Pittsford, Dover, Medina and Adrian, convened in the village of Hudson to constitute the new church. Abiathar Powers represented the new church in the council.

On the 14th day of February, 1844, the church called the Rev. Jacob Ambler to the pastorate for one year. May 19th the church appointed the Rev. Mr. Ambler, M. S. Lathrop and Abiathar Powers delegates to set in council with the Jonesville church, for the purpose of ordaining their pastor.

On the 10th day of June, 1845, the church called the Rev. Lauren Hotchkiss to the pastorate "for the ensuing year, one-half of the time." On the 14th day of March, Samuel Eddy, Samuel R. Close, A. Coats, A. Wadsworth, Wm. Ames and Abiathar Powers, were appointed to meet the Dover church in council, for the purpose of ordaining Mr. Pack to the ministry. The same day they extended a call to Mr. Pack to become their pastor. August 7th, 1847, the church invited Peter Houghwout to preach to them one year from the first of October. Mr. Houghwout was at that time a student, and resided in Medina.

In the summer and fall of 1847, the church succeeded in putting up and covering the frame of a church building, and in the winter of 1847-8 they finished it. It stood about where William B. Ames' store now is.

February 3d, 1848, the church met and passed the following resolutions:

Resolved, That P. B. Houghwout is well qualified to preach the gospel, and we desire to see him fully set apart to the work of the ministry; therefore

Resolved, That we will call a council to determine the qualifications of P. B. Houghwout, and for the purpose of ordination.

By a vote of the meeting the following churches were invited: 1st and 2d Rollin, Wheatland, 2d Rome, Medina, Dover, Medina and Wright, Adrian, Fairfield and Seneca. It was also determined to dedicate the church on the 23d day of that month, and that the ordination council convene on the 24th.

The house was dedicated on Wednesday, the 23d day of February, 1848, Elder Tucker, of Adrian, preaching the dedicatory sermon. The Baptists had the first dedicated house of worship in Hudson. For some reason, Mr. Houghwort was not ordained on the day designated. On the 10th day of June the church called Peter B. Houghwout to the pastorate, and fixed his salary at three hundred and twenty-five dollars. At a church meeting held Sunday, April 22d, 1849, it was resolved to call a council for the ordination of Peter B. Houghwout on Tuesday, the 15th day of May next, and churches were invited as follows: Medina, Wright, Wright and Medina, Wheatland, 1st and 2d Rollin, 2d Rome, Adrian, Clinton, and Dover. Samuel R. Close, Samuel Eddy and Abiathar Powers were appointed delegates to the council. The church was now vacant from May or June, 1849, to May 19th, 1850, and on the 16th day of September, 1849, it was voted "to invite the Methodists to preach in the Baptist house until such time as we get a pastor." Upon this invitation the Methodists occupied the house until they occupied their own house in the spring of 1850.

May 19th, 1850, Elder Samuel Jones, jr., was called to the pastorate for one year. On the 26th day of October following, twenty-six persons united with the church—twenty-five by profession of faith and baptism. On the 2d day of November twelve persons were received, and on the 9th thirteen persons were received, all by baptism.

April 27th, 1851, Elder A. P. Howell was called to the pastorate for one year, at a salary of three hundred dollars, to commence on the 18th day of May then next. In the month of December, 1851, the church building was consumed by fire. But the church were not easily discouraged; they at once set about re-building, and on the 8th day of October, 1852, the new house was dedicated, Rev. U. B. Miller preaching the dedicatory sermon. Elder Howell was continued in the pastorate a second year.

In the spring of 1853, the church enjoyed more than usual revival influence, and many persons were received into membership. On the 30th day of November, Elder Howell tendered his resignation, which was accepted.

January 6th, 1854, Elder Volney Church was called to the pastorate of the church. It seems that Elder Church preached on Sundays, but attended to his own business on week days. At the close of his first year he was re-engaged on a salary of two hundred and fifty dollars, he to give one-half of his time to the service of the church. Increased labor worked good to the church, for on the 19th day of May following seven persons were baptised and received into the fellowship of the church.

Some time in the summer of 1856, Elder William Pack became pastor of the church. May 18th, 1857, Elder William Pack resigned the pastorate of the church. His resignation was accepted.

Late in the summer, or in the fall of 1857, the Rev. Jas. G. Portman became the pastor of the church, on a salary of four hundred dollars, and the use of a house for residence. The winter of 1857-8 was another revival season for the church, upwards of thirty persons uniting with the church on profession of faith. In May, 1858, this church had an attack of Masonry, as witness the following resolution:

WHEREAS, We believe that all secret societies are inconsistent with the principles of the gospel; therefore

Resolved, That we disclaim all church fellowship with such societies, and we affectionately entreat our brethren to withdraw from and disclaim all such connection, for in so uniting and continuing with such societies will bring a grievous burden upon the brethren, and cause the Zion of God to mourn, and the hand of fellowship to be withdrawn from them.

After adopting the above resolution, the church appointed Bros. Wright, Wood and Van Epps a committee to labor with a brother accused of being a Free Mason. At a subsequent meeting Brother Wright reported that the offending Brother expressed affection for the church, but said his being a Mason was none of their business, or words to that effect. The church was sensible enough to refrain from excommunication, but in lieu thereof gave him a letter of dismissal, stating his relation to Masonry. But the proceeding seems to have had a bad effect upon Wright and Van Epps, for since then they have become both Odd Fellows and Masons.

The ministry of the Rev. J. G. Portman extended through 1858 and until December, 1859, and was very successful so far as accessions to the church was concerned, until about June 1st, 1859, his further usefulness was destroyed by charges preferred against him. He was accused of adultery with a young girl—a member of his church—and with unchristian conduct in his intercourse with the ministers of the other village churches. He was tried on the charge of seduction in the Circuit Court, but the jury failed to agree. The remainder of the year was occupied with church meetings and councils. As is usual in such cases, there were two parties, and the church was well nigh rent asunder. The action of the majority toward the minority was severe, and produced feelings of resentment that were never effectually healed until the first year of the ministry of the Rev. C. T. Chaffee, when the church once more resumed her proper work, and was rewarded with more than old time prosperity. The house was found too small for them; it was enlarged and improved, and under his successors—Cressey, Osborn and Shanafelt—it has been marching on to victory. The history of the church is dropped with the year 1859, for the same reasons that the modern history of the other churches was left unwritten.

THE ROMAN CATHOLICS—CHURCH OF THE SACRED HEART.—Very early in the settlement of this township and Medina, Roman Catholic families formed a part of the population, and at quite an early date—just when we have been unable to ascertain— a church was built on the line between the two towns, where occasionally the priest from Monroe would officiate.

About the year 1858 or '59 the Rev. Father Van Erp was sent here, and he at once set about transferring the church to Hudson. A building was purchased and fitted up for a church, services were held each Sunday except the last in the month, on which day services were held in the Medina church. During the ministry of Father Van Erp a priest's residence was built, and then a church commenced, and so far finished as to be used before his departure. Recently a spire has been added, which greatly adds to the beauty of the structure. The parish has increased in numbers, until it has become the largest religious body in the town.

OTHER CHURCHES.—At a very early day there was a Baptist church in Dover, which has now become one of the Clayton churches, and is located in this township, but we have not the materials at hand for a sketch.

There were from the beginning a number of persons very restive under Congregational rule, and these, being reinforced by several new arrivals, several years ago organized a Presbyterian church. They purchased the house built by the Free Will Baptists several years since, and refitted it. They are not numerous enough, however, to maintain worship all the time; indeed, for the most part their pulpit has been vacant.

In 1860 a Protestant Episcopal parish was organized and named Trinity. There was but little done, however, until the Rev. Mr. Smythe became rector in 1869, since which time the parish has been reasonably prosperous. Under the ministry of the Rev. Mr. Webster a church was built and finished, except the tower. But this church being one of the modern institutions of the township, does not come within the purview of this work.

THE SCHOOLS OF HUDSON VILLAGE.

For want of records we shall not be able to give a full and complete history of the schools of the village of Hudson. The founders of the village took a deep interest in the education of the young; schools were established on each side of Tiffin river at an early day. The main building on the West Side was erected in 1860, at a cost of $6,000. In 1874 the West Side put up a fine branch building with two rooms, north of the railroad, at a cost of $3,000. The East Side school building was erected in 1862, at a cost of about $3,000. By an act of the Legislature in 1866, the East and West Side were united and became a chartered school under the appellation of The Public Schools of the Village of Hudson. After being united for several years, the East Side, by a legislative act, was set off from the public schools of the village of Hudson, and organized as a graded school under the primary school law. This separation was effected May 1st, 1869. In 1873 an effort was made to reunite the schools, but at an election held in June to decide the matter, it failed by a small majority. Since that time no effort at union has been made. The number of children of school ages in the West Side district at the time of the last enumeration, was 475.

Among the early Principals of the West Side school, may be mentioned Prof. James, now Assistant Superintendent of the Cleveland schools, and Prof. Carson, of

Hudson, formerly Principal of the Medina Academy. In October, 1860, Prof. F. B. McClelland, now at the head of the Albion Union School, became Principal. He remained in charge until April, 1862, when he took charge of the East Side school, which position he held until July 1st, 1867. Rev. C. Van Dorn had charge of the school a large part of the time while they were united. He was succeeded by Prof. E. G. Reynolds, Jan. 5th, 1869, who held the position until June 23d, 1869.

Prof. C. D. West, of Blissfield, was the next Principal. He held the position two years. Mr. West was succeeded by Capt. C. T. Bateman, former County Superintendent of Schools for Lewanee county, who took charge of the school Sept. 1, 1873. The first class of graduates left this school in June, 1875. The class consisted of Miss Hattie Beach, Miss Clara Boies, Miss Lillie Galusha, Miss Ida Harris, Miss Allie Perkins, and Mr. Edmund Childs. The organization of the School Board, at present, is W. F. Day, president; J. M. Scarritt, secretary; R. J. Eaton, treasurer; J. K. Boies, W. J. Mosher, A. Loyster.

The following extract from the Superintendent's report for the school year of 1875 and 1876, is given:

I submit the following brief report of the condition of the Public Schools of the Village of Hudson, and of the work done in them during the past year.

Number of weeks of school during the year.. 40
" " children between the ages of five and twenty in the district.......... 475
" " pupils enrolled... 435
" " foreign pupils.. 43
Enrollment in Grammar and High School... 127
" " Second Intermediate... 60
" " First Intermediate... 48
" " Second Primary... 48
" " First Primary.. 76
" " North Branch.. 74
Number of teachers employed... 9

The corps of teachers at present consists of Prof. C. T. Bateman, superintendent and principal; Miss Ezoa Phelps and Mrs. C. E. Richards, assistants in grammar and high school. The other assistants are Miss Delia Carpenter, Miss Della Hutchins, Mrs. Maria L. Graves, Mrs. C. Plympton, Mrs. Anna Chapman and Miss Alice Perkins.

Among the principals of the East Side school since Prof. McClelland left may be mentioned Prof. Carson; Prof J. C. Dutton, now in Europe, from September, 1872, to June, 1873; Prof. Overholt, September, 1873, to April, 1874; Prof. Luther W. Covell from September, 1874, to June, 1876. Prof. Coleman Williams, aided by three associate teachers, has charge of the school at present. The school officers consist of the following named persons: Ira Swaney, director; M. R. Hazlett, moderator; D. Carpenter, assessor; B. Wright, J. Van Akin, T. J. Hiller.

The schools of Hudson have generally been in good hands, and have been prosperous to a marked degree. In the management and support of their schools the people of Hudson and vicinity have shown prudence, economy and wise generosity, and they may well be proud of their schools, which have done and are still doing good work for the youth of our community. May the good work of education in our beautiful village ever prosper.

BENEVOLENT ORDERS.

ODD FELLOWS.—In 1847 Hudson Lodge No. 26, I. O. O. F., was chartered. It worked for a number of years, and then suspended. Subsequently it was resuscitated, and has worked prosperously since. A list of its officers has been furnished, but as rotation in office has been the general rule, a list of Noble Grands, as the presiding officer is called, only is given, it being premised that the subordinate offices were filled, with but few exceptions, by the same men preparatory to the more exalted station.

Noble Grands.—Edward D. Larned, Henry M. Boies (two terms), J. B. Tucker, Augustus Thomas, Judson R. Hyde, Beriah H. Lane, Joseph M. Johnson, Dr. David

P. Chamberlin, John C. Hogaboam, Reuben A. Beach, William W. Morrous, Jesse
Maxson, Jackson M. Wood, Alexander H. Hall, Jabez J. Daniels, David R. Stroud,
Dr. Leonard G. Hall, Edwin M. Hulburd, Henry G. Stevens, Levi Saulsbury, Dexter
Gray, Robert B. Piper, William T. B. Schermerhorn, Benjamin Wright, Allen J.
Skutt, Perry Shumway (two terms), Henry G. Frank, John K. Boies, John Weed,
Hiram Mann, John V. Munger, Gamaliel I. Thompson, William C. Merrell (two
terms), William R. Weaver, Chester C. Pease, Lawrence Van Epps, Stephen T.
Dawes, Charles H. Putnam, Lawrence E. Halran, John Spaulding, William G. Don-
aldson (two terms), Marion F. Isbell, C. H. Hubbard, John T. Mann and John R.
Wirts. The only persons who have held the second office (Vice Grand) and failed of
election to the presiding officer's chair because of removal or other causes are the following: Charles E. Niles, James Lowe, John V. Goodrich, Dr. Thomas B. Minchin,
Samuel H. Perkins, William Smith and John Butts.

About ten years ago an Encampment was organized, called Wood Encampment, to
confer the higher degrees of the order. It has been successful. The Hudson Lodge
has furnished one Grand Master of Odd Fellows of the State of Michigan—Mr. Dexter
Gray.

FREE MASONRY.—In 1848 Morning Star Lodge F. & A. M., commenced work under
a dispensation, Jesse Maxson, Worshipful Master. The Lodge was chartered at the
next session of the Grand Lodge and numbered 26, and continued to work until 1859.
It had Worshipful Masters as follows: 1848, '49 and '50, Jesse Maxson; 1851, Robert
B. Piper; 1852 and '53, Jesse Maxson; 1854 to 1856, Dr. David P. Chamberlin; 1857
until it suspended, November 7, 1859, Hamilton W. Grennell.

On the 21st day of November, 1859, Maxson Lodge F. & A. M. commenced work
under dispensation, Jesse Maxson, Worshipful Master. The lodge was chartered in
January, 1860, and given the old number of Morning Star Lodge (26), and it has continued in working order since. It has had Worshipful Masters as follows: 1859,
Jesse Maxson; 1860 and '61, Dr. D. P. Chamberlin; 1862 to '64, David R. Stroud;
1865, Francis D. Beach; 1866, David R. Stroud; 1867, '68 and '69, Allen J. Skutt; 1870,
Jas. J. Hogaboam; 1871, Allen J. Skutt; 1872, '73 and '74, Francis D. Beach; 1875 and
'76, David R. Stroud.

On the 24th day of September, 1863, Warren Lodge F. & A. M., commenced work
under dispensation, Dr. Benjamin J. Tayer, Worshipful Master. Worshipful Masters—1863 and '64, Benj. J. Tayer; 1865, Hamilton W. Grennell; 1866 and '67, Edward
A. Gay; 1868 and '69, Charles Lowe; 1870, Robert Worden; 1871, Charles Lowe; 1872
to '76, Lawrence E. Halran.

In January, 1863, Hudson Chapter Royal Arch Masons was chartered and numbered
28, and continued to work until the fall of 1873. High Priests—1863, '64 and '65, Enos
Canniff; 1866, Jas. J. Hogaboam; 1867, Allen J. Skutt; 1868 and '69, Hamilton W.
Grennell; 1870, Jas. J. Hogaboam; 1871, Allen J. Skutt; 1872 to suspension, David R.
Stroud.

In the summer of 1876 Phœnix Chapter R. A. M. commenced work under dispensation; John M. Osborn, High Priest.

A council of Royal and Select Masters commenced work in 1865, and continued until the suspension of the Chapter in 1873 deprived it of material. Presiding officers—
1865, U. D., Jas. B. Pratt; 1865 (after charter), Enos Canniff; 1866, Allen J. Skutt;
1867 and '68, Chas. H. Putnam; 1869, Joseph D. Darling; 1870, Allen J. Skutt; 1871,
Myron M. Maxson; 1872, Jas. J. Hogaboam.

OFFCIIAL REGISTER—LEGISLATORS.

Senators—Henry M. Boies, William Baker and John K. Boies. Representatives,
John W. Turner, Augustus W. Childs and John K. Boies. County officers—Benj.
Turner, register of deeds; Andrew C. Mercer, Clement C. Weaver and Seth Bean,

prosecuting attorneys; Jas. J. Hogaboam and Perry Shumway, circuit court commissioners.

Supervisors: 1836, Simeon Van Akin; 1837 and '38, Augustus Finney; 1839 and '40, Henry Tibbetts; 1841, Hiram Kidder; 1842, L. Hutchins; 1843, Simeon Van Akin; 1844, Lemuel P. Whitney; 1845, Daniel R. Daniels; 1846, Simeon Van Akin; 1847, Oliver S. Colwell; 1848 and '49, Silas Eaton; 1850, Oliver S. Colwell; 1851, Benjamin Turner; 1852, Augustus W. Childs; 1853, Lorenzo Palmer; 1854, Enos Canniff; 1855, John Bean; 1856, Lorenzo Palmer; 1857, John H. Carleton; 1858 and '59, Lorenzo L. Brown; 1860 to 1863, inclusive, Lorenzo Palmer; 1864, Titus Babcock; 1865 to 1872, inclusive, Lorenzo Palmer; 1873 to 1876, inclusive, Ira Swaney.

AGRICULTURAL SOCIETY.

About the year 1859, the Hillsdale and Lenawee Union Agricultural Society was organized. It held fairs until 1864. That year it had a rainy season for the fair, and, could not pay its premiums. It died.

THE VILLAGE OF HUDSON.

PLATS—*Bowlsby's.*—Levi N. Bowlsby, proprietor; acknowledged June 7th, 1842.

Gibbon's Survey.—Platted by Isaac A. Colvin, Dudley Worden, W. H. Johnson, Hiram Osborn, Harrison Lindenbower, E. Conant, Stephen M. Wirts, Erastus Lane, J. C. Benedict, E. D. Larned, Chas. Parrish, Roswell Rose, M. S. Lathrop, W. H. H. Van Akin, W. L. Larned and B. H. Lane, January 23d, 1843.

ADDITIONS—*Van Akin's, South.*—Platted March 25th, 1850, by W. H. H. Van Akin, W. H. Johnson, Aaron Loomis and Thomas Daniels.

Laird's—Platted June 2d, 1855, by Robert Laird.

Wirts'—Old survey, platted September 3d, 1855, by Dr. Stephen M. Wirts.

Church's—Platted November 14th, 1855, by Rev. Volney Church.

Goodrich's—Platted November 28th, 1855, by Heman R. Goodrich.

Johnson's—Platted April 5th, 1856, by W. H. Johnson, Wm. B. Ames, Ann B. Cobb, Edward Cobb and Harvey J. Cobb.

Johnson and Conger's—Platted May 5th, 1858, by W. H. Johnson and John Conger.

Power's—Platted June 8th, 1858, by Dr. Jas. S. Power.

Van Akin's, East—Platted by W. H. H. Van Akin, November 5th, 1858.

Wirts'—New survey, platted November 21st, 1859, by Dr. Stephen M. Wirts.

Cobb's—Platted July 3d, 1860, by Ann B. Cobb, Edward Cobb, Jas. H. Cobb and Susan B. Whitney.

H. N. Johnson's—Platted August 9th, 1860, by Silas Eaton.

Wilcox's—Platted April 5th, 1864, by Welcome Aldrich.

The village was incorporated in 1853. The following named persons have filled the office of President: Caleb C. Cooley, Henry M. Boies, David P. Chamberlin. Stephen A. Eaton, Wm. Baker, Hamilton W. Grennell, Samuel DeGolyer, John J. Beck, Beriah H. Lane, Warren A. Jones, Levi R. Pierson, John K. Boies, Luther C. French, Russell M. Gillett, William A. Whitney, Ira Swaney, Augustus Kent and John Bean.

CLAYTON.

Platted by Chauncey and Reuben E. Bird, October 10th, 1843.

ADDITIONS.—*Waterman's*—Platted May 5th, 1864.

Graves and Reed's—Platted May 1st, 1865, by Burrit W. Graves and Jacob Reed.

Waterman's Extension—Platted by D. R. Waterman, February 19th, 1867.

Graves'—Platted June 10th, 1871, by Burrit W. and Albert H. Graves.

Bird's—Platted by Reuben E. Bird, April 14th, 1872.

The village was incorporated about 1869.

G

NECROLOGY.

Cobb—Harvey, May 15th, 1842, aged 46 years; Ann B., wife of Harvey, July 24th, 1864, aged 52 years; Carroll C., son, Oct. 27th 1854, aged 24 years; Susan B. Whitney, daughter, July 15th, 1863, aged 26 years; James H., son, Sept. 17th, 1869, aged 35 years.

Finney—Augustus, July 19th, 1857, aged 61 years; Huldah Foot, wife, August, 1843, aged 55 years; Alfred A., son, Sept. 8th, 1871, aged 52 years; Harriet C. Kidder, wife of Alfred A., Sept. 5th, 1857, aged 33 years.

Wirts—Dr. Stephen M., Nov. 1st, 1871, aged 64 years; Mary, wife, April 10th 1860, aged 46 years.

Pratt—Rev. David, March 26th, 1845, aged 56 years; Sarah Smith, daughter, March, 1856, aged 36 years; Elizabeth A., daughter, Jan. 16th, 1853, aged 19 years; Mary D., daughter, June 11th, 1869, aged 34 years; James B., son, Dec. 13th, 1875, aged 51 years; Dolly R., wife of James B., Jan. 8th, 1865.

Van Akin—Lydia, wife of Simeon, July 5th, 1868, aged 63 years; Sarah Amelia Boies, daughter of Lydia Van Akin, formerly Spear, and wife of Hon. John K. Boies, Jan. 2d, 1871, aged 39 years.

Carleton—John H., February, 1872, aged 70 years; Mary Ann Kidder, daughter, April 16th, 1861, aged 27 years; Henry, son, died April, 1865.

Osborn—John, April 28th, 1867, aged 78 years; Mercy, wife, July 15th, 1865, aged 72 years.

Eaton—Silas, Aug. 20th, 1876, aged 81 years; Constantine C. S., son, Nov. 11th, 1848, aged 21 years; Hervey U., son, April 21st, 1852, aged 22 years.

Johnson—Capt. W. H., Sept. 16th, 1865, aged 48 years; Celinda S. Hathaway, wife, June 2d, 1846, aged 25 years.

Cady—Lydia, wife of Nelson O., June 7th, 1851, aged 37 years; Levina, daughter, Aug. 12th, 1851, aged 16 years; Kleber W. died in the army.

Griswold—John, April 17th, 1874, aged 86 years; Sabra, wife, April 8th, 1872.

Kidder—Hiram, May 11th, 1849, aged 49 years; Julia G., daughter, Nov. 8th, 1856, aged 18 years; Maria J., daughter, Jan. 5th, 1857, aged 26 years.

Lane—Nathaniel, father of B. H. Lane, esq., March 16th, 1844, aged 73 years; Mary, first wife, Sept 17th, 1839, aged 68 years; Martha, second wife, March 2d, 1871, aged 85 years; Phebe, wife of Beriah H., May 22d, 1839, aged 35 years; Anna Maria, daughter of B. H. Lane, March 9th, 1851, aged 23 years.

Palmer—Lorenzo, Oct. 17th, 1874, aged 71 years; Ruth Wells, wife, Feb. 25th, 1853, aged 50 years.

Treadwell—William C., Dec. 27th, 1856, aged 42 years; Eliza, wife, March 22d, 1849, aged 29 years.

Wells—Thomas, Aug. 17th, 1847, aged 42 years; Helen, daughter, Sept. 10th, 1847.

Trask—Deacon Salmon, April 22d, 1851, aged 50 years; Zeruiah, wife, Nov. 15th, 1842, aged 35 years; Susan A., daughter, Sept. 28th, 1850, aged 20 years.

Worden—Dudley, March 28th, 1859, aged 54 years; Phebe, wife, Jan. 30th, 1851, aged 34 years.

Straw—Thomas, Dec. 25th, 1855, aged 59 years; Rhoda, wife, Oct. 29th, 1851, aged 55 years.

Orcutt—Silas, Feb. 19th, 1856, aged 45 years; Clarinda, wife, March 6th, 1855, aged 41 years.

Treadwell—Alzina P., wife of Urias Treadwell, Jan. 30th, 1863, aged 42 years.

Colwell—John, April 30th, 1860, aged 57 years.

Taylor—John L., Nov. 9th, 1862, aged 60 years.

Hall—Nancy K. Wells, wife of Dr. Leonard G. Hall, Oct. 12th, 1853, aged 33 years.

Baldwin—Samuel D., Feb. 10th, 1873, aged 62 years.

Brownell—John S., Dec. 26th, 1856, aged 37 years.

Rose—Ira, May 7th, 1875, aged 75 years.

Beasom—Philip, Sept. 9th, 1874, aged 68 years; Mary B., wife, Feb. 28th, 1876, aged

74 years; Milton, son, died July 12th, 1862, aged 32 years; Francis B., son, Jan. 22d, 1876, aged 43 years; Marcia, wife of Francis B., Jan. 31, 1876, aged 40 years.

Bush—Eli, Oct. 5th, 1872, aged 66 years.

Jones—Dr. Bela B., March 5th, 1865.

Wheeler—Rev. Judson, July 9th, 1855, aged 51 years.

Palmer—Hannah, wife of Wray T., April 9th, 1875; Laura M. Turner, daughter, and wife of Benjamin Turner, July, 1860, aged 32 years.

Leisenring—David, April 18th, 1872, aged 76 years; Sally, wife, Aug. 21st, 1854, 61 years; Mary, daughter, July, 1852, aged 24 years; Eliza Gibson, daughter, November, 1852, aged 26 years; Jesse B., son, July 10th, 1854, aged 22 years; Wm. H. H., son, Nov. 19th, 1869, aged 29 years.

Mills—Randall, May 6th, 1870, aged 52 years.

Baker—William, June 5th, 1870, aged 52 years.

Fenton—Horace, April 9th, 1876, aged 71 years.

Perkins—Stephen, June 29th, 1874, aged 76 years.

Close—Samuel R., Feb. 8th, 1865, aged 65 years.

Hume—Moses, June 16th, 1864, aged 77 years; Sarah, wife, Nov. 26th, 1868, aged 84 years; Geo. P., son, April 8th, 1865, aged 38 years,

Hulburd—Col. Edwin M., burned to death in Milburn Wagon Works, Toledo, O., Sept. 29th, 1876.

Kent—Augustus, Oct. 4th, 1876, aged 56 years.

V. ROLLIN.

The second township meeting of the township of Rollin, the first under State authority, was held at the house of Jacob Foster, on the 4th day of April, 1836. The several offices were filled by the election of the following named persons, viz: Matthew Bennett, supervisor; William Beal, township clerk; Daniel Rhodes, Joseph Steer and Lester C. Bennett, assessors; Elijah C. Bennett, collector; John T. Comstock and David Steere, overseers of the poor; John T. Comstock, Joseph C. Beal and Asa R. Bacon, highway commissioners; Matthew Bennett, Brayton Brown, Orson Green and Leonard G. Hall, justices of the peace; William Hathaway, Ephraim Sloan, Elijah C. Bennett and Joseph S. Allen, constables. There were no school inspectors elected, as appears from the records of that meeting. The electors voted to pay three dollars for bear, and two dollars for wolf scalps.

At the election held September 12th, 1836, to elect delegates to the convention to meet at Ann Arbor on the 26th day of that month, to consider the boundary question proposed by Congress, there were only eleven votes cast. The township took no part in the second or party convention which did assent to the boundary proposition.

During the winter of 1835 and '36, material had been prepared for the proposed grist-mill, and in the spring the work was pushed forward.

William Beal returned to his farm, Azel Hooker opened a store in Mr. Beal's vacated house, and placed it under the management of a man named Allen. Samuel Comstock was appointed postmaster, and to Ephraim Sloan was awarded the contract to carry the mail.

In the spring of 1836 the first religious society was organized at the house of Matthew Bennett. It was a Baptist church, and in its organization Mr. Bennett was the prime mover, and he held the office of deacon. Of this good man, one of his neighbors, Mr. Page, writes as follows: "Deacon Bennett was peculiarly well fitted to settle in a new country. Possessing a strong religious temperament and a keen sense of moral right, he used his influence for the best interests of the community in which he lived; never meeting his friends or neighbors without giving the friendly hand-shake and kind, cheering words. Like the good Samaritan, he never passed by the poor and the needy without relieving their distress as far as was within his means.

Though some time gone to his final rest, (a rest of which he so much delighted to talk,) he still holds a warm place in the hearts of those he left behind."

In the winter of 1836 and '37, the grist-mill was put in motion. It was the second in the Valley, the Talbot mill at Peru having commenced to grind in August of 1836; but as its capacity was insufficient for the needs of even the northeast part of the Valley, this new mill was hailed as a harbinger of approaching civilization.

It would indeed be pleasant to follow, in description, the rapid development of the township, in population and in wealth, until it has come to be one of the finest and most wealthy townships in the county, inhabited as it is by an intelligent and enterprising class of people, but the limits prescribed for this little volume will not permit; that must be deferred to some other time, and perhaps the task will fall to other hands. With brief mention of some of her representative men, we must close this sketch.

The Hon. Orson Green has lived in the township since 1834, and during his sojourn there, has been frequently called upon to fill offices of trust and honor. He has twice represented his district in the Legislature of the State. He was elected to that office in 1858, and again in 1870. He was a Whig, and now is a Republican in politics. Having an innate sense of justice, he is a Republican because he believes equal rights to be one of the cardinal principles of the party, and that the country will be safer under its control. Mr. Green is a leading member of the Methodist Episcopal church of his township, having enjoyed the privileges of its communion for forty years. His house was the home of the early circuit riders, who were always satisfied when lodged under his roof.

The Rev. William Rhodes settled in the township in 1834. He married his wife in Massachusetts, at the age of nineteen, before coming to Michigan. He was a Methodist from early childhood, and tells of going with his wife forty miles to attend a quarterly meeting. Mrs. Rhodes rode a horse, but Mr. Rhodes traveled the whole distance on foot. Upon his invitation, the Rev. Mr. Jackson, the junior preacher on the Tecumseh circuit, visited the Bean Creek country and preached in its several settlements. He was accompanied by Allen Staples, then a local preacher, residing at Adrian. The services in the township of Rollin were held at the house of Daniel Rhodes and Dobson Page. William Rhodes is said to have taught the first public school in the township of Rollin, in the winter of 1836 and '37, at his own house. There are some, however, who think Lucretia Beal taught a school at the house of William Beal in the summer of 1836. Mr. Rhodes was licensed to preach in early life, and afterwards was received into the itinerancy and ordained to the ministry. After traveling a few years, he located and returned to his farm in Rollin. In subsequent years he was engaged in business in New York city, and then in Hudson. He is now living in the city of Detroit, engaged in the insurance business.

Daniel Rhodes, the father of William, was also one of the earliest settlers of Rollin. He lived on his farm in Rollin until about the year 1860, when becoming too old to labor, the farm was sold, and Daniel and his wife, Abigail, moved to Hudson, where they lived until their decease.

John T. Comstock, also, was one of the earliest settlers of Rollin, and has resided on his farm ever since his settlement in 1834. Mr. Comstock belongs to the Society of Friends, and has won considerable reputation as a poet. Several years ago his wife —the companion of his youth, and the joy of his heart in pioneer days—departed this life, and he subsequently married Mrs. Elizabeth Wright, a preacher among the Friends. Mrs. Comstock is a woman of great excellence, distinguished for simplicity of manners, a fervid eloquence, and an untiring zeal in the prosecution of her mission. She has traveled largely, is extensively known, and everywhere welcomed— alike among the Friends or other religious bodies, as a true disciple of their common Master.

There are many other worthy pioneers of the township, some of whom have served their township faithfully in minor capacities, and others of them have adorned the paths of private life.

The following named gentlemen have represented the township on the Board of Supervisors: Matthew Bennett, 1835 and '37; Elijah Brownell, 1838; David Steere, 1839; Daniel Rhodes, 1840; William Beal, 1841; Thomas Kealey, 1842 and '43; William Beal, 1844; Orson Green, 1845 and '46; Jas. Patrick, 1847; Orson Green, 1848 to '52, both inclusive; William Beal, 1853; A. H. Raymond, 1854 and '55; Felix A. Wilcox, 1856 and '57; James Patrick, 1858; Orson Green, 1859; H. Rawson, 1860; Porter Beal, 1861 and '62; Orson Green, 1863; Felix A. Wilcox, 1864 to '67, both inclusive; Avery A. Dolbear, 1868 to '75, both inclusive; Orson Green, 1876.

The township of Rollin is a handsome faced country, has rich soil, and is well watered. It produces bountiful crops of all the important farm products. Its dairy interest is large, and its fruit among the finest in the country.

The people have not been inattentive to the claims of education or religion. It has a sufficient number of neat and commodious school houses, and its district schools are of a high order. It has four churches within its borders—one each in the villages of Rollin and Addison, one at the centre of the town, and a Friends' meeting-house on section sixteen.

VI. WOODSTOCK.

The first township meeting of the township of Woodstock was held at the house of Jesse Osborn on the fourth day of April, 1836. The officers elected were: Nahum Lamb, supervisor; Thomas McCourtie, township clerk; David Terrell, Samuel Dunn and Joseph Younglove, justices of the peace; Israel Titus, Ezekiel W. Sanford, and William Joslin, assessors; Jesse Osborn and John Binns, directors of the poor; Charles McKenzie and Jedediah P. Osborn, constables; Nelson Terrell, Michael Chool and Isaac Titus, commissioners of highways; William Western, Joseph Younglove and Mitchel Gue, commissioners of schools; Alonzo Smith, William Babcock and Wardell W. Sanford, school inspectors; Ezekiel W. Sanford, pound master; Benson Hulin, sealer of weights and measures.

In December, 1835, John Talbot commenced preparations for building a mill on Bean Creek, near the outlet of Devil's Lake. The mill was finished in August, 1836. The mill is said to have been situated near the southwest corner of section thirty-three. This was the pioneer grist mill of the Valley, and proved a great accommodation to the settlers. It was a small affair, however, and when run to its full capacity it was unable to do the grinding for even the northern portion of the Valley. In a short time there was quite a collection of houses, shops, etc., around the mill, which received the name of Peru.

In the fall of 1837, Mr. Talbot concluding he could obtain a better power farther down the stream, commenced a new race and mill. Although the mill property is nearly all within the limits of Woodstock, yet the mill was located just south of the township line, in the edge of Rollin, at the middle or unused flume between the present grist and saw mill. The new mill commenced operation in the month of July, 1838, and very soon after, all the denizens of Peru moved to and settled around the new mill.

During the political campaign of 1840, because nearly every voter of the burgh was a Whig, and coon skins (one of the Whig campaign emblems) were displayed at nearly every door, Thomas McCourtie nicknamed it "Coon Town," an appellation it has not entirely outgrown. In 1847, April the eighth, it was platted by the name of Harrison, but soon after became generally known as Addison. The village is situated in two townships; perhaps the greater part in Rollin.

In 1840 Jesse Osborn and David Terrell built a saw mill on Goose creek, in the northern part of the township. The mill at the village now called Addison was sold to Darius C. Jackson in 1842, and about that time the saw mill was built. The present grist mill was built in the fall of 1848.

Woodstock, like Rollin, is wholly an agricultural township. The face of the country is considerably broken and profusely sprinkled with small lakes; there are fifteen, fourteen of them wholly within its limits. Besides these lakes, there are numerous small streams. Indeed, it may be said of it, "It is well watered everywhere." In 1870 there were 11,851 acres of land under cultivation, and the valuation of its farms and live stock exceeds one million of dollars. It has some splendid farms and elegant farm houses, and taking it altogether, it is one of the best of our agricultural townships. Of churches, it has not a great number. There is a Methodist Episcopal church in the village of Addison, but it stands within the borders of Rollin. A little north of the village, on the north half of section thirty-one, there is a Friends' meeting house, and on section twenty-one there is a Congregational church.

The earliest settlers have all passed away, and those of the second and third years are counted among the oldest men and women of the township. Cornelius Millspaw, the first settler, moved into the township of Somerset before 1837, and after a while moved on still farther west. Mrs. Rachael Osborn died in 1851. In 1857 Mr. Jesse Osborn moved to Coffee county, Kansas, where he died in 1865.

The township of Woodstock has been the scene of two foul murders, or more properly, of five, for one was a quadruple murder. Mr. and Mrs. Bivins had long been residents of the township, and had won the respect and esteem of all their neighbors. They had but one child, a boy named David. He was not different from other boys, except that he was noticed to have a very revengeful disposition. At an early age he married a daughter of Ezra Sanford. She died July 5th, 1862, and it was afterwards thought that David was instrumental in her "taking off." At the time of her death she was but nineteen years of age. In February following he married his second wife, a daughter of Mr. Thomas Brownell, a citizen of Rollin township. Miss Laura Brownell was a young lady of great personal attractions, and appeared to be much attached to her husband, and they lived happily for a time. David took a notion that he ought to have a deed of his father's farm, and to induce him to deed it, David enlisted in the army. His idea was that his parents would rather deed him their home than have their only son go into the army. In this he was mistaken. Learning his mistake, he hoped he would not receive his commission and appeared disappointed when it came. He subsequently deserted the army, and at the house of his father-in-law had an interview with his father, who besought him with tears to endeavor in some way to earn an honorable living. As it was not safe for David to stay there, his father gave him one hundred dollars, expressing the hope that it was the last money he would ever ask of him. David went to Grafton, in the State of Ohio, and engaged in the sale of Blackman's medicines, and earned some money. While thus employed, he made the acquaintance of Miss Myra Hart, the daughter of a dry goods merchant of Grafton. He was smitten with her charms, and it is believed made some progress in gaining her affections. But there was a Woodstock lady in the way of a consummation of his wishes. He resolved to be rid of this encumbrance, and at the same time secure the property he would need to support Miss Hart.

With this thought uppermost in his mind, he left Grafton for Michigan, in January, 1865. He went to his father's house and had an interview with his parents and wife, and then to Hudson the same day. At the livery stable of Green & Johnson he applied for a saddle horse. Mr. Johnson informed him that they had none, but could furnish him a light buggy. It was winter, but the ground was bare. He gave orders to have the horse and vehicle ready on the arrival of the night train from the east. Having made these arrangements he went east on the afternoon train. He returned on the night train, took the horse and buggy, and driving to the vicinity of his father's house, hitched the horse among some bushes by the roadside. Going into the house he found that his father and mother were absent, taking care of a sick neighbor. His wife was alone. He sent her for his father, saying he must see him immediately-

Mrs. Bivins accompanied her husband home. David seated himself beside his father under pretense of private conversation, and thus held his attention while he presented a pistol to his head and fired. The old man dropped dead. His mother was next slain, and then he faced his wife. She plead with him for the sake of their unborn child to spare her life, but the image of Myra Hart was before his eyes, and the brute at once murdered his wife and their child. He then set fire to the house and retraced his steps to Hudson. He arrived there in time to take the morning train eastward. A robe dropped from the buggy, told who the murderer and incendiary was, and he was immediately arrested. He died in the Michigan State prison.

The other murder was that of Rhoda Pennock, who was killed by her husband, James P. Pennock, on the 22d day of April, 1865. Mr. Pennock had formerly lived in the city of Adrian, and there owned the McKenzie farm. He removed to Woodstock about the year 1854, He was upwards of six feet in height, and in 1865 he was sixty-seven years old, and his hair was perfectly white. He owned one hundred and sixty acres of land on the shore of Devil's Lake, on section thirty-four. He was a profane man, excitable and passionate, but had never been intemperate, and although penurious, had never been deemed dishonest. On the question of domestic economy Pennock and his wife had had frequent quarrels. Their son-in-law had been living with them, and most of the household furniture belonged to him and to his wife. They had determined to live apart from the old folks, but the old man objected to a removal of the furniture. Mrs. Pennock took sides with the young folks, and the result was a series of family quarrels. On the afternoon of the 22d, just before dark, the neighbors discovered Pennock's barn to be on fire. They rushed over there and succeeded in extinguishing the flames. When this was done, the house was discovered to be on fire. This fire also was extinguished, but while they were engaged there Pennock succeded in firing the barn so effectually that it was destroyed. When this third fire was discovered it first occurred to the neighbors that Pennock was the incendiary. Mrs. Pennock was nowhere around, and as darkness had now come on, they procured lights and went in search of her. They found her lifeless body under a bridge which spanned a small stream running into the lake. He had killed her by blows on her head with some blunt instrument.

The following named citizens have served as supervisors of the township: 1836, Nahum Lamb; 1837, Jesse Selleck; 1838, Samuel Driggs; 1839 to '47, both inclusive, Joel F. Knapp; 1848, Orsamus Lamb; 1849, Samuel Dean; 1850 to '67, both inclusive, Orsamus Lamb; 1868 to '72, both inclusive, Lewis Sanford; 1873 and '74, Manson Carpenter; 1874 to '76, both inclusive, A. M. Sickly.

VII. WHEATLAND.

Harvey McGee and family settled in the township of Wheatland late in 1835, and Lyman Pease in February, 1836. Pease had lived for some years west of Adrian, in Lenawee county.

At the township meeting held that year, Heman Pratt was elected supervisor, Jno. McKnight clerk, and Heman Pratt, Nelson R. Rowley, Elias Branch and Aaron VanVleet, justices of the peace.

Mr. Edson Witherell had, in 1835, located 160 acres of land in Wheatland, and in 1836, in the month of July, he moved his family on to the land. They came from Adrian through Rollin, and were three days making the journey. Their place was at the end of the road; all beyond was wilderness.

In 1836 occurred the first birth and death in town six south: or, as it was then organized, the south part of Wheatland. Mrs. Cook gave birth to a son, and a few weeks afterwards died. Elder Parker preached the funeral sermon.

It is not perhaps known where or when the first couple were married, or who they were, but there was a marriage in 1836. It was necessary, then, to obtain a license of the township clerk before consummating the marriage contract. The township was possessed of a clerk that year who thought a record of the license of no value, but he demanded and obtained the written consent of the bride's father before granting the license, and this he recorded. In this instance it is as follows:

"This may certify that I, Silas Carmichael, of the county of Hillsdale, Michigan Territory, do give my consent for Nancy Carmichael, my daughter, to marry Henry B. Smith, of Logan, Lenawee county, Michigan Territory.

SILAS CARMICHAEL.

In presence of
Henry Carmichael,
Squire Carmichael."

Dec. 26th, 1836.

Mark, too, this clerk was a strict constructionist; he called Michigan a territory, although it had been a *de facto* State for more than a year. Legally, however, it was a territory.

The Nokes school house was probably built in 1836. By this is not meant the present house, but its log predecessor. All agree that it was the first built in town, and the next was built in 1837. This last, the house in No. 2, was built by Charles Carmichael. He took the job for $70, began it in June, and finished it July 4th. When the house was completed, he prepared to go to Adrian to buy some flour, as the bread timber was about to give out. Two of his neighbors also sent for a barrel each. When he arrived in Adrian there was only one barrel for sale in the village, and they wanted $18 for it. A man told him if he would wait until next day he would sell him three barrels of flour for $14 a barrel; he expected a car load of flour next morning; (horse cars were then used on the Erie and Kalamazoo railroad.) Carmichael agreed to wait. Soon after, Zebulon Williams, who then lived south of Adrian, came along, and pressed Carmichael to go home with him for the night. Carmichael consented, but before going, deposited the money for the flour with the landlord, and apprised the merchant of the fact. Coming back to the village next morning, he saw the man unloading a car load of flour, but the man did not recognize him. Stepping up to him, he asked, "Have you any flour to sell?" "No," said the merchant, "I have none to spare; it is all promised." Carmichael looked blue enough, for well he knew the flour barrel at home must before then be empty. The man noticing his disconsolate looks, continued, by way of apology, "They are nearly starving out in the Bean Creek country; there is a man from there, here, and I have promised him three barrels; the money is deposited with the landlord, and it is all I can spare. My customers must have the rest." "All right," said Carmichael, "I am the man." To yoke his oxen, bring the wagon up, load the flour and start for home, was but the work of an hour, and busily he jogged along until the flour was in the houses of the hungry settlers.

Mrs. Charles Carmichael went East on a visit that summer. She started June 8th, and traveled from Adrian to Toledo by horse power, but when she returned, the horses had been exchanged for steam power, and she made the trip to Adrian behind a locomotive.

In 1839 Stephen Knapp raised the first frame barn in the township. It stood for several years without doors, and it began to be thought among his neighbors that he hurried it up before he was able to finish so he could say it was the first. Chas. Carmichael built his in 1842. The blacksmith who made the hinges advised him to build his doors first, as barns in Wheatland were liable to stand without doors. But Stephen Knapp was a stirring man, and kept well in advance in all farming work. He sowed the first wheat in 1835. He bought his seed wheat of Charles Ames, traveling a woods road as far as Jesse Smith's when going for his seed. The family also claim he marketed the first corn.

The farmers of Wheatland complain of the hard times of 1837, '38 and '39. Times were very hard in that new township, and much of it was due to the want of a market. They drew wheat and oats to Adrian and sold them, the first for 47 cents, and the last for 14 cents, per bushel. Perry Knapp took a load of oats to Adrian, and driving into the hotel yard broke a man's wagon tongue. He sold his oats for 14 cents per bushel, and paid a dollar for the tongue. He thinks there was but little profit on that load of oats.

When the Wheatland people use to go to Adrian to mill, it took four days to go and come; but if the Adrian mill was full, or had broken down, which was sometimes the case, and they had to go to Tecumseh, it took longer.

A story has been told of old-time milling, which was in this wise: In 1834, '35 or '36 —no matter which, but before money went out of fashion—a boy of the Valley went to Adrian to mill. He must needs be in a hurry because bread timber was scarce at home, but when he came to Adrian the mill was full. There was not even room to get his grist into the mill until room was made by departing teams. He went to the miller and laid his case before him. The miller shook his head; first come first served was the rule, and it could not be varied. "Can't it be ground at some odd spell?" "No, it must wait its turn." "Well," said the boy, "I would like to go home in the morning," and at the same time dropped a silver dollar into the busy man's hand. When he went to the mill in the morning he saw at a glance that his grist was ground. After breakfast he drove his team around, and without asking any questions loaded his grist. The others gathered around, and the question "How is this?" was on every tongue. The miller was too busy to heed their queries. and the boy merely said, "Guess there is some mistake about it, but I am darned glad of it." The boy thinks he saved about four days' time.

The farmers of Wheatland were almost overjoyed when the Talbot mill started, but when the Rollin mill was put in operation a few months later, they thought themselves out of the woods. The township of Wheatland is entirely an agricultural town; with trivial exceptions, no other business is carried on within her borders. Of churches, she has a sufficient number to accommodate her church-going people. It seems to be conceded that the first church organization was the Free Will Baptist. It was organized by Father Whitcomb and the Rev. Jonathan Thomas, in 1837. Both branches of Methodists had church organizations and buildings in an early day. The class organizations of the Methodist Episcopal church were effected very soon after the first settlement was made, probably in 1836, or not later than 1837. In a very early day, the Rev. Mr. Parker settled in the township, and, soon after, the Rev. Mr. Doolittle, both of them local elders, and they did much to promote the growth of the church. With such laborers as these to supplement the regular work, it is no wonder that Methodism flourished, and as early as 1844 had church buildings in use. The membership of other churches were not idle. The early Lanesville Presbyterian and Congregationalist preachers were self-constituted itinerants, and at first gave half of their time to the Wheatland appointment; but very soon such labors were too infrequent for the Wheatland work, and they set up for themselves. At first, a very large portion of the Hudson church was made up of citizens of Wheatland, but these, with only a few exceptions, in 1842, transferred their membership to the Wheatland church, which has become a very influential body of christians. The Baptists (the regulars), also, several years ago, effected an organization in the township, and in the early literature of the denomination the Wheatland church was often mentioned as being called upon to give counsel to sister churches.

In the matter of schools, Wheatland is not one whit behind her neighbors. Her schools, from very early times, have been considered in the van for learning, management and ability. The people have showed their appreciation of good schools by building excellent buildings and sustaining them liberally, and lately an institution has been opened to teach the higher branches of learning, and it is to be hoped that it will prove a success.

The farmers of Wheatland have never been over-anxious for political preferment, but they have furnished the State two excellent legislators in the persons of Mr. Robert Cox and Albert B. Slocum. They have also, for years, furnished the Board of Supervisors with a presiding officer. Her supervisors have been the following: 1835,

Heman Pratt, probably; 1836, Heman Pratt; 1837, '38 and '39, John Bailey; 1840 and
'41, Lyman Pease; 1842, '43 and '44, John Humphrey; 1845, '46 and '47, Zebulon Williams; 1848, John Humphrey; 1849 and '50, Zebulon Williams; 1851 and '52, John L.
Taylor; 1853 and '54, John Humphrey; 1855, Ebenezer Trumbull; 1856, John F. Taylor; 1857 and '58, John McLouth; 1859, Albert B. Slocum; 1860 and '61, Jno. McLouth;
1862, Thos. Robbins; 1863, '64 and '65, Jno. McLouth; 1866, Benjamin F. Tabor; 1867,
John McLouth; 1868, '69 and '70, Benjamin F. Tabor; 1871, John McLouth; 1872 and
'73, Myron McGee; 1874, '75 and '76, Benjamin F. Tabor.

VIII. PITTSFORD.

The first township meeting of the township of Pittsford was held at the house of
Alpheus Pratt, on Monday, the second day of May, 1836. Why it was not held in
April does not appear. Robinson H. Whitehorn was moderator, and Urias Treadwell clerk of the meeting. These, with John L. Taylor, a justice of the peace of the
township of Wheatland, but residing within the limits of the new township, were
the inspectors of the election.

Officers elected:—Elijah B. Seeley, supervisor; Urias Treadwell, township clerk;
John L. Taylor, Robinson H. Whitehorn, Elijah B. Seeley, and Sidney S. Ford, jus-
tices of the peace; Cyrus King, Austin Nye and Jesse Smith, assessors; Ozen Keith,
John Williams and Ira Rose, commissioners of highways; David Strunk, collector;
David Strunk, Jesse Kimball and Reuben Mallory, constables; Alpheus Pratt and
Daniel Loomis, poormasters; Cyrus King, Daniel Loomis and Gaylord Tabor, school
commissioners; Urias Treadwell, Sidney S. Ford and Robert Worden, school inspec-
tors.

The town was divided into four road districts, Charles Ames, Robert Worden,
Ozen Keith and Abraham Britton were the overseers, and each district was six miles
long. In consequence of some of the officers failing to qualify, a special township
meeting was held September 12th, and Daniel Loomis elected school commissioner,
and Elijah B. Seeley and Robert Worden justices of the peace.

OFFICIAL REGISTER FOR 1837.—Supervisor, E. B. Seeley; township clerk, Eldad
B. Trumbull; justice of the peace, Russell Coman; assessors, R. H. Whitehorn, Henry
Ames, Ira Rose, Benjamin Estes, Royal Raymond; commissioner of highways, John
Williams, Gaylord B. Tabor and Daniel Loomis; collectors, Jesse Kimball and Calvin
Pixley; constables, James S. Sprague, Calvin Pixley, Jesse Kimball and Geordious
Houghton; overseers of the poor, Charles Ames and Alpheus Pratt; school inspectors,
Urias Treadwell, Robinson H. Whitehorn and Laban J. Aylesworth.

The business of 1837 having all been disposed of, the record of that year closes with
this announcement: "The meeting for the year 1838 is now adjourned to the quarter
stake on the section line between sections fourteen and twenty-three, or at the school
house to be built thereat, to be held on the first Monday in April next."

At that time persons desiring to be married had to procure a license of the township clerk. Mr. Trumbull licensed four couples for that business during the year.
As a reminder of olden times and ways, one of the entries is here given:

Whereas, Robert O'Mealy applying for a license, according to law, to be united to
Sarah Peters in the bonds of matrimony. this is to certify that I see no reasons why
the said Robert O'Mealy and Sarah Peters should not be united in the holy bonds of
matrimony, and accordingly grant the same.   E. B. TRUMBULL, Town Clerk.
Pittsford, Sept. the 18th, 1837.

In like manner Christopher Clement and Alice Fish were licensed Sept. 21, 1837,
Edward Edgerly and Lucinda Britton, December 8th, and James Fuller and Esther
Stuck, December 30th.

OFFICIAL REGISTER, 1838.—Supervisor, Elijah B. Seeley; clerk, Eldad B. Trumbull; assessors, Isaac A. Colvin, Timothy Johnson, Calvin Pixley and Ira Rose;

commissioners of highways, Ozen Keith, George Goodrich and Lester Monroe; collector, Willard F. Day; school inspectors, Laban J. Aylesworth, Cyrus P. Lee and Urias Treadwell; constables, Willard F. Day and Cyrus P. Lee; overseers of the poor, Charles Ames and Samuel Day.

The reader will perhaps have noticed that some of the officers elected in 1837, and also in 1838, were residents of town eight south, one west (Wright). Such was the case with Russell Coman, elected justice of the peace, and Calvin Pixley, elected assessor in 1837, and Timothy Johnson and Calvin Pixley, elected assessors in 1838; but then it will also be remembered that Pittsford then extended to the State line.

OFFICIAL REGISTER, 1839.—Supervisor, Isaac A. Colvin; clerk, Willard F. Day; treasurer, Ozen Keith; assessors, David Strunk, Peter Clement, Lester Monroe; collector, Willard F. Day; inspector, Robinson H. Whitehorn; directors of the poor,. Samuel Day and Alpheus Pratt; commissioners of highways, Jams Earl, Gaylord Tabor and Linus Monroe; justices of the peace, Abiathar Power and George Goodrich.

Here is an item, the last clause of which is respectfully commended to modern undertakers:- "Voted that the town should pay for the coffin which was procured for Henry Prentiss, *five dollars*."

Some time during the summer of 1839, the government removed the Indians from Squawfield. They had encamped on the little St. Joseph for years, and this village was the home of the Chief, Bawbeese. Mr. E. E. Maxson had now become the owner of the land, and of course he wanted possession. By the treaty of Chicago,. 1821, the Indian title had been extinguished to the land in Hillsdale county, but the Indians had not yet been removed to their trans-Mississippi reservation. Mr. Maxson was very anxious to have the government move the Indians, but as long as they were peaceably disposed and injured no one the government was not swift to act. About this time occurred a trivial circumstance which was made the lever to effect their removal. Warren Champlin was then quite a lad, in his teens, perhaps, and was a great favorite with the Indians. He shared their sports and felt quite at home with them. One evening he went down to bathe in Mallory Lake; his younger brother, then a child, accompanied him. Leaving his brother on the shore of the lake, with a white companion and two young Indians he took a canoe and pushed out into deeper water. While bathing he heard a scream, and looking up he saw a young Indian brandishing a knife and in mimicry passing it around the scalp lock of the little boy. Warren at once came to the shore. He found the boy almost dead with fright; but Bawbeese, who had come out on hearing the cry, explained that the Indian was only showing his companions how to scalp an enemy.

Maxson took advantage of this incident, it is said, to represent to the government that the Indians were troublesome, and an order was made for their removal. The detachment of soldiers arrived in the neighborhood in the evening, secured guides, and late in the night, when it was supposed all the straggling parties would be in,. proceeded to the village. The approach was stealthy, and a line of troops had been formed around it before the alarm was given. When the Indians were awakened by the officers they were very much alarmed. The squaws and pappooses rushed as if they would gain the woods, only to meet a line of bayonets. Then they turned back and made night resound with their lamentations. But lamentations were useless; the troops were there for a purpose, and that purpose must be accomplished. The squaws and pappooses were loaded in wagons, and the Indians, unarmed, were compelled to march with the soldiers. All were taken except Bawbeese and his squaw. She had recently been confined, and they were left until she should be able to go. After she had recovered and they had bade adieu to their friends among the whites, they, too, turned their faces toward the setting sun.

Although the township had had white inhabitants for six years, it still might (in 1839) be called a wild country. Many quite extensive fields had been brought under cultivation, yet the largest part of the township was forest,—gigantic forest,—and.

wild game was still abundant. Eldad B. Trumbull, who worked on the Lanesville mill at its building in 1834, and settled in Pittsford the following year, has, ever since his first settlement, kept a daily journal of his business affairs and those things which more nearly appertained to himself and family. In looking over the entries from 1835 to '40, one is astonished at the amount of game he killed, and still did a day's work every week day and attended worship nearly every Lord's day. Mr. Trumbull tells that his wife was provoked at him because once when they were out of meat and a deer came into their door-yard on Sunday, he refused to shoot it. Mrs. Trumbull says she yet thinks it would have been excusable.

But the scene has changed; fields are the rule, and woods the exception; but many of the brawny arms that felled the forests are dust, and others have ceased the active duties of life and await the summons. Their labors have made the township of Pittsford one of the finest in Southern Michigan. It is mostly agricultural, as its many fine farms attest. Indeed, it might be said to be entirely so, as its manufactures are only those necessary to change the form of farm products to fit them for the table and market. Lowe's mill, in the southeastern, and Wood's mill, in the western part of the township, are almost entirely employed with farmers' grinding. Pittsford has had many saw mills within her borders, but as her fine forests have disappeared, so also her saw mills have decayed or been removed nearer growing timber.

Pittsford has furnished the State with legislators and the county with executive officers. In the legislative office, Elijah B. Seeley, Robert Worden and John M. Osborn, as Representatives, and John M. Osborn as Senator, have served the State; in the county, Robert Worden has guarded the treasury, and Wray T. Palmer and Willard F. Day have recorded indentures.

Politically, the township is at present Republican. From 1836 to 1842 it was strongly Whig; afterwards the parties were more evenly divided, so it was not difficult to elect a good man on either ticket, as the frequent election of such men as Seeley, Keith and Day shows; but in 1854 a large part of the Democrats became Republicans, and since then it has been strongly Republican.

The following have been its supervisors: 1836, '37 and '38, Elijah B. Seeley; 1839, Isaac A. Colvin; 1840, Elijah B. Seeley; 1841, Ozen Keith; 1842, Elijah B. Seeley; 1843, Jesse Kimball; 1844, Henry Ames; 1845 and '46, Ozen Keith; 1847, Jesse Kimball; 1848, Ozen Keith; 1849, Elijah B. Seeley; 1850 and '51, Ebenezer Stewart; 1852, Nelson P. Nye; 1853 and '54, Ozen Keith; 1855, Martin H. Webb; 1856, '57 and 58, Willard F. Day; 1859, '60 and 61, Eli Bush; 1862 to '65, both inclusive, Sidney Green; 1866 to '69, both inclusive, Truman N. Wadsworth; 1870, '71 and '72, Henry Lane; 1873, Truman N. Wadsworth; 1874 and '75, Henry Lane; 1876, Truman N. Wadsworth.

As a reminder of the days when men used to be licensed to sell liquors, the following item is given:

We, the undersigned, the township board of the township of Pittsford, county of Hillsdale, and State of Michigan, do hereby grant unto George Miller, of the township of Pittsford aforesaid, license to sell wines and spirituous liquors by retail, in a certain building owned by him, near the school house on the northeast corner of section No. 4, in said township, from this date until the 13th day of April next, provided that the wines and liquors so sold be not drank on or about the premises aforesaid of said Miller. Given under our hands this 30th day of Aug., 1845.

OZEN KEITH, Supervisor.
WM. EDMONDS, Justice.
J. C. HOGABOAM,   "
DAVID KEMP,   "
R. D. WINEGAR, Dept. Clerk.
Township Board.

Some of the early settlers of Pittsford have died, among whom are:

Champlin—William, March 15th, 1873, aged 73 years; Rhoda, wife, Oct. 18th, 1866, aged 68 years.

Ames—Charles, Sept. 4th, 1873, aged 74 years; Sarah, his wife, Dec. 24th, 1869, aged 72 years.   [For deaths of other pioneers of this town see Necrology of Hudson.]

IX. SOMERSET.

The surface of the township of Somerset is broken into numberless conical shaped hills, and interspersed with numerous small lakes and large springs of the purest water. The highest land in Southern Michigan is within its borders, yet in some parts it needs the services of a drain commissioner to adapt the soil to more perfect cultivation. In quality of soil and beauty of scenery it ranks with the best townships of Southern Michigan.

In the winter of 1836-7 John McLouth built a saw mill on the north branch of Posey creek, a tributary of the Bean, and in 1837 William Webster built another saw mill on the same stream; both were long since abandoned.

The township of Somerset was organized in the spring of 1837. It had formerly belonged to the township of Wheatland. At first the settlement along the Chicago road in town five south was the strongest, but the emigration of 1835 and '36 centered mostly in town six south, giving it the advantage in point of numbers, and in consequence each part desired a separation. The northern people sent a petition, asking that the towns might be divided and that the northern town might be allowed to retain the old name and organization. They were met in committee on townships by a petition of the southern people, asking for a separation and that the southern town might be allowed to retain the old name and organization. The Legislature decided in favor of the southern town, and five south became the new town and was named Somerset.

The first township meeting was held at the house of Cornelius Millspaw, on Monday, the third day of April, 1837. The Legislature directed it to be held at the house of Thomas Gamble. Why it was changed is not known. Officers elected:—Heman Pratt, supervisor; John McKnight, township clerk; Amos Fairchild and William Weaver, justices of the peace; William Mercer, Alvah Foster and Orson Herrington, assessors; Daniel Strong, Chauncey Kennedy and Jonathan Haynes, commissioners of highways; Samuel A. Clark, collector; Cornelius Millspaw and David Weatherwax, directors of the poor; Warner Bunday, Alvah Foster and Arza Finney, school inspectors; and Samuel A. Clark, Daniel Millspaw and William Howard, constables.

At a subsequent election, that is to say, in 1839, Timothy Gay was elected a justice of the peace.

As late as 1842 the township paid bounties for the destruction of wolves. Indeed, the township seems to have been noted for its abundant supply of game. Elias Alley, esq., relates that he killed seventy-six deer within six weeks' time.

Cornelius Millspaw built a saw mill on Goose creek, a tributary of the Raisin, in the winter of 1838. The saw mill has gone to decay, and now a flouring mill occupies its place. This last was built by Harrison Fitts, in 1851 or '52. It is now owned by Jesse Tucker & Son.

There was a Presbyterian church organized in 1836, at what is called Somerset Center, and worship was maintained there for many years; but the society, which was considerably scattered, was partly absorbed by the church at Gambleville and partly by a church in the west part of the township, and the house was sold to the Methodists.

In 1841 Newton C. Wolcott commenced manufacturing rakes on the head waters of Goose creek, and the business developed extensively, and for a time it was the leading rake factory in Michigan; but of late the prison makes rakes so much cheaper than he can, that he has ceased manufacturing.

The township has furnished Hillsdale county two judges, (Heman Pratt and William Mercer,) and the State one legislator, in the person of Dr. Root, of Gambleville.

Supervisors—1837, Heman Pratt; 1838, William Weaver; 1839, Elias Branch; 1840, William Weaver; 1841, Azariah Smith; 1842, '43 and '44, William Mercer; 1845, Jabez

S. Mosher; 1846 and '47, Chester Hunt; 1848 and '49, William Mercer; 1850 and '51, Chester Hunt; 1852, Daniel C. Crane; 1853, '54 and '55, William Mercer; 1856 and 57, William P. Richards; 1858, William Mercer; 1859, William P. Richards; 1860, George A. Smith; 1861 and '62, Sanford Hopkins; 1863 and '64, Newton C. Wolcott; 1865 to '73, both inclusive, Sanford D. Hopkins; 1874, '75 and '76, Andrew N. Westcott.

Township Clerks—1837, John McKnight; 1838 and '39, W. S. Branch; 1840, James Gowans; 1841 and '42, Charles Farnsworth; 1843, George L. Moore; 1844, Jabez S. Mosher; 1845, George L. Moore; 1846, John M. Munson; 1847, George L. Moore; 1848, '49 and '50, Oliver Lathrop; 1851, Charles Farnsworth; 1852 and '53, Orson Herrington; 1854, H. H. Davis; 1855, Charles B. Moore; 1856 and '57, Roswell R. Farnsworth; 1858 to '62, both inclusive, Aaron Bickford; 1863, Dennis Clancy; 1864, Aaron Bickford; 1865 and '66, Dennis Clancy; 1867 and '68, Warner Bunday; 1869, David A. Terrell; 1870 to '76, both inclusive, Oscar D. Brown.

X. MEDINA.

The mill, commenced building in 1835, was finished in the spring of 1836, by Laban Merrick, and the first lumber was sawed on the 12th day of April. William Walworth built a small mill on Lime creek, section 21. It was a patent arrangement, and ground coarse grain only. Tyler Mitchell was the carpenter and millwright, and the mill commenced grinding in June, 1836. Walworth died in August—the second death in the township, the first having been Loren, a son of John Knapp, April seventh. In the spring of this year Mr. George W. Moore became an inhabitant of the township; he had purchased his land in the spring of 1834. The Rev. David Smith preached in the township. He was a Presbyterian clergyman sent out as a missionary, and supported by the Presbytery of Western New York. He lived in a small house on the farm of Simon D. Wilson, in Seneca, and preached in private houses. He removed to Illinois in the spring of 1837. In June the Rev. Edward Hodge became the pastor of the Baptist church, organized at Canandaigua in January of that year. He had a salary of two hundred dollars. He lived in the township of Dover.

The spring of 1836 was a very severe one for the inhabitants of this part of the Valley. The most of them had moved in, in 1835, and as yet had not raised a crop, and provisions were very scarce and dear. Even had there been provisions that could have been bought, many of the settlers could not have purchased, as they had used up their means in purchasing land and moving in. One man who had planted some potatoes in the spring of 1836 was obliged to dig them up and eat them. It was all they could get to eat. Flour, when obtainable, was sixteen dollars a barrel; pork, thirty to thirty-two; oats, one dollar and seventy-five cents a bushel; and salt, ten dollars a barrel. Some families were obliged to live for weeks together without bread, and depended upon the rifle for their daily subsistence. Said the Rev. William E. Warner to Mr. Moore, one day in the fall of 1836, "We are having snug times at our house; for our breakfast this morning we had nothing but *pumpkin sauce* to eat and Mrs. Warner thinks *these are rather hard times*."

The hard times, however, did not have the effect to suspend the execution of the Divine command, Gen. 1: 28. On the 14th day of July, 1835, a son was born to Charles A. Prisbey. The boy afterwards died at Murfreesboro, Tenn., June 27th, 1863, while a member of the 24th Wisconsin infantry. On the 14th day of November, Orrin Green was born. On the 18th day of February, 1836, a child was born in the family of Lewis Shepardson, and on the same day a child was born in the family of a Mr. Bayless, in the south part of the township. On the 24th day of August, 1836, Henry C. Foster was born. He, also, died in the service of his country, at Athens, Alabama, Sept. 24th, 1864, a member of the 18th Michigan infantry. In the summer of 1836, Ansel Coats and Phœbe York were married, Daniel H. Deming officiating, and September 18th, J. D. Sutton and Abigail Knapp were married.

This young town must have begun to feel the curse of intemperance, for on the fourth day of July, 1836, Dr. Hamilton delivered a temperance lecture at Canandaigua.

The Rev. Lorenzo Davis having been sent to the newly organized Bean Creek mission of the Methodist Episcopal church, preached in Mr. John R. Foster's house. Mr. Foster had already built his second house, and the pioneer building was used as a church and school house. Mr. Davis continued to preach in that house once a month during that conference year.

Mrs. Dr. Hamilton taught the school in the Canandaigua school house in the summer of 1836, and that fall a frame school house was built in that village. Then Canandaigua aspired to be the metropolis of Medina township. The same fall a log school honse was built on the farm of Benjamin Rogers, southeast quarter of section twenty-three. Medina had three schools in the winter of 1836-7; the third was taught by Miss Colgrove, in John R. Foster's house, near the northeast corner of section three.

In December, 1836, the Baptist church of Canandaigua voted to hold their meetings in the village of Medina. The meetings were held at the dwelling house of Deacon Cook Hotchkiss during the winter of 1836-7 and the summer of 1837.

Medina village, as it then began to be called, had no physician, and, ignoring the Divine command, they coveted their neighbor's doctor. Dr. Hamilton had built a new frame house in the village of Canandaigua, and to induce him to move to their village, the people of Medina purchased the house, and the doctor moved in December, 1836. As the villages are only about one mile apart, it practically could make but little difference whether he lived at one or the other of the places; but for the oldest village to lose her only doctor to enrich her rival, was rather humiliating. But their cup of humiliation was not yet full. The only frame dwelling house in the township was within her borders, and this the Medina people determined should not be,—they would remove it. Twenty of her most stalwart men went down there, with fifteen yoke of oxen collected from among the farmers of Medina and Hudson, to accomplish the removal. Shoes were placed under the building, the oxen hitched to it, and "Whoa," "Haw," "Get up, Bright," and away the house went towards Medina. To avoid the bridge, they cut a road through the woods, north of the creek. The route they were compelled to take to avoid the bends of the creek made the road nearly two miles long, and the house was two days in transit; but at last Medina had one frame house, Canandaigua none.

In the winter of 1836-7 the Medina Mill Company built a saw mill in the village of Medina. They commenced sawing lumber April 1st, 1837.

On the eleventh day of March, 1837, the Legislature set town eight south, one east, off from Seneca, and gave it the name of Medina. The act directed the township meeting to be held at such place in the township as the sheriff of Lenawee county should by proclamation designate. Accordingly, the sheriff issued a proclamation as follows:

PROCLAMATION.

Notice is hereby given to the electors residing in township eight south, of range one east, to meet at the house of John Dawes, in said township, on the first Monday in April next, at ten o'clock A. M., and there proceed to elect township officers for the year coming, agreeable to law. Given under my hand at Adrian, this 29th day of March, 1837.   J. H. CLEVELAND, Sheriff of Lenawee County.

On the 20th day of March, 1837, the Legislature passed a supplemental act detaching fractional town nine south, one east, from Seneca and attaching it to Medina. But the action of the Legislature was probably unknown to the sheriff, hence the notice is only to the voters residing in town eight.

At that time the following named persons were voters in the township of Medina as it was then actually organized, although only those living in town eight south participated in the township meeting: Nathaniel W. Upton, John R. Foster, John Knapp, Cook Hotchkiss, Charles Prisbey, Samuel Fincher, Ebenezer Daniels, John C. Hotchkiss, Artemas Allen, Dr. I. S. Hamilton, Rev. William E. Warner,

Abel Platts, Patrick McKenny, Tyler Mitchell, Patrick Dillon, William Cavender, Samuel Gregg, S. Dewey, Orrin Pixley, Charles Baldwin, Lawrence Reubottom, Hiram Lucas, Asa Farley, Lewis Shepardson, Amasa Converse, N. K. Green, John Dawes, Levi B. Wilder, Benjamin Holmes, James McQuillis, Ben Rogers, Abner Rogers, Chester Savage, Justus Coy, Orvill Woodworth, Cassius P. Warner, John Powers, Ethan Barns, Seneca Barns, Rollin R. Hill, Orlando Whitney, John S. Sweeney, John D. Sutton, Henry S. Smith, Samuel Kies, Horace Garlick, E. H. Johnson, Levi Goss, Benjamin Hornbeck and Hiram Wakefield, heads of families, and Eli Upton, George W. Moore, Andrew McFarlane, James Burns, Patrick Trumer, Levi Daniels, James Rogers, Charles Stone, Newton Dawes, Alonzo S. Hume, Benjamin Converse, Nathan Stone, John Seeley, J. M. Baggerly, and Zebedee Baggerly, unmarried men.

In accordance with the sheriff's proclamation, the township meeting was held on Monday, the 3d day of April, and officers were elected as follows: Rollin R. Hill, supervisor; John Dawes, township clerk; George W. Moore, Noah K. Green and James A. Rogers, assessors; Orlando Whitney, John S. Sweeney and John Powers, commissioners of highways; Asa Farley and John D. Sutton, school commissioners; Benjamin Rogers and John Knapp, overseers of the poor; Asa Farley, James A. Rogers, Henry S. Smith and Samuel Kies, justices of the peace; Charles Stone, Cassius P. Warner, Horace Garlick and E. H. Johnson, constables; Charles Stone, collector.

The justices elect drew for term, with the following result: Henry S. Smith, four years; Samuel Kies, three years; James A. Rogers, two years; Asa Farley, one year. The voters thought it necessary to offer a five-dollar wolf bounty.

The new township government did not start off very smoothly. Hitherto, there had been both school commissioners and school inspectors, but the Legislature abolished the office of school commissioner at their session in 1837. The people evidently thought it was the inspectors that were abolished, for they elected school commissioners but no inspectors. Then, also, they were in a muddle with their justices.

In 1836, Cook Hotchkiss was elected a justice of the peace for the township of Seneca, which then included Medina. The Medina people thought it not best to have a Seneca officer hold over amongst them, and persuaded Hotchkiss he had better resign his Seneca office and be elected anew, and they evidently supposed he consented to do so, and had done so, for at their election they elected the full complement of justices, but omitted Hotchkiss from the list. When the election was over, the new justices learned, to their dismay, that Cook Hotchkiss had not resigned, and did not propose to resign. Here was a muddle. The law provided for four justices, and no more. Four had been elected on a general ticket, and now that there was room for only three, how could they tell which one was not elected. Thus reasoning, they called a special township meeting to rectify the errors. The special township meeting was held on the 20th day of June, at the house of John Dawes. Dr. I. S. Hamilton, Rollin R. Hill and Noah K. Green were elected school inspectors, and Asa Farley, Noah K. Green and John Dawes, justices of the peace. Henry S. Smith and John Kies were left out of the deal this time, and now it became a question who was elected to the office. As to Farley, there could be no question; but Smith and Kies, or Green and Dawes—which? Recourse was now had to the prosecuting attorney, and he advised them that there was nothing in the law to prevent their having five justices in such cases, and that the first was the valid election. Later in the season, Samuel Kies removed from the township. Another special meeting was held, and Samuel Gregg elected justice to fill the vacancy.

Early in 1837, the wounded honor of the people of Canandaigua was somewhat healed by the coming of Dr. Angell, a botanic physician; but soon after, a new wound was inflicted. A Mr. Stephenson prepared the timber for a new hotel building which he proposed to put up in Canandaigua, but being somewhat impecunious, he mortgaged the timber. Afterwards, being unable to pay off the mortgage, he sold the timber to Charles A. Prisbey and C. P. Warner, of Medina village, without disclosing the fact that it was mortgaged. Prisbey and Warner drew the timber to Medina and constructed the tavern now owned by Mr. Allen. The mortgagee made them pay his debt, but Medina had a frame hotel.

Another little incident occurred about that time, which tended to even matters up a little. In the fall of 1836, an itinerant fruit tree vender brought some apple trees to Canandaigua to sell to the farmers of Medina and Seneca. He had fifty more than he could dispose of, and these he buried in Cavender's field. In the winter, a Medina man coming by the field, discovered the tree tops covered with snow, and asked Burns Cavender what it meant. He said Gregg had thrown a drunken Indian out of his bar-room, he had died from exposure, and his body was buried lightly and covered with brush. The Medina man went home, revolving in his mind the tragic death of the Indian. He called a secret council, and it was determined that the matter must be investigated and Gregg punished. In the dead of the night, six of Medina's most valiant sons sallied forth, armed with axes and spades, for a march on Canandaigua. They came to the spot and attempted to remove the brush, but their butt ends had sank in the mud and frozen down. The axes were called in requisition, and the brush cut away even with the ground. Then the digging commenced, and in the course of an hour's hard work the bodies and roots of the trees were exhumed. They went home sadder and wiser men, desiring above all things to keep their agency in the matter a secret. But "murder will out," and they had to pay for the trees; and what was of more consequence to them, be jeered at by the Canandaigua folks.

On the 7th day of March, 1837, a church was organized in the south part of the township, and called the First Congregational church of Medina. It had eleven members, and the Rev. Paul Shephard was its first pastor.

On the 20th day of May, the name of the Baptist church was changed to "The Baptist church of Medina," and in the fall a small church building was built. A post-office was established at the village of Medina this year, and Artemus Allen was made postmaster. Mr. Lauren Hotchkiss came into the township from Adrian, whither he had come in 1831.

In the summer of this year, 1837, the Medina Mill Company built a grist-mill. The building was one and a half stories high, and 24 by 36 feet. In it were placed two run of stones. I. H. Luddon, was the millwright, and J. C. Lewis built the wheel. The old building now forms the north and lower portion of the Kerr mill. The first flour was ground in this mill on Thanksgiving day, 1837. In the fall, George W. Brower built a saw-mill on Lime Creek, on section twenty-three, and commenced sawing in December, 1837.

Canandaigua was platted October 26th, 1835, by Ira White, but Medina village was not platted until a year and a half later. The plat was made and acknowledged by Asahel Finch, Cook Hotchkiss, Artemus Allen and L. Hotchkiss, March 30th, 1837.

In 1838 B. F. Hutchinson purchased the Canandaigua saw-mill, and built an addition to it in which he put the Walworth grinding mill. Dr. Rufus Kibbie settled in Canandaigua this year, and resided there and practiced medicine until he removed to Coldwater.

The Legislature, at its session in 1838, chartered the Medina & Canandaigua Railroad Company. Cook Hotchkiss, John Knapp, B. F. Hutchinson, Samuel Gregg, William Billings, Artemus Allen and Ebenezer Daniels, were the corporators named in the act. The subscription books of the company were to be open two days each in the villages of Medina and Canandaigua. Thirty days' notice of the time when, and place where, such books would be open, should be published in the *Constitutionalist* or *Watchtower*. The route was to be from Morenci, through Canandaigua and Medina, to some point on the Southern Railroad in Lenawee county.

In the fall of 1837 the new township furnished the State a legislator in the person of Lauren Hotchkiss. The subsequent year, 1839, he was ordained to the ministry of the Baptist church, and was the pastor of the Medina church several years on a salary of $125 a year; and if times were hard, and his people could not well pay, he did not exact all of that. In 1840 he built a saw-mill, at what is now Tiffin, and about 1844 or '45 a mill was built by Nathan Bassett for carding wool, and, later still, for fulling, shearing, coloring and pressing cloth. Weaving and spinning were also carried on to some extent in the establishment. About 1854, Mr. Hotchkiss bought the property, exchanged the machinery for flouring apparatus, and began grinding grain. The mill was afterwards the property of Morse and Christophers, and now is owned by C. C. Morse & Sons.

This year, 1839, Medina had its first celebration of American Independence, at Canandaigua. The committee of arrangements were A. L. Downer, B. F. Hutchinson, F. H. Hagaman, John McGowan, John D. Wolf, Philo Wilson, Orlando Whitney, Hiram Lucas, Lawrence Rheubottom, William Billings, Samuel Kies and Robert Sloan; president of the day, Samuel Gregg; chaplain, Rev. Mr. Bacon; orator, Wheeler M. Dewey; readers, Philo Wilson and John M. Bird. They had militia companies in those days, and Capt. Drown and his Bean Creek Rangers did the escort duty of the day. The dinner was free, and of course ended with regular and volunteer toasts. Here is a specimen of the volunteer kind, and is given as tending to show the humble bearing of the men of those times: "We, the citizens of Bean Creek, unrivalled in industry, unsurpassed in virtue and morality, and unremitting in our efforts to fulfill the Divine command to multiply and replenish the earth."

August 28th, 1839, one of the settlers of 1834 died. It was Cook Hotchkiss, the founder of the Baptist church of Medina, the first blacksmith and the first justice of the peace in the township. One of his neighbors said of him, "He was a consistent christian, a kind neighbor and a true friend."

In 1839, Mr. Hutchinson built another addition to the Canandaigua mill, and put in one run of stones. Penniman and Ashley bought this property about 1844, and in that and the following year built a new mill three stories high, 40 by 60 feet, costing $10,000. It was burned Nov. 19, 1856, and a few years since a small mill was built.

In 1840, to '44, the villages of Medina and Canandaigua were at the height of their power, grandeur and glory. The two villages did the most extensive milling business in the Valley, if not in the county. The Medina mill alone, in 1840, floured 40,000 bushels of wheat, besides custom work, and the store of Allen Daniels & Co. was the most complete in Lenawee county, outside of the village of Adrian. The original merchant of the township of Medina was a Mr. Saulsbury, at Canandaigua, in 1835. He was succeeded by Green in 1836, also at Canandaigua, and Allen Daniels & Co., at Medina, were the third in the mercantile succession.

In 1841 or '42, the people of Medina township had another evidence of the advance of the country from infancy to maturer growth in the establishment of a distillery at Canandaigua by Franklin Smith, then lately of the village of Hudson. The distillery continued in operation for several years, and, it is said, made a very poor article of corn whisky. Mr. Smith, while there, was made Colonel in the Michigan militia, and hence derived his military title. He returned to Hudson about 1853, and for a while run the Wirts steam mill, and suddenly developed into a temperance man; and as he formerly aided in the manufacture of drunkards, so now his temperance views were of the strictest and most uncompromising kind. After the death of his wife, a daughter of the Rev. David Pratt, he went West and engaged in building railroads, and became very wealthy. He has since lost his only daughter, helped to bury every member of his father-in-law's family, except the old lady, and he now makes frequent visits to Hudson to care for her. His only hate seems to be against dealers in, and drinkers of intoxicating drinks, and those who aid or encourage them. In the manifestation of this hate, he sometimes seems unreasonable.

About 1845 or '46, Mr. and Mrs. Barrows opened a select school in the central part of the township. They boarded their pupils who came from a distance, and exercised parental care over them. The school was rather under the auspices of the Congregational church, was largely patronized by members of that church abroad, and was a good school. The Congregational society at that point built a church building on section twenty-six. It was dedicated in 1849. The Rev. George Barnum was its pastor for nine years, and under his ministrations the church prospered. In 1858 and '59, many of its most substantial supporters removed from the township, others transferred their membership to the new churches at Canandaigua and Morenci, and the church became extinct. The building was afterwards taken down, rebuilt at Prattville, Hillsdale county, and re-dedicated as a Congregational church.

About the year 1844 a Methodist class was organized near the southwest corner of the township, and built a church on the west side of section thirty, but afterwards it became the property of the United Brethren.

In the year 1844, Dr. Hamilton removed from Medina to Adrian. He afterwards removed to Tecumseh, where he still resides. Dr. David Brown succeeded him. Dr. Brown was a son of father Elisha Brown, of Hudson. He read medicine with Dr. Hamilton in Medina, and graduated at a Massachusetts college in the spring of 1843. He returned to Medina and commenced practice with his preceptor, whose removal in 1844 left him a large practice. He died in Medina in 1858.

About this time, also, (1844), Judson R. Hyde came to Medina, where he lived until about 1850. He married the daughter of Mr. Cornelius DeMott. Miss DeMott should have been mentioned as bringing, in 1839, the first piano into the township of Medina. On leaving Medina, Mr. Hyde and family went to Hudson. He afterwards resided in New York, then in Omaha, again in Medina and Hudson, and finally again in Omaha, where he became the land agent of the Union Pacific Railway Co., and there Mrs. Hyde died.

In 1846, a new Baptist church was built in the village of Medina. It was remodeled and re-finished in 1875.

In 1848, a Dutch Reformed church was organized at Canandaigua. The Rev. Mr. Hermans preached there two years as a missionary. The church is extinct.

In 1848 or '49, Chester Savage built a saw-mill on Bean Creek, in the southeastern part of the town. Medina has had several steam saw-mills, mention of which will be made in this connection. Benjamin Durffe built a mill in the western part of the town, about the time under consideration, 1848; John Johnson built a mill near the residence of his father-in-law, Orville Woodworth, esq.; Orris R. Baker, a mill on section seven, in town eight south; C. H. Baldwin, a mill in Canandaigua, and George Beach a mill in Medina village.

As before stated, a postoffice was established in Medina village in the spring of 1837. A weekly mail was received until 1840, and subsequent to that date a semi-weekly mail. In 1850 the postoffice was removed to Canandaigua, and Samuel Gregg appointed postmaster. A petition was sent to Washington to have the office returned to Medina. No action was taken, however, until 1851, when a new postoffice was established at Medina, and Ebenezer Daniels appointed postmaster, and the two offices have existed within a mile and a half of each other until the present time. Since 1854 there has been a daily mail run between Clayton and Morenci, by the way of Medina and Canandaigua.

In 1853, the inhabitants of Medina, feeling the need of better school facilities than could be obtained in the district schools, organized a joint stock company and built an academy building, 30 by 50 feet, two stories high. Alonzo M. Carson and wife, of Hudson, taught the first year, and were succeeded by Mr. O. L. Spaulding, since Gen. O. L. Spaulding, of St. Johns, in this State. Among the instructors employed at the Oak Grove Academy, as it was named, were Prof. Edwin Cook, of Chicago; Gen. Byron Cutcheon, of Manistee; Prof. Swan, of Exeter, N. H.; Prof. John Drake, New York; B. F. Boughton, Wis.; Edwin B. Sayers and Henry W. Norton, of this county. The Academy was incorporated in 1872. Its students adorn every path of life, from the honorable Congressman to the independent farmer. The Hon. John Baker, member of Congress from Indiana, was one of its earliest students. Eleven of its students have graduated at the various State colleges, and more than seventy-five were officers or soldiers in the war of the rebellion.

In 1853 or '54, Dr. Rufus Kibbie left Canandaigua and went to Coldwater, in this State. Dr. Todd, now of the city of Adrian, settled in Canandaigua in 1853, and remained four years, when he removal to Adrian. Dr. Chappell came in 1844, and is still in practice there. Dr. Brown died in Medina, in 1858, and was succeeded by Dr. Weeds, who remained until, in 1861, he was commissioned a surgeon in the United States army. Dr. Jas. S. Power succeeded Dr. Weeds, and remained until 1866. Dr. Ely, an eclectic, and Dr. Dodge, an allopath, are the present practitioners in the village of Medina. In addition to the physicians already named, Drs. Titus, Hampton and Kendall, have practiced medicine in Medina. Dr. Titus came to Medina about 1845, and for a time was a partner of Dr. Brown. He removed to the State of New York, thence to Missouri, returned to Medina in 1862, and staid one year. He was a skillful practitioner, but his intemperate habits unmanned him for business. Dr. Carlos G. Hampton practiced in company with Dr. Brown two or three years, and afterwards, for some time, lived on a farm near the village. He removed to Texas about 1859 or '60, but on account of Union sentiments, was driven out of the South in 1861 or '62. After his return, he practiced medicine in Hudson for a time, and then removed to Muir, in this State. He married a daughter of Capt. Drown, of Medina. His oldest son enlisted in the 18th Michigan Infantry, was taken prisoner at Athens, Ala., confined in a rebel prison, and, after exchange, was killed by the explosion on the steamer Sultana, in April, 1865. Dr. Kendall lived on a farm in the south part of the township, and practiced medicine for many years. He is now selling drugs in Fayette, Ohio.

About 1858 or '59, the Methodist societies at Medina and Canandaigua built churches. In 1858, a Congregationalist society was organized in Canandaigua, and the Rev. Geo. A. Nichols, a Presbyterian clergyman, preached to them one year. In 1859 the church was organized, and a church building erected, which was dedicated in July, 1860. The Rev. Mr. Hyde was the first pastor; he remained two years, and was succeeded by the Rev. Herman Bross. In the summer of 1870 the society built a brick parsonage.

No township in the Valley has furnished the State so many legislators as Medina. She has furnished one Senator, Dr. Rufus Kibbie; five Representatives, who served an aggregate of eight terms, as follows: Lauren Hotchkiss, Ebenezer Daniels and Charles A. Jewell, one term each; Philo Wilson two, and Noah K. Green three terms. Ebenezer Daniels was a member of the constitutional convention of 1850, and Jacob C. Sawyer of that of 1867. Philo Wilson served one term as county judge. Supervisors: 1837 and '38, Rollin R. Hill; 1839, Rufus Kibbie; 1840 and '41, Geo. W. Brower; 1842 to 1849, both inclusive, Noah K. Green; 1850 and '51, Edward C. Perkins; 1852, Noah K. Green; 1853, Edward C. Perkins; 1854, Jacob C. Sawyer; 1855, John Dawes; 1856, Carlos D. Hampton; 1857, Joseph Hagaman; 1858, '59 and '60, Noah K. Green; 1861 to 1869, both inclusive, Charles A. Jewell; 1870, '71 and '72, Chas. C. Morse; 1873, Edwin Haff; 1874, Chas. C. Morse; 1875, Chester R. Lyon; 1876, Chas. C. Morse.

By the kindness of Mr. George W. Moore, the following list of officers and soldiers furnished by Medina to the armies of the Republic during the war of the rebellion, is given.

Old First Infantry.—Returned, James Donaldson, Louis Heath, Wm. C. Moore.

New First Infantry.—Returned, Thomas Hannan; killed, Edward P. Brown, at second battle of Bull Run, Va., Aug. 30th, 1862.

Second Infantry.—Returned, Benj. F. Heydenberk, Lester Culver.

Third Infantry.—Died, J. S Weeds, at St. Louis, Mo., Jan. 15th, 1862.

Fourth Infantry.—Returned, Harrison Hamlin, Royal Hamlin, Albert Wilbur James Brogan, Geo. Donivan, Irwin P. Perry, Cyrus Millins, Chauncey Heath, Edgar Heath, Thos. C. Williams, Jonathan Fink, John Townsend, Alfred Townsend, Sterling Chatfield, John C. Hotchkiss. Killed, J. S. Bailey, Malvern Hill, Va., June 20th, 1862; L. L. Kenyon, Malvern Hill, Va., July 1, 1862; W. H. Palmer, Petersburg, Va., June 14th, 1864; Henry S. Lawrence, Chancellorsville, Va., May 5th.

1863. Died, L. Cox, Huntsville, Ala., Feb. 22d, 1865; E. H. Wheeler, Georgetown, D. C., Aug. 29th, 1861; Geo. W. Millins, of starvation, Andersonville, Ga., May 16th, 1864; Peter Gahagan, of wounds received at Gettysburg, Pa.; Chas. Heath, New York city, March, 1863; Moses Rose, at Fredricksburg, Va., May 9th, 1864; Hiram Rose, at Washington, D. C., July 9th, 1864; Harvey Warn, at Libby prison, 1864.

Seventh Infantry.—Returned, Lieut. James Donaldson, Horace Rice; died, Geo. Knapp, Washington, D. C., 1863.

Eleventh Infantry.—Returned, *Capt. Lewis Heath, Andrew McFarland, Peter Malarny, Levi Manning, Sumner Manning, Henry Lawrence, John Osborn, Alonzo Kinney, Henry Spring, Ira Baker, Leroy Coats, Oliver Converse, James Culver, Geo. Savage, Marvin Wood, Henry Lewis. Killed, David Edwards, Stone River, Tenn.; L. P. Wilkins, near Atlanta, Ga., Aug. 16th, 1864. Died, Horace Osborn and William Sutton, in Kentucky, 1862; Geo. Peters, Nashville, Tenn., 1863.

Fifteenth Infantry.—Returned, Thomas Rooney, Timothy Creeden, John O'Connor.

Seventeenth Infantry.—Returned, John Moriarty; died, Thos. McKenney, Knoxville, Tenn., Nov. 16th, 1864.

Eighteenth Infantry.—Returned, *Capt. W. C. Moore, Lieut. C. A. Jewell, John Creen, Andrew J. H. Gove, jr., Ira L. Forbes, Nelson Rice, Hope Welch, Jas. Holmes, William Gunderman, Henry Clark, Freeman Gould, Benson Gray, Harlow S. Hilliker, Wm. H. Hawkins, Wm. Hughes, Frank Drown, Emmons Hyde, Samuel Bothwell, Jas. Bothwell, Wm. Bennett, Lewis Converse, Geo. J. Johnson, Andrew J. Jewell, Warren Bennett, Wm. McCarty, Cyrus Baldwin, Allen Paulding, Chas. Barber, Chas. Wheeler, Alvin Wilbur, DeWitt Garlick, Henry Emmons, Ephraim Sloan, Geo. Bebee (deserted); Mark Goss (now in U. S. Insane Asylum, Washington, D. C.), Killed, Henry C. Foster and Fernando Wheeler, Athens, Ala., Sept. 24th, 1864; Henry Chatfield, near Huntsville, Ala., Nov. 28th, 1864. Died, N. Bailey, Lexington, Ky., April 22d, 1863; Orrin S. Upton, Nashville, Tenn., Sept. 1st, 1864; George W. Proper, Camp Chase, Ohio, June 20th, 1865; A. W. Gould, Danville, Ky., March 7th, 1863; H. Ogden, Nashville, Tenn., May 13th, 1864; Peter Hoyt and Henry Baker, Nashville, Tenn., Nov. 20th, 1864; John Bennett and Joseph Bennett, Nashville, Tenn., 1864; Herman Higley, Stevenson, Ala., November, 1864; Joshua Kinne, Stevenson, Ala., Dec. 27th, 1864; Milford Graham, Nashville, Tenn., Jan. 19th, 1864; Charles E. Greer, 1867; James H. Main, 1865, at Medina, of disease contracted in the army; Jeremiah Spring, H. H. Vancourt, James W. Bradish, Warren Upton, Frank Hampton and Seymour H. Main, April 27th, 1865, on the steamer Sultana.

Twenty-Third Infantry.—Died, Edward M. Spaulding, Bowling Green, Ky., Feb. 10th, 1863.

Sixty-Eighth Ohio.—Returned, Martin V. Palmer, David Palmer and Lewis Smith.

Fifty-Second Ohio Infantry.—Killed, Horace B. Jewell, near Atlanta, Ala., July 19th, 1864.

Ninth Cavalry.—Died, Robert W. Campbell, at Medina, of injuries received in the army.

Eleventh Cavalry.—Returned *Benj. F. Heydenberk, David Stuck, Henry Lawrence, Marvin Rogers. Killed, Samuel F. Smith, supposed at Saltville, Va., Oct. 2d, 1864. Died, Charles Wood, in Kentucky, 1864.

Fourth Battery.—Charles Lewis (deserted).

Sixth Battery.—Died, Geo. A. Graham, Grand Rapids, June 9th, 1864.

Eighth Battery (DeGolyer's)—Returned, Lieut. Edward Luce, Laban Shaw, Isaac Rose, Orrin Smith, Decatur Belden. Died, David Farewell, Vicksburg; J. Joughin, Memphis, Tenn., Feb. 14th, 1865; A. Dutcher, Marietta, Tenn., Aug. 28th, 1863.

Ninth Battery.—Killed, G. L. Baker, Atlanta, Ga., Aug. 7th, 1864. Died, Eli Bennet, Detroit, 1864.

Berdan's Sharpshooters.—Returned, E. C. Farnsworth, Edwin Cramer. Albert Jewell, Edwin Walton, Andrew Walton, Estel Hoag. Killed, Elbridge Jewell, at Kelley's
*Re-enlisted.

Ford, Va., Nov. 8th, 1863; Otis Higley, Gettysburg, Pa., July 2d, 1863. Died, Simon Rose, Philadelphia, Aug. 25th, 1863; Eugene Smith, Virginia, February, 1863.

First Mechanics and Engineers.—Returned, Martin Johnson. Killed, William Johnson, on steamer Sultana, April 27th, 1865.

XL. SENECA.

Notwithstanding the many purchases of land in 1834 and 1835, in Seneca, considerable of her domain was Government property in the spring of 1836. During that year, purchases of Government land were made, as follows: Ira L. Mills, March 28th; William Camp, May 20th; James Mather, Nov. 7th; Jacob L. Roy, Sept. 26th; Nelson Camp and John Camp, May 20th; Augustus Ford and Robert Furman, June 1st; John R. Willis, July 4th; Henry V. Mann, June 16th; George Packard, May 14th; Oliver Furman, June 20th; Samuel Jordan, February 19th; John B. Norvis, July 24th; Josiah Randolph, May 28th; Lois Morey, January 18th; Japheth Cross, March 17th; John McVicker, June 1st; Gedatha Cross, June 18th; Moses Legon, April 25th; Stephen W. Powell, March 16th; William Service and Warner Wing, March 17th; Asa Arnold, February 18th; George Dunlap, March 21st; George L. Church, March 24th; Edward Rice, April 19th; William Bancroft, Jan. 19th; Jedediah Jessep, Jan. 25th; Elkanah Briggs, Jan. 25th; Daniel Tuttle, Feb. 6th; Edward Willis, Feb. 24th.

Work had been commenced on the territorial road in the winter of 1834-5, and in 1836 was passable, but never was a good road.

In the spring of 1836, Japheth Whitman settled in, or where Morenci now is, built a log building and opened a frontier store, the stock consisting of articles in the dry goods, hardware, grocery, drug and saloon line. Some time afterwards, Wm. Sutton kept a tavern in a log building, the first hotel in Seneca township.

Franklin Cawley came to Morenci in 1836. He bought his land in 1850, of James Armitage, of Monroe, and a large part of the village of Morenci is on the land thus bought.

In 1838 a postoffice was established, and Mr. Whitman made postmaster. Its name, Morenci, was given by Mr. Simon D. Wilson.

In 1841, David M. Haight came here and opened the second store within the territory denominated Seneca. Morenci, however, was but little more than a country postoffice until about the year 1850, when it took a new growth.

Almost immediately after his coming here, in 1836, Mr. Franklin Cawley purchased the pioneer saw-mill on the Bean, about one and a half miles above the site of Morenci. It had been built in 1835, by Jacob Baker and Horace Garlick. About the year 1850, Franklin Cawley purchased the land on which Morenci is principally built, and himself, Dennis Wakefield and George W. Wilson built the saw-mill, and afterward the grist-mill, and also opened a store.

In 1852, there were four stores in Morenci. The original store had ceased to exist. Mr. Haight was still selling a few goods. Asa A. Kennedy and Moses S. Worth had each little stores, and the store of the mill company made the fourth. In the fall of that year, Silas A. Scofield came to Morenci, built a building, with steam power, and commenced the manufacture of furniture. He afterwards, the community seeming to demand it, added planeing machinery, and extended his business in any direction the need of the place seemed to demand, sometimes to his own detriment financially. Mr. Scofield has been one of those useful men which every new village needs, who work hard and disinterestedly to build up the place, but who fail to amass fortunes. They are of more use in building up a place than money-lenders; while they fail, their work remains to enrich others. But Mr. Scofield is yet a young man; he has acquired a respectable fortune which, it is to be hoped, will develop into wealth.

In 1854, the Hon. James P. Cawley bought the store of the mill company and com-

"The family of Mr. Russell Coman spent the winter of 1835-6 in the midst of an American Forest, miles from any neighbors." (p. 119)

"The covered wagon was backed up close by the cabin and the boys lodged there." (p. 120)

menced business on his own account. He continued in business until 1860, by him-self; at that time he formed a copartnership with Messrs. Rothrock & Green. In 1873, having become involved by reason of his connection with the Morenci Woolen Mill Co., he was declared a bankrupt, and his estate wound up. He afterwards removed to Detroit, and is now interested in the house of L. H. Dean & Co., commission mer-chants. Mr. Cawley is a very competent business man, a prominent member of the Methodist church, and a useful member of society. For one term he represented Lenawee county in the State Senate.

About the same time, Pegg & Swindle built the tannery. It afterwards became the property of Wilson & Swindle. It was burned in 1874, but has been rebuilt.

About 1855, the Rev. John Crabbs came to Morenci and established himself here as a tailor. He remained in that business, preaching on Sunday a part of the time, un-til the war of the rebellion. He was commissioned chaplain in an Ohio regiment, and was stationed the most of the time with Gilmore, on the Island before Charleston, South Carolina. Since the war, he engaged for a time in the life insurance business, but latterly has resumed his old business.

David M. Blair came to Morenci about the same time, and engaged in blacksmith-ing. This business he has developed, until he now has one of the finest carriage man-ufactories in Southern Michigan.

The village of Morenci now has four churches, in which the Methodists, the Bap-tists, the Congregationalists and the United Brethren, worship.

Since 1860, the village has made rapid progress, more especially since the comple-tion of the Chicago & Canada Southern Railway gave them railroad communication with the rest of the world. The village sensibly feels the pressure of hard times, es-pecially in the loss of her woolen mills, and the consequent embarrassment of some of her best business men. The village, a few years since, became incorporated, but the hard times have prevented any great municipal improvements. The township has sufficient milling privileges. Besides its original water-mill, and the Morenci mills already spoken of, it has a steam mill in the northeastern part, and the Canandaigua mill, near its northwestern boundary, are easily accessible to its inhabitants.

Its official list is not large. It has furnished one sheriff to the county, Col. S. B. Smith, and one Senator to the State, the Hon. James P. Cawley.

Besides its religious organizations, the township has a lodge of the Independent Order of Odd Fellows, a Masonic Lodge and Chapter, and a Farmers' Grange.

The old men and women are fast passing away. Baker, Cawley, Dr. Swaney, Mrs. Wilson and others, are gone. Simon D. Wilson and Elias J. Baldwin linger in feeble health. Coomer, Wakefield and a few others, perhaps, of the settlers of 1834, are yet strong, but a few more years will have removed them all. How important, then, that some willing and competent hand, living in the township, collect more of the facts of the history of the early settlements of the township, that they may be pre-served to posterity.

XII. WRIGHT.

The family of Mr. Russell Coman spent the winter of 1835-6 in the midst of an American forest, miles from any neighbors. The nearest neighbor to the north ward was Mr. Whitbeck, on the town line between Medina and Hudson, and the next, east of him still, the Rev. Mr. Warner. On the Hudson, or county line road, there was none nearer than Lowe's mill, and it is believed none nearer than Samuel Davis, northwest corner of section thirty, Hudson. It was a lonely winter—not even Indians for neighbors.

Mr. Michael Lickley and family settled in the northwest corner of the town in May, 1836. As soon as spring opened, Mr. Samuel Coman put his family in motion towards the wilds of Michigan. The party consisted of himself and wife, his son, Curtis

Coman, and wife, his daughters, Lydia and Orpha, and sons, Samuel P., Stephen W.,. Francis H. and William E. The journey from Toledo was made by team, the women of the party walking nearly the entire distance. From Canandaigua they were directed to Hudson; arrived there, they took the south road and encamped at its end, on the top of the hill south of Lowe's mill. A family had lately arrived there and built a shanty. The boys from here went to look for Russell, and having found him the family was piloted in. They arrived on the twenty-third day of June, and for a time that little cabin buzzed with life, for until another cabin could be built fifteen persons lived in and around that one. The covered wagon was backed up close by the cabin and the boys lodged there. But so many hands made light work, and soon a second cabin was ready. Curtis Coman and wife took possession, and divided the large family.

Between the arrival of Russell's family, in December, 1835, and the arrival of the other Comans, it is believed that the following named families settled in town eight south, one west, forming a part of the township of Wheatland before April the fifth, and of the township of Pittsford subsequent to that date: Royal Raymond, Joseph Pixley and Truman Bown. Raymond settled on the farm William Bradley now owns, Joseph Pixley where the widow Root lives, and Bown where the late Timothy Johnson so long lived.

About that time, or soon after, James Wilson commenced a settlement in town nine south, and the country filled up rapidly. That is to say, the purchasers of 1835 for the most part came in and built cabins on their lands. The town was densely timbered, and each cabin was in the woods, no other house in view, and before neighbors could be in sight acres of timber must be felled. At it they went, and before winter set in, the most of them had their door-yards clear of logs. The Comans sowed one acre of wheat that fall, and from it in 1837 reaped fourteen bushels of wheat. Before leaving the East, Curtis had purchased a small patent mill, for which he paid twenty-five dollars. He now built a frame for it. In this mill he ground the wheat he had raised, and the old man assured the writer he never felt so independent in his life. The frame of the mill is still in existence, and is kept as a *souvenir* of the days of 1836.

The settlers of towns eight and nine south, one west, experienced great hardships during 1836, '37 and '38. When they came there in 1836 their towns were one vast wilderness, broken only by the door-yard of Russell Coman. These trees had to be chopped and the timber burned before a crop could be raised. The Comans raised a little corn among the logs, and perhaps a few others did also, but the winter of 1836 set in with gloomy prospects. The settlements to the north of them had not raised sufficient for their own subsistence, and imported food was both dear and of poor quality. The most of the farmers exhausted their means in the purchase of that winter's provisions, and in the spring of 1837 were entirely destitute. The most of them had cows, and the pasturage was excellent, the only drawback being that sometimes the cows would stray and be gone several days. As illustrating the peculiar hardships of pioneer life, the following incident is given. Its truthfulness is vouched for by a prominent member of the first family. The exact date of the occurrence is not known, and it matters not, for such a thing could have occurred in any summer from 1836 to 1840. Do doubt, however, it occurred soon after the advent of the family to the settlement.

Mr. Farnham's family, at the time of its arrival in the Valley, consisted of himself and wife, two daughters and his mother. They brought two cows, and those cows were the main dependence for nourishing the family. These cows, like other cows of the settlement, strayed off occasionally, and to use the peculiar language of the frontier, "laid out." At one time Mr. Farnham's cows were gone several days, until, indeed, the family were reduced to the verge of starvation. Farnham had traveled miles through the wilderness, looking in vain for his cows. At last Farnham and his wife started out for another look. After several hours search, they had lost themselves and were unable to find their way out. They sat down and talked the matter over. They were lost in the woods, but they might as well die there as at home. They would die of starvation in either place, for they had not a mouthful of food, and gaunt starvation stared them in the face; and talking the matter over, they cried. Reader, pardon the tears; none can sympathize with them but those who know something of pioneer life. But the thought of that aged mother and those loved daughters induced them to make another effort to find, not the cows, but themselves. While they were in the woods, hunger impelled the grandmother of the family to look about for a crust, "that she might eat it and die." Rummaging the contents of an old trunk, she found the string ends of several pieces of dried beef. While the beef was drying it had been suspended by strings down through the flesh at the small end or corner of the strips. When sufficiently dried it had been packed in this old trunk for trans- portation. In using the beef it had been sliced off, until but little was left but the string, or as the historic Irishman would say, nothing but the string and hole, and these strings and fag ends were allowed to remain in the trunk. The old lady gathered the pieces, chopped them very fine, soaked them soft, and then with a little salt and wild herbs she succeeded in making a very savory dish of pottage, and had it just ready for the table when the lost cow hunters appeared at the door.

April the twelfth, 1837, the first child was born in the township,—Marion, daughter of Russell and Ann Coman. Marion grew to womanhood in the township, was educated in its public schools, and after teaching several years went to California, whither an elder sister had preceded her, married Mr. Harrison Dayton, and died February 28th, 1870, leaving three children.

The Rev. William E. Warner preached the first sermon in the township on the occasion of a funeral in the family of Mr. Pixley. For the early ministrations of the Word the pioneers were chiefly indebted to the Rev. Peter Foote, a preacher of the Protestant Methodist church.

At the township meeting of the township of Pittsford, held in the spring of 1837, Russell Coman was elected a justice of the peace, and Royal Raymond was elected assessor, and Calvin Pixley constable.

In the winter of 1837-8 the inhabitants met to take the preliminary action looking to the organization of a township. They were unanimously of the opinion that it would be for the interest of the people to have towns eight and nine south organized into a separate township, and then the question naturally came up what it should be called. The Comans and their relatives formed a large part of the voting population, and these and some others were in favor of calling the township after the first family settled in the town. Some were in favor of calling it Comansfield, and others simply Coman, but a vote decided in favor of Coman. The petition was drawn up and signed, ready for transmittal to the Honorable Legislature, then in session in Detroit. William K. Johnson, a man living near Lime Lake, and commonly called "Bill Johnson," was entrusted to carry the packet as far as Ypsilanti, and there mail it.

At the township meeting held in the township of Pittsford in April, 1838, Timothy Johnson and Calvin Pixley, of town eight south, were elected assessors; but a few days after, they learned that the Legislature had, on the sixth day of March, organized their township and called it Canaan. The Comans were surprised and chagrined. Some of the others laughed over the change of name. Poor Bill Johnson was charged with forgery, but he stoutly denied the impeachment. In after years it was found out that his asseveration was only partly true. A niece of his did the mischief by con-- verting the o of Coman into an a, and forming another a on the last stroke of the m, with his guilty knowledge, if not by his direction.

But Coman or Canaan, it was best to accept the situation; so the inhabitants were notified, and a township meeting held on the 24th day of April, 1838, at the house of Samuel Coman. Joseph Pixley was moderator, and Samuel Coman clerk. Officers elected: Timothy Johnson, supervisor; Arthur Lucas, town clerk; John M.

Lickley, Calvin Pixley and Ransom T. Crofford, justices of the peace; Royal Raymond and William K. Johnson, assessors; Ebenezer Pixley, collector; Evat Barber and Ebenezer Pixley, constables; Calvin Pixley, William Bennett and Michael Lickley, commissioners of highways; W. W. Johnson, Curtis Coman and Russell Coman, school inspectors; Joseph Pixley and Samuel Coman, directors of the poor. The justices were allotted terms as follows: Calvin Pixley, one year; Ransom T. Crofford, two years, and John M. Lickley, four years. Russell Coman was elected justice of the peace at the Pittsford town meeting in 1837, and as he had served one year and had three more to serve, but three justices were elected, none of them allotted the three year term.

The first school in the township was in the Coman neighborhood, afterwards designated the Black school house, now Prattville. The township now has excellent schools and school buildings. The forests have disappeared, and the township is fast developing into one of the finest in Hillsdale county. A large part of the township has a heavy clay soil, which only needs a generous system of underdrains to make it the most desirable wheat land in Southern Michigan.

It has before been remarked that the people of this township were largely indebted to the Rev. Peter Foote for ministerial services. His earnest representations made to the Protestant Methodist conference induced the sending of Father Milligan, in 1843, to organize a permanent work. Under his ministration many persons were converted, and a church organized. He was succeeded by the Rev. D. C. Oaks, and then other ministers followed until, for some cause, the Protestant Methodists withdrew from the field.

By act of the Legislature approved February 24th, 1844, Canaan became Wright.

On the 11th day of March, 1855, a Wesleyan Methodist church was organized at the school house in district number four. The persons participating in the organization were Hiram N. Barstow, Philo H. Stroud, J. N. Wilcox, J. L. Farnham, Rev. J. B. Hart, Rev. C. M. Preston, Stephen W. Coman, Matilda Barstow, Amelia Coman, Rebecca Hart, Ann Eliza Preston. Hiram N. Barstow was appointed leader, and J. N. Wilcox and S. W. Coman stewards. From this beginning the Wesleyan Methodist denomination has grown into a numerous body. They have a church at South Wright, and still keep up their appointments in district number four.

But earlier than this Wesleyan organization, the Baptists organized a church in the northwestern part of the township, at what is known as Lickley's Corners, and about 1855 they erected a church building.

The other churches of the township are the Disciples, or Campbellites, the United Brethren, at South Wright, and the Congregationalists, at Prattville.

South Wright is the elder village of the township, and has besides the three churches mentioned, a mill, two stores and a hotel. The farmers of the township have a grange organization which holds its meetings at South Wright.

Prattville is quite a modern village and has one mill, a store and a church.

The township has furnished the county a county clerk, W. W. Brewster, and has given the State two legislators, Hon. Russell Coman and Hon. Leonidas Hubbard. Its list of supervisors has the following names: 1838, Timothy Johnson; 1839, Russell Coman; 1840 and '41, John M. Lickley; 1842, Thomas C. Sawyer; 1843, Russell Coman; 1844, Timothy Johnson; 1845, '46 and '47, Russell Coman; 1848, Thomas C. Sawyer; 1849, Timothy Johnson; 1850, '51 and '52, Sawyer B. Downer; 1853, Russell Coman; 1854, William W. Brewster; 1855, Ira C. Smith; 1856, Lawrence Rheubottom; 1857 and '58, William W. Brewster; 1859, Lawrence Rheubottom; 1860 and '61, Edward C. Brewster; 1862 and '63, Leonidas Hubbard; 1864 and '65, Amos W. Clark; 1866, Edwin Johnson; 1867 and '68, Leonidas Hubbard; 1869 and '70, Edward C. Brewster; 1871, Ambrose M. Burroughs; 1872, Jacob Shaneour; 1873, Ambrose M. Burroughs; 1874, Jacob Shaneour; 1875, Hial Johnson; 1876, Edward C. Brewster.

XIII.   RANGE TWO WEST.

As announced in the introduction, sketches of the townships of Moscow, Adams, Jefferson, Ransom and Amboy will now be given.   They are only sketches, however, and do not pretend to exhaust the subject—the history of the early settlements:

MOSCOW.

The first settler in the township was Peter Benson, in 1831.   The second was Judge Lyman Blackmar, 1832; he lived in the township until his death.   Next followed Benjamin Fowle, Charles Fowle, Aaron Spencer, Daniel Aiken, etc.   Mrs. Brown, mother of Mrs. Daniel Aiken, died in 1834.   That summer Delilah Blackmar taught a school in a private house.   That fall a school house was built, and Seth Kempton taught the winter school.   Thus much by way of *resume* of what has preceded.

RELIGIOUS SOCIETIES.—The Rev. Mr. Colclazer is said to have been the first preacher of the gospel in the township of Moscow.   But previous to this, however, Judge Lyman Blackmar, then a licensed Methodist exhorter, had gathered a class on Moscow Plains and held services in a small frame barn.   This class was organized in 1835 or '36.   Only one member, Mrs. Sarah Camburn, is now living.   A church building four miles west of the village of Moscow was begun in 1853 and finished in 1854. Another class was formed, at the village of Moscow, in 1852; in 1854 they built a church, which in 1874 was refinished, making it as good as new and adding greatly to its beauty.

A church of the Associate Reformed Presbyterians was formed in 1838 or '39 and a church building was erected some two years later.   They were firm believers in Divine decrees of election and reprobation, believed in infant baptism, and were close communion.   The church became extinct by deaths and removals.   Their building yet stands, but is used for other purposes.

A Baptist organization was formed about the same time, (1839,) but they built no church.

The Moscow Mills are situated on the east branch of the Kalamazoo river, one mile south of Moscow village, on the site of the first saw mill in this part of the country, built by Benjamin Fowle in 1836.   The saw mill was rebuilt in 1859, and a run of light stones added, which did some grinding.   The present flouring mill was built in 1865, by Orrin Fowle, son of the original mill man.   The water power was afterward supplemented by steam power.   The engine being a Woodbury No. 8, has of itself sufficient power to drive all the machinery, therefore the mill is never idle; when water is plenty it is used as a matter of economy, but usually the saw mill furnishes sufficient fuel for the steam power.   The mill is only a little more than a mile from Jerome, a station on the Detroit, Hillsdale & Southwestern railroad, and with an additional run of stone might greatly increase its business.

SUPERVISORS.—The township was organized in the spring of 1835, but the records of the township meetings for the years 1835, '36 and '37 appear to have been lost.   Subsequent years the township was represented on the board of supervisors as follows: 1838, Zachariah Van Duzer; 1839, Orthnill Allen; 1840, Daniel A. Wisner; 1841, Zachariah Van Duzer; 1842, '43 and '44, Brooks Gale; 1845, Zachariah Van Duzer; 1846, Osmon B. Blackmar; 1847 and '48, Joel Moore; 1849, Zachariah Van Duzer; 1850 and '51, Wallace H. Godfrey; 1852, Benjamin Fowle, 1853, Orlando C. Gale; 1854, Benj. J. Kenyon; 1855, Horatio N. Rowley; 1856, Abram Ramsdell; 1857, Horatio N. Rowley; 1858, Henry C. Mallory; 1859, Horatio N. Rowley; 1860, Wallace H. Godfrey; 1861 and '62, Joel Moore; 1863, '64 and '65, Horatio N. Rowley; 1866 and '67, Albert Kenyon; 1868 to '72, both inclusive, Elisha C. L. Mumford; 1873, '74 and '75, Parker B. Shepard; 1876, William Armstrong.

The township has furnished one judge for the bench of Hillsdale county.

ADAMS.

This township was settled principally through Moscow. It was for a year a part of the township of Moscow, and therefore the history of the two are somewhat blended. Adams was organized as a separate township in the spring of 1836. It is believed the following named persons were then residents: Salmon Sharp, Abijah Smith, Henry N. Wilcox, Alpheus Hill, W. W. Jackson, John M. Foote, Milton Foote, Stephen Birdsell, William Cutler, Peter Sprowls, Henry Huff, Joseph B. Dowley, Luke Bross, David Bagley, Roswell Parker, Reuben Fuller, R. J. Fuller, Nicholas Worthington, John O. Swift, William C. Swift, Easton Wilbur, James Kirby, Horace Hitchcock, Seth Kempton, Roderick Wells, Orrin Blackmar, Benjamin Moore, Joseph W. Atard.

The first township meeting was held on Monday, the fourth day of April, 1836. Salmon Sharp was moderator, and Nicholas Worthington clerk. Officers elected:— Salmon Sharp, supervisor; Seth Kempton, clerk; Benjamin Moore, William Cutler and William W. Jackson, assessors; Nicholas Worthington, William W. Jackson and Easton Wilbur, commissioners of schools; Stephen Birdsell and Joseph W. Atard, commissioners of highways; Joseph B. Dowley and Julius O. Swift, directors of the poor; Easton Wilbur, collector.

At a special election held on the 12th day of September, to elect a delegate to the State convention, sixteen votes were polled.

It will be perceived by scanning the list of officers elected that the people of the township of Adams were strict constructionsits and elected officers under the Territorial laws, and not under the State constitution. This may account for the absence of justices of the peace and school inspectors.

The first mill built in the township was built by Swift & Co., in 1837 or '38. Soon after, another mill was built, on section five. Afterwards mills were built, one at North Adams by John Lane, one in the east part of the town by L. H. Updyke, and one in the south part of the town by Kerney & Howe.

Supervisors:—1836 to '40, both inclusive, Salmon Sharp; 1841, David Bagley; 1842, Ethel Judd; 1843 and '44, Peter Gates; 1845 and '46, David Bagley; 1847, Norman S. Sharp; 1848, Easton Wilbur; 1849, Andrew Wade; 1850, Asa S. Edwards; 1851, Norman S. Sharp; 1852, John M. Foote; 1853, Easton Wilbur; 1854, Peter Gates; 1855, Nelson Nethaway; 1856, William Cutler; 1857, Nelson Nethaway; 1858, Andrew Wade; 1859, Nicholas G. Vreeland; 1860 and '61, James S. Fowler; 1862 and '63, Nelson Nethaway; 1864 to '68, both inclusive, Ethel Judd; 1869, John Phillips elected, resigned and Ethel Judd appointed to vacancy; 1870 to '74, both inclusive, James Foote; 1875, Albert Kenyon; 1876, Saxton Bagley.

Township Clerks:—1836 to '39, both inclusive, Seth Kempton; 1840, Nicholas Worthington; 1841, '42 and '43, William D. Moore; 1844 to '48, both inclusive, Nelson Nethaway; 1849, David Bagley; 1850, Warner Spooner; 1851, David C. Fuller; 1852, James H. Fowler; 1853, Nicholas G. Vreeland; 1854, Firman Huff; 1855 and '56, Allen Kinney; 1857 to '61, both inclusive, Saxton S. Bagley; 1862, '63 and 64, Henry Wade; 1865, Darius J. Thompson; 1866, Saxton S. Bagley; 1867 and '68, John B. Kemp; 1869, David M. Foote; 1870, '71 and '72, Thomas J. Nethaway; 1873 to '76, both inclusive, George Kinney.

The first school house was built in 1838, in the district now known as number six, and Mary Driscoll taught the first school. Now the township has nine school houses, and the people are proud of their schools.

The Methodist Episcopal church is the oldest, having an organization older than the township. The other churches are the Baptist, Congregationalist, Christian, and Wesleyan Methodist.

The township has one hotel and one saloon, both in the village of North Adams. The village, which was nothing more than a country four corners until the completion of the Detroit, Hillsdale and Indiana railroad, is growing rapidly, and bids fair to become a business point of some importance.

JEFFERSON.

This town, first named Florida, was first a part of the township of Moscow, and afterwards of Adams, but the Legislature of 1837 organized towns seven, eight and nine south into a new township, named it Florida, and directed the first township meeting to be held at the house of William Duryea. Mr. Chauncey Leonard gives the following list as containing the names of every voter in the township at the time of its organization: John Perrin, John Perrin, Jr., S. W. Perrin, J. H. Thorn, M. B. Howell, William Duryea, Peter Failing, James Bullard, R. McNeil, Jr., Rev. Jacob Ambler, Chauncey Leonard, W. S. Coon, Rowland Bird, J. H. Springer, James P. Howell, H. P. Adams, H. Hadley, William Heacox, O. B. Coffin, William Green, Frederick Duryea, H. Bullard, R. McNeal, Sr., A. McNeal, Fourtelett O. Anderson, H. Black, Perez Demmick, A. Orcutt, John M. Duryea.

The township meeting was held April third, 1837, on a log near William Duryea's house. The proceedings of that meeting, as related by Mr. Leonard, are very amusing. There was but one party, no ballots or ballot-box, and they held the caucus simultaneous with the election. They caucused among themselves as to whom it was best to have for supervisor, and having determined that point, a motion was made that he be elected, which of course was carried, the vote being *vive voce*, and then the same process was gone through with for each of the other offices.

The official records show the following officers elected: Henry P. Adams, supervisor; Chauncey Leonard, township clerk; James Ballard William Heacox, Alonzo McNeal, assessors; John M. Duryea, collector; Horatio Hadley and Michael B. Howell, directors of the poor; Orrin Anderson, Frederick Duryea and Robert McNeal, Jr., commissioners of highways; Wait Chapin, William S. Coon and John Perren, Jr., school inspectors; William Duryea, William S. Coon, Henry P. Adams and Horatio Hadley, justices of the peace; John M. Duryea and Orrin Anderson, constables.

The justices drew terms as follows: Horatio Hadley, one year; Henry P. Adams, two years; William S. Coon, three years; William Duryea, four years.

A special township meeting was held on the fourth day of May to elect a supervisor, and the Rev. Jacob Ambler was elected.

The first school house was built on section four, in 1837, and Emeline Sears taught the first school. The first frame school house was built in district number two, in 1840 or '41.

In 1849 the name of the township was changed to Jefferson.

The township is well supplied with mills for sawing and grinding. Chauncey Leonard owned a saw mill on the present site of the Wood mill, in 1846. The grist mill was built by Wood about seventeen years ago. There are several other mills in the township.

Supervisors:—1837, Henry P. Adams to May 4th; from May 4th, Jacob Ambler; 1838, Jacob Ambler; 1839 and '40, William Heacox; 1841, William Duryea; 1842, Chauncey Leonard; 1843, William Heacox; 1844, Chauncey Leonard; 1845 and '46, James H. Thorn; 1847 and '48, Warren Thompson; 1849 and '50, James H. Thorn; 1851 and '52, Charles D. Luce; 1853, William Heacox; 1854, James H. Thorn; 1855 and '56, Henry F. Sutton; 1857, Moses Rumsey; 1858 and '59, Henry F. Sutton; 1860, Charles D. Luce; 1861, Joseph Slaight; 1862, Silas A. Wade; 1863 and '64, James Leonardson; 1865, Moses Rumsey; 1866, '67 and '68, James Leonardson; 1869 '70 and '71, Charles D. Luce; 1872, Moses Rumsey; 1873, James Leonardson; 1874, '75 and '76, Charles D. Luce. Mr. Luce has also represented his district in the State Legislature.

TOWN EIGHT SOUTH, TWO WEST.

The town described in the title to this section was first a part of the township of Moscow, 1835, of Adams, 1836, and of Florida, 1837–40.

Rowland Bird was the first settler in the town, his advent to its wilds bearing date

March the eighth, 1836, while the town was yet a part of Moscow, but it is fair to presume the authorities of Moscow knew nothing of his coming. Mr. Bird was a native of Massachusetts. In 1832, after a sojourn in the State of New York, he came to the Territory of Michigan and settled in or near Sylvania. During the Toledo war he determined to be an inhabitant of Michigan at all hazards, removed from the disputed territory, and settled in town eight south. Mr. Bird's family consisted of his wife and seven children,—three sons and four daughters,—and a young man named Leander Candee. The next family settled in the town was Orrin Cobb, on the west line. Thomas Burt, family and brother, settled in 1837 or '38 probably, as he speaks of stopping over night at the Medina tavern and with Augustus Finney at Lanesville. The Burts were English people. Thomas, when he first came to America, settled on the Maumee river, near Perrysburgh. A few years after, he returned to England, and then his wife and brother came over with him. Having sold his Ohio possessions, he sought a home in the wilderness of Michigan. When they came to Medina, on their way in, they were penniless. Mr. Burt explained his situation and was cared for as well as though he had money. At Lanesville the same course was pursued with like results. The family carried their own provisions, and only needed shelter for themselves and shelter and provender for their beasts. Near the northwest corner of Pittsford the family were left while the men pushed on to build a cabin, and very soon they were settled on their own land. A few years later they were able to repay the worthy landlords for their kindness.

The way having been opened, the town was settled quite rapidly, and some settlers found their way into town nine south.

The first school was taught in a shanty on the northwest quarter of section eight, by Lucinda Bird, in the summer of 1838. Three families sent to this school,—Orren Cobb, Israel S. Hodges and Rowland Bird.

The same year, Mr. Bird built the first frame barn. Some of the men who helped at the raising came from Jonesville for that purpose.

Indeed, the settlers of that town know what hardships and privations mean. One of them desiring sash for the windows of his new log house, walked to Jonesville, bought five sash, paid all his money, lashed the sash to his back, and returned without having a mouthful to eat. Another man desiring some seed oats, started out, accompanied by his thirteen-year-old boy, in search of some; he bought three bushels three miles west of Hudson. Two bushels were put in one bag and one bushel in the other. The bags were shouldered respectively by father and son, and carried the whole distance home.

In the year 1839 a child was born to Mr. and Mrs. Babcock,—the first birth in the township. March the eighth the first death occurred. It was Allen Bird, aged sixteen years. He died just three years after the arrival of the family in the town. The Rev. Jacob Ambler, of Osseo, preached the funeral sermon,—the first sermon in the town.

In March, 1840, occurred the first marriage in the territory now embraced within the limits of Ransom. Leander Candee and Miss Lorinda, eldest daughter of Mr. Rowland Bird. It is said to be the first because, although Miss Drake, of town nine south had been married the year previous, yet as both towns were then Florida, and the scene of the marriage is now in Amboy, it is difficult to see how it can be credited to Rowland or its successor, Ransom.

The inhabitants having become numerous,—about one hundred,—the the Legislature of Michigan, at its session in the winter of 1840, was petitioned to organize towns eight and nine south into a new township. By an act approved April 1st, the township was organized and named

ROWLAND.

The first township meeting was held on the sixth day of April, 1840, at the house of Alexander Palmer. James H. Babcock was moderator, and Israel S. Hodges secretary, (so says the record), and Rowland Bird, Orrin Cobb and Rufus H. Rathburn were inspectors of election. Officers elected: Leander Candee, supervisor; Israel S. Hodges, township clerk; Rowland Bird, treasurer; Matthew Armstrong and Rowland Bird, assessors; Alexander Palmer, collector; Matthew Armstrong, Israel S. Hodges and James H. Babcock, school inspectors; Joseph Howe and William Phillips, directors of the poor; James H. Babcock, Alexander Palmer and Henry Cornell, commissioners of highways; Rowland Bird, James H. Babcock, Matthew Armstrong and Henry Cornell, justices of the peace; Alexander Palmer, Joseph Phillips, Amos S. Drake and Alexander Findley, constables. The justices elect drew terms as follows: Henry Cornell, one year; Matthew Armstrong, two years; Rowland Bird, three years; and James H. Babcock, four years. The township voted five dollars bounty for wolves, and one hundred and twenty-five dollars for contingent expenses.

On the ninth day of April, 1840, Mrs. Candee died,—the bride of a month filled the second grave in the township. The same day her sister, Eunice, the youngest daughter of Mr. Rowland Bird, died. In the September following, the 18th day, Mr. Bird's youngest son died, aged six years, and on the 22d day of the same month Rowland Bird died, aged forty-seven years.

In 1839 or '40 the first school house in the township was built. It was in district number two, near the site of the present school house. There are now eight school districts in the township, numbered from one to nine, except there is no number four. Three of these districts have brick, and five have frame school houses. The first frame school house was built in district number seven in 1844.

In October, 1841, the first fire occurred in the township. C. B. Shepard, then of Adams, was preparing to become an inhabitant of this township. He had put up the body of a house and covered it; he hauled a load of lumber for doors and floors from the Kidder mill in the township of Hudson. This he unloaded near the shanty he had built for a temporary shelter, and went to Adams to spend the Sunday and bring a load of goods on his return Monday. But when he returned, his shanty and lumber were ashes. He supposed it to have been occasioned by the accidental explosion of some gunpowder he had deposited in a boiler.

In 1848 began a series of skirmishing for township name, and it was not until 1850 that the township had a settled name. From April 1st, 1848, to April 2d, 1849, it was known as Ransom; from April 2d, 1849, to March 28th, 1850, it was called Bird, but since 1850 it has uniformly been known as

RANSOM.

In 1848 a Congregationalist church was organized, and 1855 that church built a house of worship, and since that, churches have been built, until now the Methodist Episcopal and the Seventh-Day Adventists have each one, the United Brethren two, and they are preparing to build a third.

Dr. Lee was the first resident physician. He settled in Rowland about 1842. He also opened the first store in the township, and Ichabod Steadman kept the second, or the first in Ransom village.

The following comparison of the Ransom of to-day with the same territory in 1836 is from the pen of Samuel B. Brown, her local historian:

"In 1836, forty years ago, Ransom was an unbroken forest,—not one acre of cleared land, but all heavy timber. Of the 19,185 acres of land in Ransom, 12,074 acres are improved, 2,111 acres are included in the highways and partial improvements, and 5,000 acres are wood. The improvements, including highways, average nine acres to every inhabitant of the town. Forty years ago people traveling in Ransom with a team had to cut and clear a road; to-day there are in Ransom seventy miles of highway, occupying 560 acres of land. The inhabitants of Ransom have invested in their highways a capital of $70,400, and are expending annually $2,000 in repairing them. (It is no part of this history to state whether the roads are as good as the investment ought to furnish.) Forty years ago there was not a rod of fence in Ransom; to-day there are 420 miles of fence, at 50 cents a rod is $160 a mile, making $67,200, the cost of fences, not including any repairs. Forty years ago there was one dwelling house in Ransom; to-day there are 341. Then there was one family; to-day there are 346. Then there were ten inhabitants in the town; latest statistics give us 1,539. The census of 1874 furnish us with items of interest, some of which we will record. In 1873 1,962 acres of wheat were harvested in Ransom, yielding 24,871 bushels, 13 bushels per acre; 1,852 acres of corn were harvested, yielding 99,660 bushels of ears, 54 bushels per acre. In 1874 there were 522 acres of apple orchards in Ransom; sheep, 1,848; hogs, 1,138; horses, 577; mules, 5; oxen, 46; cows, 886; wool sheared in 1873, 16,070 lbs.; pork sold, 183,504 lbs.; cheese made, 49,882 lbs.; butter made, 89,580 lbs. In comparing the productions of Ransom in 1873 with the productions of Hillsdale county in 1840, we have the following results: In 1840 Hillsdale county produced 80,250 bushels of wheat; Ransom in 1873 produced 24,871 bushels of wheat. In 1840 the county produced 82,757 bushels of corn; Ransom in 1873 produced 99,660 bushels of corn. The dairy product of Hillsdale county in 1840 was worth $5,626; the dairy product of Ransom in 1873 was $21,152.75."

Ransom furnished for the armies of the Republic, during the great rebellion, one hundred and forty-three men, forty of whom were killed, or have died of wounds received, or disease contracted in the service. The following were among the number enlisted: James Tarseney, Riley Ainsworth, Hiram Hartson, Ira Williams, Emery Yost, —— Yost, John Williams, Horace Doty, Darius Howe, Marshal Tooth, Ephraim Baker, Charles Baker, C. Button, Samuel Wheaton, William Kelley, John Durgan, William Palmer, William Britton, Sidney Palmer, —— Hall, Andrew Booth, Hollis Hammond, —— Higley, Charles Coppins, Samuel Halsted, Geo. Dewey, Orrin Olds, E. H. Goodrich, J. M. Bailey, William Doyle, Oscar Barnes, William Clark, Amos Smith, Charles Hartson, Edgar Ainsworth, Richard Hart, James Burt, William Pettit, S. Bliler, John Smatts, Hiram Hurd, H. Perkins, Chas. Olds, Capt. Hill, Wm. Rose, Geo. W. Van Gauder, Loren Hammond, Geo. H. Cornell, John Palmer, Isaac Brown, James H. Thiel, Kincade Shepardson, D. W. Litchfield, J. Schermerhorn, William H. Shepard, Michael Howland, Lewis Deuel, John Croop, Alfred Deuel, Wm. Liddall, Willis Woods, Loren Whitney, John Williams, Sidney Dodge, Daniel Clemens, Sheldon Carey, Daniel Brogan, Henry Common, John C. Cooper, William Manning, John Tarseney, Thomas Plumley, George Brewster, Thomas Tarseney, Andrew Tarseney, Quincy Britton, Aaron Boyer, Michael Helmick, James D. Cornell, Horace Gay, Warren Perham, William Mapes, Geo. Mapes, Aaron Smith, Cornelius Boington, James Hoover, Samuel Kingsley, Geo. R. Palmer, Benj. S. Ward, Collins Wilcox, William Youngs, T. C. Baker, Chas. Hannibal, Isaac Smith, H. Bailey, Orsamus Doty, Harry Mott, David Litchfield, John Ainsworth, William H. Allen, Samuel Cressey, Edwin Camp, George Casterline, Jeptha Casterline, Henry Tary, John Hosman, Geo. Hart, Frank Hoover, Elias Hoover, Thomas Lozier, Israel Lozier, Benj. Olds, Asahel Parks, Charles Parks, Frank Runell, Lewis Smith, Orville Thompson, E. W. Warner, Fred Olds, Jacob Rorrick, William Agnew, George W. Booth, William Lile, Andrew Crandall, Aaron Stocker, Jonas Smith, William Young, A. Howell, W. Young, E. P. Barson, George N. Sacrider, I. C. Hinds, Frank Smith.

ACCIDENTS.—In 1851, Mr. Featherly was killed by a falling limb while in the woods east of Danforth, Bugbee's Corners. In 1860, Mr. Joles was killed by lightning. Not far from that time, old Mr. Siddle was killed while falling a tree in the southwest part of the town. A young man by the name of Ward was killed by falling on to a pitchfork, in the south part of the town. The explosion of a steam boiler in a sawmill, on the farm of Charles Burt, in the southeast part of the town, in 1872, killed four, and injured a number of others.

But one case of homicide has occurred. February 6th, 1876, Jacob Stevick killed Horace A. Burnett. He was tried in the Hillsdale circuit court, convicted of manslaughter, and sentenced to ten years' imprisonment.

Supervisors of Rowland: 1840, Leander Candee; 1841, Nelson Doty; 1842, Thomas Burt; 1843 and '44, Nelson Doty; 1845, Israel S. Hodges; 1846 and '47, Thomas Burt. RANSOM—1848, Leander Candee. BIRD—1849, William Burnham, jr. RANSOM—1850, Thomas Burt; 1851, John J. Andridge; 1852, William E. Warner; 1853, Thomas Burt; 1854, Israel B. Norris; 1855, Jared B. Norris; 1856 and '57, Nelson Doty; 1858, Lemuel J. Squire; 1859, Ephraim C. Turner; 1860, Warren McCutcheon; 1861, Henry W. Russell; 1862 to '68, Warren McCutcheon; 1869 and '70, Miles G. Teachout; 1871 and '72, Warren McCutcheon; 1873 and '74, Samuel B. Brown; 1875 and '76, William H. H. Pettit.

AMBOY.

Only the eastern part of this township comes within the scope of our undertaking. Amos S. Drake settled in town nine south, two west, in December, 1838, but the town settled quite rapidly.

In February, 1839, Sarah N. Drake died; her funeral sermon was preached by Elder Stout, who, at that time, lived in the vicinity of Bird Lake. It was the first sermon preached in that town.

In December, the same year, Samuel Carl and Jane Drake were married by Mr. Fowler, of Camden.

When Rowland was organized, town nine south was attached, and shared in all the mutations that township endured.

In 1850, all that part of towns nine south, ranges two and three west, lying within the State of Michigan, and one tier of sections off the south side of town eight south, ranges two and three west, were organized into a new township, and called Amboy. Nearly all the improvements have been made since that time.

The grist-mill, owned by Waldron & Hall, was built about thirty years ago, but there was a saw-mill there several years earlier. Besides this, there is the Higby & Osborn mill, the Manly or Lewis mill, and the Bryan mill. There has been a Chilson mill, but it has ceased to work.

There are two churches, the Baptist and Methodist, and both have neat and commodious houses.

The first township meeting was held on the 22d day of April, 1850, at the house of Amos Drake. John King was moderator, and Gideon G. King clerk. Amos S. Drake and John P. Corey were inspectors of the election. Officers elected: Nathan Dewey, supervisor; Gideon G. King, clerk; Charles Clark, treasurer; Nathan Edinger, John King and Charles S. Baker, justices of the peace; Henry Prestage, John Goforth and Gideon F. King, commissioners of highways; Charles Farley and William Drake, school inspectors; Amos S. Drake and John King, directors of the poor, and Joseph Philbrick, Charles H. Barton and Paden Marshal, constables.

Supervisors: 1850, Nathan S. Dewey; 1851 and '52, Gideon G. King; 1853, William Gay; 1854, Charles S. Baker; 1855, William Gay; 1856 and '57, Gideon G. King; 1858 and '59, Charles Farley; 1860, Gideon F. King; 1861 and '62, William Drake; 1863 to '67, both inclusive. Augustus G. McClellan; 1868 and '69, William Drake; 1870, Augustus G. McClellan; 1871 and '72, William Drake; 1873, Augustus G. McClellan; 1874, Augustus G. McClellan, until he died, and then William Drake; 1875, James M. Baker; 1876, James Battel.

SUPPLEMENT.

HUDSON.

Boots and Shoes.—In the early years of this township, the articles mentioned at the head of this article were found in all general stores, and there were several shoe-makers who made to order such articles in this line as could not be supplied from the stores; but there was no distinctively boot and shoe store until Hiland and Clark R. Beach came to the village, in the spring of 1849, and opened a boot and shoe house. The house first took the name of H. Beach, and has been continued by one or the other of the brothers under various styles, sometimes with partners, sometimes alone, until the present time it bears the name of C. R. Beach.

Alfred A. Finney, the only child of Augustus Finney, esq., settled on a farm on section seven, Hudson, about the time of his marriage with Miss Harriet Kidder, eldest daughter of Hiram Kidder. Soon after the discovery of gold in California, perhaps in 1849, he went to that State. He made the journey by sail vessel, around Cape Horn. Soon after his return, he established the old Elephant boot and shoe house. He served one term as justice of the peace, but the most of his time was devoted to his store. He died Sept. 8th, 1871, but his business has been continued by his only child, Mr. Byron A. Finney.

Carriage Manufactories.—In the early years of Hudson township, several men worked at wagon-building, but the first establishment that deserved the name of a manufactory was that began by Alexander M. Ocobock, on the present site of the spoke factory, in or about the year 1852. Mr. Perley Chase was associated with him until the spring of 1857, when Chase was succeeded by Munson. The same spring, carriage-building was abandoned by Ocobock & Munson, and they turned their attention to the manufacture of hubs and bent work.

George W. Carter, in September, 1854, came to Hudson, and commenced black-smithing. He did the ironing of carriages for Ocobock & Chase, until, in the spring of 1857, he bought out their carriage business and commenced manufacturing on his own account. He yet continues the business. His original one-story wood buildings have given place to large two-story brick buildings. The change was necessitated by the increase of his business, managed with skill and care, always under his own personal supervision.

The original foundry was erected by Samuel Eddy for Loren Chapin, and it now forms a part of the Elliott House. The original drug store was kept by Hall & Wells.

Among the business houses of to-day are the following: Two banks; four dry goods, eleven grocery, four hardware, four drug, two furniture, four boot and shoe houses; one hat, one tobacco, one tea and one jewelry house; three clothiers, two bakeries; six millinery, four barber, one gun, three cooper, five blacksmith, one tailor and two paint shops; one pump, one fanning mill, one tub, two carriage, one wheelbarrow manufactory; one machine shop, three planing mills, three lumber yards, two liveries, one saw mill, eight physicians, two dentists, eight lawyers, two artists, two hair-dressers, four insurance offices, five saloons, three meat markets, one butter and egg store, four hotels, two book stores and two printing offices.

By the census of 1874, Hudson township had 3,927 inhabitants, of which 1,946 were males and 1,981 were females; excess of females, 35. Of the males, 25 were between seventy-five and ninety years of age; 433 between forty-five and seventy-five; 602 between twenty-one and forty-five; 452 between ten and twenty-one years of age, while

434 were under ten. Of the females, 41 were upwards of seventy-five years of age; 474 between forty and seventy-five; 722 between eighteen and forty; 361 between ten and eighteen years of age, while 383 were under ten.

Eight hundred and fifty of the males over twenty-one years of age were married; 51 were widowers or divorced persons; 159 had never been married, and one person only, under twenty-one years of age, was living in the marriage relation. Of females over eighteen years of age, 824 were married; 171 widows or divorced persons; 274 had never been married, and 9 persons under eighteen years of age were living in the marriage relation.

We had enough marriageable maidens to mate our bachelors and 83 more, while we had maidens and widows enough to mate our bachelors and widowers, and 203 more.

Against the 451 unmarried males under twenty-one years of age, being prepared by time for the marriage state, we had only 352 females under eighteen years of age.

In 1873, there were 26 marriages, 37 deaths and 77 births. There were 4 deaf and dumb persons, 1 blind and 4 insane. Twenty-six persons were of African descent.

In 1873 there were 3,470 acres of wheat and 1,938 acres of corn harvested. There were 3,346 acres of wheat to be harvested in 1874.

It had 614 acres of peach, pear, apple, plum and cherry orchards; 10 acres of raspberry bushes; 11 of strawberry vines; 5 of currant and gooseberry bushes, and 30 acres of melons and garden vegetables.

In 1873, 10,432 lbs. of wool were sheared; 288,020 lbs. of pork, 44,945 lbs. of cheese and 209,502 lbs. of butter were marketed.

In the same year, 42,365 bushels of wheat, 96,945 bushels of corn and 21,000 bushels of other kinds of grain; 35,525 bushels of apples, 71 bushels of pears, 51 bushels of cherries, 27 cwt. of grapes, 27 bushels of strawberries, 35 bushels of currants and gooseberries, and 463 bushels of melons and garden vegetables were harvested.

There were 20,650 pounds of fruit dried; 4,380 pounds of maple sugar made; 7,555 bushels of potatoes raised; 830 barrels of cider made, and 2,586 tons of hay raised and cut.

It had 214 persons employed in its manufacturing establishments, and the amount of capital invested was $185,500.

It had only two flouring mills, with two run of stone each, and four saw mills, worth $7,300, which sawed in 1873, 530,000 feet of lumber.

CORRECTIONS.—As was stated in the introduction to this book, it is impossible to make it free from errors, especially in dates and in Christian names. A few have already been discovered. That many more exist, seems very probable. There are also some typographical errors, but they are few, and easily corrected by the reader.

Hudson: On page 84, the last clause of the eighth paragraph reads that sundry persons were "admitted to membership on probation." It should have read, "were admitted to membership on profession of faith."

Page 81: In second line of fourth paragraph, for "Tuesday" read "Wednesday."

Page 91: Fifth paragraph, last clause, for "made it," read "it made."

Medina: Page 51, first line of Western Fairfield, instead of "March, 1835," it perhaps should read "October, 1834," but this is a disputed point.

Page 52: The fourth paragraph should read, "In 1835, William Cavender bought the land owned by William Walworth—the site of the Canandaigua mills—and in the fall of the same year sold it to Laban Merrick, who commenced building a saw-mill."

Page 112: Close of first paragraph, for "Levi Daniels" read "Lemuel Daniels;" for "Patrick Trumer," read "Patrick Trainer;" for "Nathan Stone," read "Nahum Stone."

Rollin: The Quaker Mill was built about 1850, by Mr. William Beal. It is now owned by Nelson Perkins.

Seneca: Page 119, at end of sixth paragraph, read "and two Representatives, Dr. Jas. H. Sweeney and Elias J. Baldwin.

TECUMSEH.

Since the first sections of this book were printed, S. C. Stacy, esq., editor of the Tecumseh *Herald*, delivered an address before the Lenawee County Pioneer Society on the early history of Tecumseh. As in some of its statements it differs from the statements contained in the opening sections of this book, it has been determined to give it to the reader in the form of a supplement. Mr. Stacy was born and reared in that village, and has opportunities for investigation, and is, by all odds, the best authority extant on the early history of the pioneer town:

In preparing a historical paper to be read before the Lenawee County Pioneer Society to-day, it occurred to me that a detailed account of some particular event in the county, or of some particular locality, would be more valuable as well as more interesting, than a general sketch covering a larger extent of territory and a longer period of time.

Accordingly, we have selected for our theme the "First Settlement of Tecumseh," and we shall endeavor to faithfully portray the principal events which transpired within the present corporate limits of this village, from the time when the first settler trod the virgin soil of the Territory in the summer of 1823, until the first formal celebration of Independence Day, on the 4th of July, 1826. This period will embrace the first two years of the settlement of Tecumseh. During this time, the civilization of the white man was planted in the then "Far West," a village was established, several families were domiciled in their new homes, a county seat was legislated into existence, and Tecumseh assumed her position as an important geographical point in Michigan.

The founder of Tecumseh was a worthy Quaker, of whom we have all heard before, named Musgrove Evans. He was a native of Pennsylvania, but for several years prior to 1823 had been residing in the town of Chaumont, Jefferson county, New York. Like many other enterprising men of that day, he caught the Western fever, and in the early summer of 1823 he left his New York home to "seek his fortune," and came to Detroit. At this point he formed the acquaintance of Austin E. Wing, who had already been a resident of the Territory for several years, which acquaintance afterwards ripened into a strong friendship and business partnership, that continued unbroken until Mr. Evans' death. After obtaining from Mr. Wing what information he could in regard to the most desirable locations in the interior, he started out to explore the Raisin Valley, for in that early day the valley of the Raisin was justly celebrated for its beauty. Shortly before this time, this portion of Michigan had been surveyed, and the Government lands had been thrown upon the market. Of this trip by Mr. Evans but little is known, as we have neither records nor tradition to enlighten us; but we know the fact that the Quaker pioneer fell in love with the beautiful oak openings around Tecumseh, and the splendid hydraulic power afforded by Evans Creek and the river Raisin, and resolved to make this section his future home. Accordingly, he returned to Jefferson county, enlisted his brother-in-law, J. W. Brown, and a few others, in the enterprise, and made preparations to remove his family West in the coming spring.

Mr. Evans spent that winter in gathering his party together, and early in 1824 a company of over twenty, under his guidance, left the town of Chaumont, Jefferson county, New York, to take up their abode among the oak openings of the Raisin Valley, in Michigan. The journey before them was no holiday trip. In fact, they consumed more time and endured more privations and hardships than a like company would to-day in traveling from New York to San Francisco.

The party consisted of Musgrove Evans, his wife and five children, General J. W. Brown, Ezra F. Blood, Peter Benson and wife, Turner Stetson and wife, two Fulsoms, father and son, Nathan Rathbone, Peter Low, John Borland, Curtis Page, George Spafford, Levi Baxter and Henry Sloate. They came up Lake Ontario to Lewiston, and from there to Black Rock, near Buffalo, where they remained for one week on account of the ice. In those days, steam navigation was in its infancy. There was but one steamboat on Lake Erie, and passenger tickets thereon, between Black Rock and Detroit, were $20 each. Most people traveling West were unable to pay the fare. The Evans party, therefore, chartered a schooner called the "Erie," (the same craft which subsequently went over the Falls of Niagara,) and as soon as the harbor was sufficiently clear of ice, they weighed anchor and set sail for Detroit. No incident particularly noteworthy occurred during the voyage, and they disembarked in safety at Detroit during the last week in April, 1824.

After a stop of three days in Detroit, the gentlemen of the party started for Tecumseh on foot, taking with them one pony and a French boy to transport their baggage and commissary stores. They followed the St. Joe trail to Ypsilanti. This trail was a narrow track, only wide enough for one man or horse, but well beaten, being worn into the earth from three to six inches below the surface of the ground. There was no mistaking the trail when once seen, nor was there any danger of losing it. It followed a general westward course, winding about among the trees and crossing streams at fordable points. The members of the party, of course, pony and all, were compelled to travel in single file, in orthodox Indian fashion, and when drawn out in that manner they made quite an imposing caravan. From Ypsilanti they followed the same trail to Saline, and thence to the river Raisin, a mile or so north of the present village of Clinton. There they crossed the river and discharged their pony, and leaving the trail, bore off in a southwesterly direction until they reached the eccentric little creek which now bears Musgrove Evans' name, which they followed to its junction with the Raisin, arriving at that point in the afternoon.

Here, on the spot where the Globe Mill now stands, they found two or three Indian wigwams. They were deserted, but were in good enough repair to afford comfortable shelter, and in the largest of these wigwams the company passed that night. The next morning they explored the section of country adjacent to Evans Creek and the Raisin, and came to the conclusion that here was the place to "settle down." Three or four days were passed in this manner, and the nights were spent in the big wigwam. Finally their commissary stores having become exhausted, they left for Monroe where they expected to meet the remainder of the party. They were one whole day making the trip, traveling on foot. They followed an Indian trail, and arrived just at night in Monroe, as hungry a set of men, probably, as Michigan has ever seen before or since. The whole village of Monroe turned out in surprise to meet them, for it was a strange sight to witness a company of white men coming into Monroe from the West. Here they met the women and children of the party, who had just arrived from Detroit in a sail boat called the "Fire Fly," commanded by Captain Harvey.

Austin E. Wing met them at Monroe, and here the partnership of Wing, Evans & Brown was entered into, and the determination formed to secure the location of the county seat at Tecumseh. Gen. Brown, and most of the men in the party, then went back to Detroit, and thence East for their families, and while at Detroit, Gen. Brown had an interview with Gov. Cass in regard to the county seat.

Evans then hired about thirty men, and they proceeded to Tecumseh, cutting a road as they went along. They followed the general course of the Indian trail from Monroe to Tecumseh, and in due time halted at the east bank of the Raisin, about thirty rods east of the present site of the Globe Mill. The river, however, was so high as to render it unsafe to ford it at that point, and so they followed the east bank about two miles north and west, and at five o'clock in the afternoon halted their wagons on the flat where the small dwelling house, barn and cooper shop, belonging to the Brownville Mill, now stands. Here the party passed that night, with a few oak trees and the blue dome of heaven as their only shelter. The next morning they commenced work on a log house, which was soon erected. Its dimensions were twenty feet square, horizontally, and about nine feet perpendicularly. There was a low garret, two logs in height above the ceiling, which was used as a bed-room for the boys and hired men. There was no floor, as the nearest saw-mill was at Monroe, and the roof was covered with bark peeled from elm trees, and until the next November it was provided with neither chimney nor fireplace. A bake-kettle served the purpose of an oven for several months. For cooking purposes a fire was made on the ground, the smoke ascending through a hole in the roof. Mrs. Benson accompanied this party of workmen to prepare meals for them. She was the first white woman in Lenawee county. In this house Evans and his wife, with five children, Peter Benson and wife, and several men, lived during the summer, Mrs. Evans and Mrs. Benson preparing food for from fifteen to twenty persons daily.

As soon as the house was completed, Evans returned to Monroe for his family. Having procured ox teams, and packed their household goods and provisions (what little they had) in rough wagons, they turned their faces once more toward the setting sun. This was a beautiful summer morning, the first day of June, 1824. The men traveled on foot, and the women and children found it convenient to rest themselves by walking a part of the distance. It was easier to walk than to ride, and just as cheap. On the afternoon of the second day, June 2d, 1824, they arrived at the Evans mansion, in Brownville, and took up their abode.

Their household utensils were but few, and of the rudest kind. They brought no bedstead with them, but a bed was made in each corner of the house by sticking two poles into a hole in each wall, and supporting the outer ends of the poles, where they crossed each other, with a block of wood. Thus a good bedstead was made out of two saplings, and with but a single leg. Tradition tells us that the lord of the house, Musgrove himself, was unceremoniously tumbled out of bed one morning by having the block, which formed the corner post, knocked from under the two saplings. They had no chairs, but used rough benches instead. In the following November a floor was laid, a chimney and an out-door oven, and two small shanties were added to the house, for two other families had arrived to occupy the mansion during the ensuing winter.

Gen. Brown returned East in July, and had brought back his wife and children, and George Spafford and wife had arrived. Brown brought a dozen chairs with him, and some other articles of household furniture, including a trundle-bed. During the winter of 1824-5, this house afforded a home for Mr. Evans, his wife and six children, Gen. Brown, his wife and six children, Peter Benson and wife, and George Spafford and wife. This log house was the first in Lenawee county, and one of the first ones in Michigan, west of Monroe and Detroit. A building was made near by of tamarack poles, twelve feet square and seven feet high, which was used for a school house, Mrs. George Spafford teaching school there during that winter.

Among the farming implements brought to the settlement by Mr. Evans, was one plow. No crops were put in the first summer, except a little corn and wheat and some garden truck, as the season was too far advanced when the new comers arrived. But there was a man in the company, named Fulsom, who was bound to have some plowing done. He wanted to see how Michigan soil looked, for he was confident he could tell by inspection whether it would produce good crops or not. He borrowed Evans' plow, hitched on an ox team, and with Ezra F. Blood to hold the plow, turned the first furrows in the virgin soil of Lenawee county.

This plowing took place on the bank of the creek, in the western portion of the village, and near the spot where A. McNeil's house now stands.

During the summer, several other families reached Tecumseh from Jefferson county, all of whom had been induced to come West from the representations of Mr. Evans. In June or July, James Patchin arrived with his family, coming by the way of Detroit and Monroe, as the pioneer party had done. He located two lots of land east of Brownville, and built a small log house thereon, where he continued to reside for many years. This farm is now owned and occupied by Jacob G. Roberts.

E. P. Champlin arrived with his family about the same time, settled on the land now owned by Elizabeth Whitney, near the Patchin farm, and a little west. These three families have long since been scattered, and the members thereof who lived in that early day have gone to their final home. Mrs. James Patchin continued to reside here until her death, which occurred within the last five years.

Turner Stetson and wife came with the original Evans party, but met them at Detroit, and were persuaded by Evans and the rest to accompany them to Tecumseh. Stetson built a house on the bluff of the creek, near the present site of the Episcopal church. He sowed a small patch of wheat in the fall of 1823, as also did Evans, some four acres.

The first land bought of the Government was in 1823, when Austin Wing entered two lots, covering the Brownville mill privilege. The next land entered was in June, 1824—one lot by Stetson, extending north and west from the present depot, and the next was two lots, entered by Ezra F. Blood, in June, 1824, about a mile southeast of the village. Upon this same farm Mr. Blood and his family still reside. He is still in good health, and we trust he may remain with us many years longer.

The next family which arrived was that of Abner Spafford. His family came on the Erie, to Detroit, where they arrived on the 4th of July, 1824. One of Mr. Spafford's daughters, Cynthia, (now Mrs. Wm. W. Tilton, who still resides in Tecumseh,) remembers that celebration vividly, as it was the first time in her life that she ever heard a cannon. Soon after, Mr. Spafford, with two of his boys, started for Monroe by land, driving eleven head of cattle, and Mrs. Spafford, with the rest of the family, five in number, took a sail boat called the Fire Fly and proceeded to Monroe by water. After a week's stay at Monroe, Spafford got two yoke of oxen and a lumber wagon, and with this rig the family started for Tecumseh. They camped out two nights, and on the third day arrived at Musgrove Evans'. They located their house on the flat near the creek, a few rods north of the present depot building. Elevating the wagon-box on crotches and poles, they camped under it until a log house could be raised. This house, like its predecessors, was destitute of floor or chimney. They had no floor until the 27th of November, when the new saw-mill had commenced operations, and enough lumber was obtained to make one.

Mr. Spafford's family continued to live here for many years. Two of his daughters, Mrs. W. W. Tilton and Mrs. Webster, still reside here, and one son, Sumner F. Spafford, esq., is a resident of Des Moines, Iowa. Abner Spafford's family lived in this house two years, and then moved upon E. F. Blood's farm.

During the fall of 1824, Mr. Blood built a log house upon his farm, the gable ends being finished with the first lumber turned out of the new saw-mill. This building still stands on the bluff of the river, a few rods north of Mr. Blood's present dwelling house. It is greatly dilapidated and rapidly going to decay, but is allowed to stand as one of the very few remaining mementoes of the first year's settlement of Tecumseh. The same fall, an Indian trader, by the name Knaggs, built a small house on the north side of Chicago street, upon the block east of the East Branch school, and during the winter of '24 and '25, that was the only place of business in Tecumseh.

In July or August, Daniel Pitman and his family, consisting of a wife and two children, arrived. He put up a small house on the present site of Dr. Patterson's residence, where he lived for several years. The next summer he erected a store on the same lot and embarked in the mercantile business. A daughter of his, Mrs. E. A. Tribou, still lives in Tecumseh, and James E. and Samuel Pitman live in Detroit.

Borland, his wife and two children, arrived the same fall, although late in the season, and took up their abode with Mr. Blood, upon his farm, where they lived for two years, and until Abner Spafford's family moved in. Borland then became the landlord of the Brown tavern.

Horace Wolcott and family came about the same time. He entered two lots north of the Evans home, in Brownville, which are now divided into several small farms, and built a small log house there. The family lived there for some years. Peter Low joined the party at Buffalo. He entered a lot on Evans Creek, between Shawnee street and the present village cemetery. He sold this lot in the fall to Jesse Osborn,.

and took up a part of P. Bills' present farm, east of the road leading to E. F. Blood's present residence, adjoining Mr. Blood's farm.

Jesse Osborn and family, consisting of a wife and five or six children, came in during that fall and purchased the lot of Peter Low. He set out a large orchard on this place, afterwards known as the Hoag orchard. His house was on the bank of the creek, a few rods north of John Whitnack's present residence. A few years after Mr. Osborn moved to the town of Woodstock, in this county. To him belongs the honor of raising and taking to mill the first wheat that was ground in Tecumseh. The house and the "old barn" remained on this place many years, and we remember the fact that in our boyhood days a favorite swimming place in the creek was behind this same "old barn."

In the original party which came with Evans was a Lawyer Rathbone, but as the pioneers were a peaceable set he had no litigation to attend to. But as there was a considerable sickness in the new settlement a physician became a necessity. Dr. Ormsby arrived in the fall of '24 and continued in practice here two years. Mr. E. F. Blood had the honor of going to Detroit after his medicine chest.

Thomas Goodrich, Sr., came that fall and located the farm now occupied by Mrs. H. R. Clark, at Newberg. On the 16th of November his family, consisting of himself, wife and seven children, Ira and George Goodrich, with their families, landed at Monroe and came direct to Tecumseh. Ira located a farm one mile north of Newburg.

We have thus enumerated (as far as we have been able to gather the dates) all the persons who came to Tecumseh during 1824 with a view of a permanent settlement. When that winter set in, the total population of the village, including men, women and children, numbered about fifty.

We will now take a brief retrospect to relate a few incidents of a general character.

During the summer of 1824 the principal business of the men in the settlement was building houses and cutting out roads. No crops of any amount were put in during the season. As often as a new family arrived all hands would turn in and help put up a log house. Nearly all their provisions, flour, merchandise, etc., were carted from Monroe in wagons. Peter Benson, who was in the employ of Mr. Evans as his teamster, did most of this work. He spent the whole summer traveling back and forth between Monroe and Tecumseh. New pieces of road had to be cut every few days, as the soil was marshy in many places and the road would soon become impassable by reason of the mud.

The entire stock of sugar, however, was purchased of the Indians. It was maple sugar, and was put up in a vessel called a "mocock." This vessel was made of bark and about the size and shape of a copper boiler. A "mocock" of maple sugar would last a family several months. The mails came up from Monroe at intervals of a week or ten days, whenever Peter Benson came over the road with a load of provisions. During the autumn of 1824 the first saw mill was erected. A dam was thrown across the river in Brownville, which dam remains there to this day, and serves as a highway across the river at the paper mill. The work upon the mill was done mostly by volunteers, the same as the log houses had been raised. Men had but little to do at home, and they were all waiting for lumber with which to finish their houses for winter. The site of the saw mill was east of the bridge across the mill-dam and south of the race leading to the Heck Bros. mill. It was completed in a few weeks, and by November was in running order. Several logs were sawed up that fall, and thus the settlers were supplied with boards with which to build floors for their houses. This mill did valiant service for several years, but it finally went to decay, and the last timber of its foundation floated down the Raisin many years ago.

Before Mr. Evans settled in Tecumseh, and during his stay of a few days in Monroe, in April, 1824, a co-partnership was formed between Austin E. Wing, Musgrove Evans and Gen. Brown, by the firm name of Wing, Evans & Brown, and very soon after the arrival of the parties, steps were taken to have the new settlement made a county seat. Gen. Brown stopped at Detroit on this mission when he started East for his family, paid a personal visit to Gov. Cass, and the Governor appointed a committee of two, consisting of C. J. Lanmon and Oliver Johnson, who visited Tecumseh and approved the location. On the last of June the Legislature was in session. The committee made their report, which was accepted and adopted. It was stipulated in the enactment that in laying out the village, the company should set apart for the public benefit four squares, viz., one for a court house and jail, one for a public promenade, one for a cemetery and one for a military parade ground, and that they should build a bridge across the River Raisin east of the village. These conditions were accepted. In the meantime Wing, Evans & Brown had entered the land, comprising the present village east of Railroad street, and extending north to the Brownville mill. Upon this tract of land the original plat of the village was made.

Musgrove Evans himself, who was a surveyor, laid out the village plat during the summer of 1824. The original plat embraced the territory bounded east by Wyandotte street, south by Killbuck street, west by the present railroad and the section line running directly north from the present depot, and north by a line about ten rods north of the street leading east from Brownville across the river. All of the territory west of the railroad has been attached to the village by subsequent additions. The cemetery square was located on the corner of Ottawa and Killbuck streets, the military square on Shawnee street, the court house and park squares on the west side of Maumee street, and upon either side of Chicago street. The cemetery square has long since ceased to be used for that purpose, but the village still improves it as public property. The park square has been turned over to the school district, and upon that the East Branch School now stands. The court house square, opposite, is still village property, but the building itself has been moved one block further east, and is now used by S. P. Hosmer as a tool handle factory. Time upsets all things. The first court house in the county is deserted by sheriffs, lawyers and judges, and given over to the manufacture of hickory tool handles.

But this talk is a digression. Returning to our task, let us trace the history of our village through 1825. During that year but few new settlers presented themselves; but many new buildings were erected and substantial improvements made. Among the arrivals were Curtis Page and William W. Tilton, two practical carpenters. Mr. Tilton came in June, 1825, and he was the man who cut the two small fields of wheat sown by Stetson and Evans the fall before. Soon after, he and Page hired out to Daniel Pitman, and were employed several weeks in building his new store upon his lot at the corner of Chicago and Ottawa streets—Dr. Patterson's present lot. In the fall Mr. Pitman opened his store, and continued in mercantile business there for several years.

Thomas Griswold, wife and four children arrived in July, 1825. He entered two lots about a mile north of Wolcotts, on the present Clinton road. The family lived with Evans until November and then moved upon their farm.

In the spring of this year Gen. Brown commenced the erection of a large frame tavern on the southeast corner of Maumee and Chicago streets, the present site of George W. Frasier's house. The house was occupied during the summer, and was kept as a public house for ten or twelve years, when it burned down. At the time it burned, it was known as the "Green Tavern."

On the 30th day of July, a child of Musgrove Evans, little Charley, aged about three years, was drowned in the river, near his father's house in Brownville.

George Griswold, who lives in this township, was with Charley when the accident happened. George was four years old. The two boys went down to the river bank directly east of the present mill cooper shop to play, and while there Charley walked out on a plank which had been placed to stand on while dipping up water, and fell off into the river. George shouted for his mother, but before any one arrived Charley was drowned.

Col. Hickson and family arrived the same fall, and took up their abode in the building owned by the Indian trader, Knaggs. They lived in Tecumseh a few years, and afterwards moved on a farm just north of Clinton, where Mrs. Hickson still resides, in a hale and happy old age. Theodore Bissell arrived the same summer, remained over one winter, and then returned East. In 1827 he came back and settled here.

The first religious service held here was in the summer of 1825, and was conducted by Rev. Noah M. Wells, then pastor of the First Presbyterian Church of Detroit. He formerly resided in New York, and Mrs. Gen. Brown was a member of his church there. He came over to Tecumseh to pay the General's family a visit, and as he remained in town one Sabbath, a meeting was held in Brown's tavern, and Mr. Wells preached the sermon.

In the fall, Rev. Mr. Bachman, a Methodist, commenced preaching here and continued regularly every two weeks for three or four years, Tecumseh being the principal point in his circuit. He received the magnificent salary of $100 per year. These services were held at first in the school house and afterwards in the court house.

During the season of 1825, the settlers were hard at work breaking up the land, tilling and harvesting their crops. A large amount of wheat was sown that fall. It was in the fall and winter of this year that Wing, Evans & Brown started the project of a new grist mill. The first winter (1824-5) had been a very mild one, but the second one (1825-6) was colder, and there was some good sleighing. At this time a sleigh ride was got up to Benjamin's tavern, ten miles this side of Monroe. There were two loads of seven persons. One load contained Theodore Bissell, Horace Wolcott, and five young ladies, from fifteen to thirty years old. They were the only single ladies of a marriageable age then living in Tecumseh.

The other load contained Dr. Ormsby, Cousin George Spafford, and five married ladies. As there were but two strings of bells in the county, each load appropriated one string. The husbands of the married ladies had previously gone to Monroe to purchase provisions, and after the two sleigh loads arrived at Benjamin's, the five husbands stopped on their return home, and very unexpectedly found their wives there. The occurrence produced much merriment, and was the theme of gossip in the village for some time afterwards.

In the fall of '25 or spring of '26, Borland made a party at his house on the Blood farm. Gen. Brown hitched up Evans' lumber wagon, put a long board across, and picked up a load of ladies to take to the party. Going home the wagon reach came apart, the board dropped down, and the women were tumbled into the ditch. Mrs. Daniel Hickson was one of the heroines of this accident.

In the fall of '25 a small frame school house was built on the north side of Chicago street where the old Michigan House was afterwards erected, the present site of S. B. Terry's residence; and in the ensuing winter, George Taylor, father of Mrs. James Pencil, of this village, taught the first regular term of school, in the new building.

The first white male child born in the county was George W. Goodrich, who now lives in the township of Clinton. The next child, or rather children, were twins, and Mrs. Peter Low was the happy mother. Peter Low was an uncle of Justus Low, who now lives in Ridgeway.

In the spring of '26, Evans commenced the building of a large frame house on the corner of Oneida and Chicago streets, and by the 4th of July, in that year, the frame was up and roof on, and it was used for the celebration. This house yet stands and is used by Peter R. Adams, Esq., as his residence.

This spring the grist mill, which had been started the previous fall, was completed. The mill was placed east of the Brownville dam, opposite the river from the saw mill, about where the paper mill is now located. But the project came near being a failure for lack of mill stones. Fortune, however, favors the brave. About a mile or so northeast was found a huge boulder of pure granite. With drill and wedges—for they had no powder—two large slabs were split off and worked into suitable size to answer the purpose. Along in June, when the mill was nearly finished, Jesse Osborn and Gen. Brown, in a bantering way, pledged each other, the one to furnish new wheat and the other to grind it on the 4th of July. They kept their word. Jesse Osborn harvested his wheat on ground north and east of Judge Stacy's present house, threshed it with a flail, took a grist to the new mill on the morning of the 4th, and from flour made that morning Mrs. Brown made some cake and biscuit, which were used at the celebration dinner in the afternoon. Sylvanus Blackmar was the miller who ground this grist, and to him belongs the honor of having ground the first flour ever manufactured in Lenawee county.

Another version is that Thomas Griswold ground the first grist. Blackmar was the regular miller, and Griswold worked in the mill. It is quite likely, therefore, that both of them had a "hand in the hopper."

For several days prior to July 4th, 1826, arrangements were making for an extensive celebration. About noon a procession formed at Brown's tavern. Daniel Pitman was marshal of the day, and rode on a small bald-faced pony. Brass bands were not plenty in those days, but music of some kind was necessary, so they got a French fiddler from Monroe, and that Frenchman with his fiddle constituted the band.

After forming the procession it was marched to Evans' new house, three blocks up Chicago street, where the exercises were held. During the march, one string of the Frenchman's fiddle broke, and the band cried out, "Stop the procession." The marshal, however, kept the procession moving, but the music after that was rather demoralized. Arriving at Evan's house, the speaking of the day was gone through with and then the company dispersed. Some of the men returned to Brown's tavern for their dinner, and others, with the ladies of the village, made some tables in Pitman's yard, on the corner opposite Evans' new house, and enjoyed a picnic dinner. Mrs. Brown had some cake and biscuit there made from the new flour ground that morning.

Cynthia Spafford, now Mrs. Tilton, was living in Pitman's family at that time, and she considers that meal was one of the best and most enjoyable picnic dinners she has ever partaken of from that day to this.

The first two years of pioneer life in Tecumseh were filled with many privations and trials. Many illustrations of this we have given, and many more will never be recorded.

An anecdote is told of Capt. Merritt, an early resident, which shows the feeling of the early settlers. Meeting a friend one day in Monroe, he was asked where he lived. "In Tecumseh," said he. "And where is that?" "It is thirty miles from Monroe," he replied, "and forty miles beyond God's Blessing." Those of us who have come up with the present generation have but a faint idea of the privations and struggles that the pioneers endured who laid on the banks of the Raisin the foundation of the village of Tecumseh.

Our allotted task is done, and upon this glorious fourth of 1826, we drop the curtain of our history for the present.

Gen. Brown, Mr. and Mrs. Tilton, E. F. Blood, Mrs. Hickson, Sumner Spafford, Sam and James Pitman, and perhaps a few others, are the only persons now living who can remember with any distinctiveness the events of those far off days, and those few persons are rapidly passing away. Peter Benson lives near Grand Traverse, and Mrs. Knaggs, his sister, is living in Monroe. We trust some abler pen may hereafter take up the thread of our narrative where we have left it, and rescue the events of the subsequent five or ten years from the oblivion which now threatens them.

INDEX.

KEY TO EVERY-NAME INDEX

Every person's name is indexed alphabetically. When various spellings are given, all are included.

Following each surname, businesses and other names are listed alphabetically.

Example:

> GREEN, Orson
> GREEN & JOHNSON LIVERY STABLE
> HADLEY, Horatio H.

Pioneer settlements, names or roads and Indian trails which no longer exist, or have been renamed, are marked with an asterisk (*).

Every person's name is listed, also Chapter Headings and Township headings.

Other categories included in this index, in the manner above stated, are:

> BUSINESSES
> CHURCHES
> HOTELS, INNS, TAVERNS
> INDIANS
> MILLS
> NEWSPAPERS
> * PIONEER SETTLEMENTS & EARLY PLACE - NAMES
> RAILWAYS
> * ROADS & INDIAN TRAILS
> SCHOOLS

BROWNELL continued
  Elijah, 17, 18, 48, 101
  John S., 73, 98
  Laura (Miss), 102
  Sands, 27
  Thomas, 102
BROWNVILLE
  ---, 11, 135, 136, 137,
    138, 139
BROWNVILLE MILL
  ---, 134, 139
BRYAN MILL
  The, 129
BRYANT
  John, 46
  N, 58
BUCK
  Samuel, 15
BUDLONG
  Alfred W., 51
  Calista, 51
  Lorenzo, 51
BUGBEE
  Eli, 44
BUGBEE'S CORNERS
  ---, 128
BUGBY
  Moses, 18
BULLARD
  H., 125
  James, 125
BUMP
  Bartlett, 54
  Harley, 90
BUNDAY
  Warner, 109, 110
BURBANK
  Gamaliel, 54
BURCH
  Frost &, 72
BURNETT
  Horace A., 128
BURNS
  Patrick, 52
  Peter, 52
BURNHAM
  John H., 92
  Warren, 36
  William, 36
  William Jr., 129
BURNS
  James, 112
BURROUGHS
  Ambrose M., 122
BURT
  Charles, 128
  James, 128
  Thomas, 126, 129
BURTON
  Samuel, 18
BUSH
  Christopher, 52
  Eli, 99, 108
  Farm, 9
BUSHBERRY
  Matthew, 44
BUTLER
  Richard, 36
BUTTON
  C., 128
BUTTS
  John, 96

CADILLAC
  De La Motte, 7
CADY
  Kleber, 98
  Levina, 98
  Lydia, 98
  Nelson O., 98
  N. O. (Mrs.), 87
  Sabra Ann (Griswold), 27
CALDWELL
  Huldah, 50
CALHOUN
  --- (Mr.), 71
CALLISON
  Alexander P., 53
CALVIN
  J., 40
CAMBURN
  Hannah, 51
  James W., 39
  John, 39
  Sarah, 123
CAMP
  Edwin, 128
  John, 118
  Nelson, 118
  William, 118
CAMPBELL
  Robert W., 117
  William, 48
CAMPBELLITES
  ---, 122
CANAAN TOWNSHIP
  ---, 121, 122
CANANDAIGUA RAILROAD CO.,
  Medina &, 113
CANADA SOUTHERN RAILWAY
  CO., Chicago &, 119
CANADAIGUA BAPTIST CHURCH
  ---, 110, 111
CANADAIGUA MILLS
  ---, 132
CANANDAIGUA SAW MILL
  ---, 113
CANDEE
  Leander, 126, 127, 129
  Lorinda (Bird), 127
  --- (Mrs.), 127
CANER
  Dolly (Elwell), 49
  Stephen (Dr.), 49
CANNIFF
  Enos., 79, 96, 97
CANIFF
  & Montgomery, 79
CAREY
  Sheldon, 128
CARL
  Samuel, 129
CARLETON
  ---, 77
  Henry, 98
  John, 65
  John H., 91, 97, 98, 87
  Mary Ann, 98
  --- (Mr. & Mrs.), 87
CARMICHAEL
  Bradford, 54
  Charles, 54, 55, 91,
    104
  Charles (Mrs.),104
  Henry, 55, 66

CARMICHAEL continued
  Nancy, 104
  Silas, 54, 104
  Squire, 104
CARPENTER
  D., 95
  Delia (Miss), 95
  Ebenezer S., 39
  Manson, 103
  Samuel, 18
CARR
  Calvin, 54
CARRIER
  Lewis, 44
CARSON
  Alonzo M., 115
  Prof., 94, 95
  William, 50
CARTER
  George W., 67, 131
  T., 39
CASE
  Martin, 44
CASS
  Gov., 134, 138
  Lewis (Gov. Col.), 8, 9, 10,
    12, 17
  --- (Mr.), 60
CASTERLINE
  George, 128
  Jeptha, 128
CATELLE
  David, 44
CAVENDER
  ---, 38
  Burns, 51, 113
  William, 23, 38, 51, 52,
    59, 112, 132
CAVENDER'S
  ---, 26
CAWLEY
  Franklin, 118, 119
  James P. (Hon.), 118, 119
CEROW
  Jeremiah, 48
CHAFFEE
  Allen, 18
  C. T., 93
CHAMBERLIN
  David (Dr.), 95, 96
  David P., 97
CHAMBERS
  Samuel, 41
CHAMPLIN
  Adelia (Miss), 65
  E. P., 135
  --- (Mrs.), 87
  Rhoda, 108
  Warren, 107
  William, 36, 108
CHAPIN
  Loren, 131
  Wait, 125
CHAPMAN
  Anna (Mrs.), 95
  John, 18
  William, 36, 66
CHAPPELL
  --- (Dr.), 116
CHASE
  Perley, 131
  Ocobock &, 131

-4-

FARMER continued
  Silas, 46
  Thomas, 46
FARMER FAMILY
  ---, 54
FARMERS' GRANGE
  --- (The), 119
FARNHAM
  Erastus, 48
  J. L., 122
  --- (Mr.), 120
FARNSWORTH
  Charles, 110
  E. C., 117
  Roswell R., 110
FARROLL
  Thomas, 50
FARWELL
  Hiram, 41
FAY
  Catherine, 18
FEATHERLY
  Daniel, 36
FELCH
  Judge, 71
FEATHERLY
  --- (Mr.), 128
FELLOWS
  Joseph, 51
FENTON
  Horace, 99
FERGUSON
  Hiram, 54
  Jeremiah, 54
  Joseph, 53
FERRIS
  Caleb D., 50
FIELD
  Pliney, 18
  Reuben G., 53
FINCH
  Asahel, 20, 113
  B. F., 113
FINCHNER
  Samuel, 40, 111
FINDLEY
  Alexander, 65, 127
FINK
  Jonathan, 116
FINNEY
  Alfred A., 98, 131
  Arza, 44, 109
  Augustus, 65, 66, 67,
    68, 72, 87, 97, 98,
    126, 131
  Augustus (Mrs.), 87
  Byron A., 131
  Harriet C. (Kidder), 98, 131
    131
  Huldah (Foot), 98
  --- (Mr.), 68, 69
FINNEY FARM
  ---,
FISH
  Alice, 106
  David, 36
FITCH
  John, 18
  Stephen, 18
FITTS
  Harrison, 109
FLAGER

FLAGER continued
  Hiram, 53
  Zachariah, 53
FLETCHER
  --- (Col.), 61
  Joseph, 9, 66
  Seth, 36
FLORIDA TOWNSHIP
  ---, 125
FLOWERS
  William, 27
FLUGHLER
  Peter, 53
FOOT
  Huldah, 98
FOOTE
  David M., 124
  James, 124
  John M., 124
  Milton, 124
  Peter (Rev.), 87, 121, 122
  --- (Rev. Father), 87
  William B., 91
FORBES
  Horatio L., 53
  Ira L., 117
FORD
  Augustus, 118
  Sidney S., 55, 106
FORSYTH
  Russell, 51, 53
FOSTER
  Alvah, 109
  Henry C., 110, 117
  J. R., 58
  Jacob, 43, 47, 99
  John, 47, 48
  John R., 40, 111
  --- (Mrs.), 40
  Phoebe, 43
  William, 18
FOSTER'S
  ---, 87
FOWLE
  Benjamin, 27, 123
  Charles, 27, 123
  Orrin, 123
FOWLER
  James H., 124
  James S., 124
  --- (Mr.), 129
FRANK
  Henry G., 96
FRANKLIN
  Amos, 39, 41
  John, 40
FRANKLIN HOTEL
  ---, 72
FRANKLIN LOT
  (The Old), 72
FRARY
  Margaret (Miss), 15
FRASIER
  George W., 138
FRATTS
  Nicholas, 36, 66
FRAZEE
  Sarah, 50
  William, 49, 50, 58, 66
FRAZER
  Joseph, 92
  --- (Rev.), 38

FREELAND
  Jonathan C., 43
FREEMAN
  Isaac, 36
FREE WILL BAPTIST CHURCH
  ---, 94, 105
FRENCH
  Isaac, 18, 27, 66, 67
  Jonathan, 56
  Luther C., 97
FRIEND BAKERY
  The., 69, 87
FRIENDS
  (Church), 11, 14, 17, 100,
    101, 102
FRIENDS CHURCH
  Rollin Twp., 101
FRIENDS MEETING HOUSE
  (Church), 11, 14, 100,
    102
FRIENDS OF THE (RAISIN)
  VALLEY, The, 17
FROST & BURCH
  ---, 72
FULLER
  David C., 124
  James, 106
  Philo C., 67
  R. J., 124
  Reuben, 124
FULSOM
  ---, 133, 135
FURMAN
  Oliver, 118
  Robert, 118

GAGE
  Elias, 50
  Stephen L., 54
GAHAGAN
  James, 86
  Peter, 117
GALE
  Brooks, 123
  Orlando C., 123
GALLOP
  William, 44
GALUSHA
  Lillie (Miss), 95
  --- (Mr.), 81
GAMBLE
  Thomas, 54, 109
  Thomas Sr., 44
GAMBLEVILLE
  ---, 31, 54, 109
GARDNER
  Henry P., 59
GARLICK
  DeWitt, 117
  Horace, 18, 39, 41, 112
GATES
  Peter, 42
  ---, 58
  Lewis, 58
  Lewis M., 52, 58
GAY
  Ebenezer, 23, 24, 27
  Edward A., 96
  --- (Father), 23
  Horace, 128
  --- (Mr.), 27, 30
  --- (Mrs.), 24, 29, 30, 31

HANNAH
  James Jackson, 41
HANNAHS
  D. P., 73
HANNAN
  Thomas, 116
HANNIBAL
  Chas., 128
HARE
  Amos, 46
HARKNESS
  David, 44
  Gideon, 44
HARNARD
  Jonathan, 18
HARRINGTON
  David, 24
  Levi W., 55
HARRIS
  Ida (Miss), 95
"HARRIS LINE"
  ---, 60, 61, 62
HARRISON
  --- (Gen.), 73
  --- (Mr.), 13
  William Henry (Gen.), 7
"HARRISON"
  ---, 101
HART
  Geo., 128
  J. B. (Rev.), 122
  Myra, 102, 103
  Rebecca, 122
  Richard, 128
HARTSON
  Charles, 128
  Hiram, 128
HARVEY
  Captain, 134
HASKILL
  E. R., 92
HASKINS
  --- (the three), 47
  John, 43, 48
HATFIELD
  Hiram, 46
HATHAWAY
  Celinda S., 98
  James, 27
  William, 43, 99
HAVILAND
  Charles, 18
HAWKINS
  John R., 43
  Richard, 50
  Wm. H., 117
HAWLEY
  Marcus, 36
  Thomas, 39
HAWLY
  Thomas, 40
HAYNES
  Hiram, 90
  Jonathan, 44, 109
HAYWARD
  Henry, 27, 39
  Judith P., 53
HAYWOOD
  Lucy R., 53
HAZLETT
  M. R., 95
  --- (Mrs.), 72

HEACOX
  William, 125
HEATH
  Chas., 117
  Chauncey, 116
  Edgar, 116
  Lewis (Capt.), 117
  Louis, 116
HECK BROS. MILL
  ---, 137
HELM
  Charles, 55
HELMICK
  Michael, 128
HENRY
  Charles M., 41
HERALD, THE
  ---, 79
HERMANS
  --- (Rev. Mr.), 115
HERRINGTON
  David, 27, 44
  Heman, 40
  Orson, 109, 110
HESTER
  ---, 82, 83
  Mary E., 80
HEWITT
  Charles M., 41
HEYDENBERK
  Benj. F., 116, 117
HEYWARD
  Roswell J., 39
HICKSON
  Col., 138
  Daniel (Mrs.), 139, 140
HIGBY & OSBORN MILL
  ---, 129
HIGLEY
  ---, 128
  Herman, 117
  Otis, 118
HILL
  ---, 86
  A. L., 85, 86
  Alpheus, 18, 54, 124
  --- (Capt.), 128
  Jesse, 46
  Rollin R., 51, 112, 116
HILLER
  David, 27
  T. J. 95
HILLIKER
  Harlow S., 117
HILLSDALE CENTER
  ---, 67, 68
HILLSDALE & INDIANA RAILROAD
  DETROIT, 124
HILLSDALE & LENAWEE AGRI-
  CULTURAL UNION SOCIETY,
  97
HILLSDALE & SOUTHWESTERN
  DETROIT RAILWAY, 123
HINDS
  I. C., 128
HITCHCOCK
  Hiram, 48
  Horace, 36, 66, 124
HITCHINS
  John, 32 (see Hutchins)
HIXSON
  Amos, 44

HOAG
  Estel, 117
HOAG ORCHARD
  ---, 137
HOBART
  --- (Mr.), 79
HOBBS
  William P., 41
HODGE
  Edward (Rev.),110
HODGES
  Israel S., 126, 127, 129
HOEG
  Amos, 19
  Stephen, 54
HOGABOAM
  J. C., 74, 108
  J. J., 82
  James J., 1
  Jas. J., 4, 97
  John C., 68, 72, 73, 96
  --- (Mrs.), 73
HOLBROOK
  Silas, 20
HOLLISTER
  Ephraim, 39
HOLLOWAY
  Ira, 39
HOLMES
  Benjamin, 112
  Jas., 117
  Manly, 46
  William, 46
HOLT
  Alvah, 39, 87
HOOKER
  Azel, 99
HOOPER
  John, 50
  Pontius, 18, 27
HOOVER
  Elias, 128
  Frank, 128
  James, 128
HOPKINS
  Orphelia B., 51
  Sanford D., 110
HORNBECK
  Benjamin, 40, 53, 112
  James, 51
HORNER
  --- (Gov.), 63
  John S., 62
HOSMAN
  John, 128
HOSMER
  S. P., 138
HOTCHKISS
  Cook, 40, 111, 112, 113,
    114
  John C., 111, 116
  L., 50, 113
  Lauran (Mr.), 113, 114, 116
  Lauren (Rev.), 92
HOTELS
  (& Taverns), 15, 16, 18, 21,
    53, 54, 69, 72, 76, 80,
    87, 126, 131, 136, 138,
    139, 40 (see names of)
HOUGH
  Olmsted, 47
  (Sheriff), 82

JOLLS continued
  Thomas, 44
JONES
  Bela B. (Dr.), 99
  Ira, 48
  John, 52
  Jonathan (Rev.), 88
  Samuel, 93
  Samuel Jr., 93
  Warren A., 97
  William, 52
JORDAN
  Samuel, 118
JORDAN'S
  ---, 42
JORDON
  Samuel, 23
JOSLIN
  Willard, 44
  William, 101
JOUGHIN
  J., 117
JUDD
  Ethel, 124
  William P., 90

KALAMAZOO RAILROAD,
  Erie &, 60,104
KEALEY
  Thomas, 48, 65, 101
KEDZIE
  William, 13, 15, 16, 17
KEECH
  C. C., 82
KEELEY
  Edward, ---
  Thomas, 50
KEENE
  ---, 58, 68, 72, 84, 87
KEITH
  ---, 108
  Cecil, 50
  Jane (Miss), 84
  Martha, 50
  Ozen, 36, 50, 56, 106, 107,
    108
KELLEY
  Elias H., 44
  Julia Ann, 84
  William, 128
  Willis, 55
KELLY
  Dolly (Elwell), Caner, 49
  Oliver, 49
KEMP
  David, 108
  John B., 124
KEMPTON
  Seth, 46, 123, 124
KENDALL
  Amos, 65
  --- (Dr.), 116
KENLY
  James, 48
KENNEDY
  Asa A., 118
  Chauncey, 109
  Philip, 27
KENT
  Augustus, 85, 86, 97, 99
  Richard, 37
KENYON

KENYON continued
  Albert, 123, 124
  Benj. J., 123
  L. L., 116
  Sylvester, 33, 36, 66
KERNEY & HOWE
  ---, 124
KIBBIE
  Rufus (Dr.), 113, 116
KERR MILL
  ---, 113
KIDDER
  ---, 31, 32
  Addison, 24
  Calista, 24
  Harriet, 24
  Harriet C., 98, 131
  Hiram, 18, 22, 23, 24, 25,
    26, 27, 33, 35, 49, 97,
    98, 131
  Julia G., 98
  Maria, 24, 29
  Maria J., 98
  Mary Ann (Carleton), 98
  --- (Mr.), 25, 28, 29
  --- (Mrs.), 24, 27, 28, 29
  Nathan, 24, 35
  Nathan B., 18, 22, 23
KIDDER'S
  (House), 25, 26
KIDDER MILL
  ---, 67, 127
KIDDER SETTLEMENT
  ---, 29, 31, 38
KIES
  Alonzo, 27
  Samuel, 112, 114
KIMBALL
  Jesse, 33, 36, 37, 56,
    106, 108
KINNE
  Joshua, 117
KING
  Calvin, 41, 52
  Cyrus, 106
  Gideon G., 129
  John, 129
  Laban, 36
  Salem T., 51
KINGSLEY
  Samuel, 128
KINNEY
  Allen, 124
  Alonzo, 117
  Amos A., 39
  Elias, 53
  George, 124
  James S., 53
  Robert, 36
KIRBY
  James, 124
KNAGGS
  (Benson), (Mrs.), 140
  "Indian Trader", 136, 139
  --- (Mrs.), 140
KNAPP
  Abigail, 110
  Amos S., 41
  Edward, 48, 50
  Geo., 117
  James, 45
  John, 113

KNAPP continued
  Joel, 103
  John, 40, 41, 110, 111, 112
  Loren, 110
  Perry, 45, 46, 104
  R., 75
  Stephen, 45, 46, 55, 104
KNAPP FAMILY
  ---, 54
KNOGGS
  James, 14

LAIR
  Jacob, 44
LAIRD
  Robert, 97
  Robert (Rev.), 84
  & Penfield, 79
LAKE SETTLEMENT, THE
  ---, 43,-45
LAMB
  Isaac, 54
  Nahum, 44, 101, 103
  Orsamus, 103
  Roswell, 43
LAMMON
  Mary, 53
  Samuel, 39, 53
  Seth, 18
LAMPHERE
  Burton, 46
LAND OFFICE
  Monroe, 23, 26
LANE
  Anna Maria, 84, 98
  B. H., 86, 97, 98
  Beriah H., 6, 33, 35, 36,
    50, 64-67, 72, 95, 97,
    98
  Erastus, 33, 35, 36, 49,
    66, 67, 97
  Henry, 108
  John, 124
  Martha, 98
  Mary, 98
  --- (Mr.), 48, 49, 50, 74,
    75
  Nathaniel, 36, 49, 67, 98
  Phebe P., 72
  Phoebe, 50, 98
LANE & CHILDS,
  Eaton, 73
LANES, THE
  ---, 35
LANESVILLE
  ---, 65, 66, 68, 69,
    72-74, 77, 87, 88, 126
LANESVILLE SAW MILL
  ---, 66, 67
LANESVILLE PRESBYTERIAN
  ---, 105
LANESVILLE SCHOOL
  ---, 65
LANNON
  C. J., 138
LAPHAM
  Stephen, 23
LA PLAISANCE BAY TURNPIKE
  (Road), 19, 54
LARNED
  E. D., 76, 97
  Edward D., 95

MOREY
   Lois, 118
MORGAN
   Harrison (Rev.), 91
MORIARTY
   John, 117
MORRIS
   Charles, 18
   James W., 51
MORSE
   C. C. & Sons, 114
   Chas. C., 116
   & Christophers, 114
MORRDUS
   William W., 96
MOSCOW
   ---, 123 (Chapter).
MOSCOW HOTEL
   ---, 21
MOSCOW MILLS
   ---, 123
MOSCOW PLAINS
   ---, 123
MOSHER
   Jabez, 108, 109, 110
   W. J., 95
   James & Co., 77
MOTHERSILL
   William, 91
MOTT
   Harry, 128
MUDGE
   --- (Miss), 73
MUDGE'S CORNERS
   ---, 23
MUMFORD
   Elisha C., 123
MUNDY
   Edward, 47
MUNGER
   Alanson, 51
   John, 36
   John V., 96
MUNSON
   ---, 131
   John M., 110
   --- (Mr.), 78, 79
   Ocobock &, 131
MURPHY
   John, 18
   Seba, 36, 51
MURRAY
   James, 51

NETHAWAY
   Nelson, 124
   Thomas J., 124
NEWCOMB
   Justus G., 43
NEWELL
   Harriet, 76
   Harriet (Eaton), 76
NEWMAN
   Philemon, 53
NEWSPAPERS
   (See name of Newspaper)
   6, 79, 80, 113, 133
NEWTON
   B., 36
   Buckley, 36
NICHOLS
   George A., 116

NICHOLS continued
   Oren C., 50
NICKERSON
   Lewis, 18, 55
NILES
   Charles E., 96
NOBLE
   Susannah, 84
NOKES
   George, 54
NOKES SCHOOL HOUSE
   ---, 104
NORRIS
   Israel B., 129
   Jared B., 129
NORTH WHEATLAND CHURCH
   (Methodist), 90
NORTHROP
   H. H. (Rev.), 85
NORTHRUP
   Burr S., 46
NORTON
   Henry W., 115
   Noah, 16, 17, 18
NORVIS
   John B., 118
NOYES
   Lydia, 39
NYE
   Austin, 106
   Nelson, 108
   Sarah, 50

OAK GROVE ACADEMY
   ---, 115
OAKLEY
   H. P., 65
OAKS
   D. C. (Rev.), 122
O'BRIEN
   John, 46, 51
OCOBECK
   Alexander, 131
OCOBOCK
   Alexander M., 78
   William, 49, 58
OCOBOCK & CHASE
   ---, 131
OCOBOCK & MUNSON
   ---, 131
O'CONNOR
   John, 117
ODD FELLOWS LODGE
   ---, 91, 93, 95, 96
ODELL
   Daniel, 18
OLD CORNER STORE (the)
   ---, 77
OLDS
   Alanzo, 54
   Alonzo, 55
   Benj., 128
   Chas., 128
   Fred, 128
   Orrin, 128
OLNEY
   ---, 58
O'MEALY
   Robert, 106
ONCANS
   George, 44
ORCUTT

ORCUTT continued
   A., 125
   Clarinda, 98
   Silas, 43, 98
ORGANIZATION OF TOWNSHIPS
   ---, 63-64
ORMSBY
   C. N., 18
   C. N. (Dr.), 16
   Caleb (Dr.), 16
   Caleb N., 27
   --- (Dr.), 137, 139
OSBORN
   ---, 14, 64, 94
   A. C., 19
   Hiram, 97
   Horace, 117
   Jedediah, 101
   Jesse, 44, 63, 101, 102,
      136, 137, 139
   John, 53, 55, 73, 98, 117
   John M., 96, 108
   John M. (Hon.), 80
   M., 82
   Mercy, 98
   --- (Mr.), 14
   Rachel (Mrs.), 102
OSBORN MILL
   Higby &, 129
OSBORN'S
   ---, 24
OSBURN
   ---, 64
   Jesse, 12, 13, 14, 19
OSGOOD
   Charles, 55
OVERHOLT
   --- (Prof), 95

PACK
   --- (Mr.), 92
   William (Elder), 93
PACKARD
   Cyrus B., 43
   George, 39, 118
   John F., 39
   Joshua, 43
PADDLEFORD
   Joseph, 54
   Zachariah, 54
PAGE
   Curtis, 133, 138
   Dobson, 100
   --- (Mr.), 99
   Prudence, 50
   William D., 39
PALMER
   ---, 51
   Alexander, 126, 127
   Almon, 51, 53
   Alonzo, 79
   Benjamin, 50
   Cornelius G., 51, 52
   David, 117
   Geo. R., 128
   Hannah, 99
   John, 128
   Juba, 52
   Laura M., 99
   Lorenzo, 76, 97, 98
   Martin V., 117
   Noah, 50

PALMER continued
  Ruth (Wells), 98
  Sidney, 128
  Silas, 50
  W. H., 116
  William, 128
  William W., 80
  Wray T., 99, 108
PARISH
  Charles, 97
PARKER
  Elder, 103
  Elkanah, 51
  --- (Rev.) (Mr.), 105
  Roswell, 124
PARKS
  Ashael, 128
  Charles, 128
PARMELEE
  Albert, 54
PARRISH
  Chas., 97
PARSON
  --- (Miss), 54
PATCHIN
  James, 135
  James (Mrs.), 136
PATCHIN FARM
  ---, 135
PATRICK
  James, 101
  Jas., 101
PATTEE
  A. H., 79
PATTERSON
  --- (Dr.), 136, 138
PAULDING
  Allen, 117
PEASE
  ---, 86
  Chester C., 80, 81, 96
  Lyman, 18, 25, 32, 35,
    48, 54, 55, 103, 106
  S. B. (Deacon), 85
  Samuel, 86
PECK
  Daniel, 48
  Rufus, 48
PEGG & SWINDLE
  ---, 119
PELTON
  Nathan, 18
PENCIL
  (Taylor) (Mrs.), 139
  James (Mrs.), 139
PENFIELD
  Henry (Rev.), 91
  Laird, 79
PENNIMAN AND ASHLEY
  ---, 114
PENNINGTON
  Israel, 46
  John, 46
PENNOCK
  James P., 103
  Rhoda, 103
  Thomas, 22, 31, 32
  Ames &, 56
PENNOCK'S
  ---, 57
PENOYER
  John, 54

PEOPLE'S BANK, THE
  ---, 80, 82
PERHAM
  Warren, 128
PERKINS
  Allie (Miss), 95
  Edward C., 116
  H., 128
  Lorenzo D., 51
  Nelson, 132
  Samuel C., 74
  Samuel H., 96
  Stephen, 25, 44, 48, 99
PERRIN
  Bethseda, 50
  Emily, 50
  John, 50, 55, 125
  John Jr., 125
  S. W., 125
  Stephen W., 50, 55
PERRY
  Irwin P., 116
  Washington, 53
PERU MILL
  ---, 100, 101
PETERS
  Cassander, 18
  Geo., 117
  Sarah, 106
PETTIT
  William, 128
  William H., 129
PHELPS
  Ezra (Miss), 95
  Oliver, 53
PHILBRICK
  Joseph, 129
PHILLIPS
  John, 124
  Joseph, 127
  William, 127
PICKARD
  Jonathan N., 51
PIERCE
  ---, 40
  J. W. (Rev.), 83
PIERSON
  Leir R., 97
PILCHER
  E. H., 87
PIONEER HOTEL
  ---, 87
PIONEER SETTLEMENTS
  (Extinct Names) (See
    Names of Settlements)
    5, 11, 14, 15, 16, 17,
    18, 19, 20, 21, 22, 23,
    24, 29, 31, 54, 56, 58,
    65, 66, 67, 68, 69, 72,
    74, 77, 84, 87, 88, 101,
    104, 107, 109, 121, 122,
    123, 125, 126, 128, 133,
    135, 136, 137, 138, 139,
    140
PIONEER SOCIETY OF BEAN C
  CREEK COUNTRY, 6
PIPER
  ---, 77
  Robert B., 96
PITMAN
  Daniel, 136, 138, 140
  James E., 136, 140

PITMAN continued
  Samuel, 136, 140
PITTSFORD
  ---, 106-108 (Chapter VIII)
PIXLEY
  Calvin, 59, 106, 107, 121,
    122
  Ebenezer, 122
  Joseph, 51, 120, 121, 122
  Orrin, 51, 53, 112
PLUMLEY
  Thomas, 128
PLYMPTON
  C. (Mrs.), 95
PLYMPTON, BEARDSELL &,
  ---, 74, 76
PORTER
  Asaph R., 52
  --- (Gov.), 60
  William R., 48
PORTMAN
  Jas. G. (Rev.), 93
POST, THE
  ---, 79
POTTER
  Peter, 36
  Polly, 36
POWELL
  Isaac N., 39
  Stephen, 118
POWER
  Abiathar, 107
  Jas. S. (Dr.), 97, 116
  John, 32
POWERS
  Abiathar, 92
  John, 18, 51, 112
  William, 44
PRATT
  Alpheus, 25, 26, 28, 32,
    50, 56, 57, 64, 83, 87
    106, 107
  Alpheus (Father), 87
  David (Rev.), 65, 83
  Charles, 31
  Daniel (Rev.), 114
  David (Rev.), 98
  Heman, 24, 27, 54, 103,
    106, 109
  Jas. B., 96
  Joseph, 18
  --- (Mr.), 35, 75
  --- (Mrs.), 31, 35
  Sarah, 98
  Sophia, 44
  William T., 51
PRATTS
  Abel, 112
PRENTISS
  Henry, 107
PRESBYTERIAN CHURCH
  ---, 17, 65, 83, 84, 85,
    86, 88, 90, 105, 109,
    110, 123, 139 (see
    Separate Listings)
PRESBYTERIAN CHURCH OF BEAN
  CREEK, 83
PRESBYTERIAN CHURCH (Hudson)
  ---, 65, 83, 84, 85, 86,
    88, 89, 90, 105
PRESBYTERIAN CHURCH OF HUDSON
  AND PITTSFORD, 83

SMITH continued
  S. B. (Col.), 119
  Samuel F., 117
  Thomas, 59
  Sarah (Pratt), 98
  Timothy S., 16
  William, 33, 58, 84, 96
SMYTHE
  --- (Rev.) (Mr.), 94
SNELL
  Reuben, 50
SOLOMON
  Wright, &, 49
SOMERSET
  (Chapter IX), 109-110
SOMERSET HOTEL
  ---, 21
SOUTH WRIGHT GRANGE
  ---, 122
SOUTHERN FAIRFIELD
  ---, 53-54
SOUTHERN RAILROAD
  ---, 67, 74, 75, 113
SOUTHWESTERN RAILWAY,
  DETROIT, HILLSDALE,
  123
SOUTHWORTH
  Benjamin, 66, 67
SPAFFORD
  Abner, 136
  Cynthia, 136, 140
  George, 13, 133, 139
  George (Mrs.), 13, 135, 136
  Sumner F., 136, 140
SPARKS
  George W., 53
SPAULDING
  Edward M., 117
  John, 96
  O. L. (Gen.), 115
SPEAR
  Charles, 55
  Lydia (Miss or Mrs.), 98
SPENCER
  Aaron, 46, 123
  D. H., 86
SPOONER
  Warner, 124
SPRAGUE
  Elizabeth (Ames), 25, 36
  James, 36, 56
  James (Mrs.), 25
  James S., 106
  Mr. & Mrs., 43
SPRING
  Henry, 117
  Jeremiah, 117
SPRINGER
  J. H., 125
SPROWLS
  Peter, 124
SQUAWFIELD
  ---, 29, 56, 107
SQUIER
  Harriet N., 84
  Sarah, 84
  Lemuel J., 129
STACY
  S. C. (Judge), 12, 14,
  133, 140
STALKER
  Thomas, 92

STALKER continued
  Thomas (Rev.), 92
STAPLES
  Allen, 100
  Allen (Rev.), 86, 87, 100
STARKWEATHER
  Erastus W., 36
  John, 39, 51
  Samuel, 55
STEADMAN
  Ichabod, 127
STEARNS
  Elvira (Mrs.), 65
STEELE
  Ebenezer, 91
STEER
  Amos, 48
  David, 22, 43, 44, 46
  Joseph, 47, 99
STEERE
  David, 99, 101
STEPHENSON
  --- (Mr.), 112
STETSON
  Turner, 11, 14, 18,
  133, 136, 138
STEVENS
  Asher, 18
  Chauncey W., 79
  Henry G., 96
  Willard, 51
STEVICK
  Jacob, 128
STEWARD
  Mayhew, 43
STEWART
  Ebenezer, 108
STICKNEY
  Benjamin F., 20
  --- (Major), 62
  Two., 62
STILLWELL
  Christopher H., 51
STOCK
  Charles, 27
STOCK STORE (the)
  ---, 78
STOCKER
  Aaron, 128
STOCKWELL
  John W., 50
  William N., 36
STONE
  Charles, 112
  Jeremiah, 18
  Nathan, 112, 132
  Nahum, 132
  Pomeroy, 18
STONEX
  William G., 92
STOUT
  Cornelius A., 16, 18
  Elder, 129
  George, 15
STRAW
  Isaiah, 54
  Rhoda, 98
  Thomas, 98
STRONG
  Daniel, 44, 109
  David, 55
STROUD

STROUD continued
  David R., 96
  Philo H., 122
STRUNK
  David, 55, 91, 106, 107
STUBLY FARM
  ---, 86
STUCK
  David, 65, 117
  Esther, 106
  Michael Jr., 55
STUDDEFORD
  William V., 67
STURGIS
  Isaac M., 59
SUPPLEMENT
  (Hudson), 131-132
  (Tecumseh), 133-140
SUTTON
  Abigail (Knapp), 110
  Henry F., 125
  J. D., 110
  John D., 51, 112
  Reed, 50
  William, 117, 118
SWAN
  Prof., 115
SWANEY
  --- (Dr.), 119
  Ira, 95, 97
SWEENEY
  James H., 39
  Jas. H. (Dr.), 132
  John S., 112
  Samuel, 41
  Samuel Jr., 41
SWEET
  Griffin, 55
SWIFT
  John O., 124
  Julius O., 124
  William C., 124
SWIFT & CO.
  ---, 124
SWINDLE
  Pegg &, 119
  Wilson &, 119

TABOR
  ---, 31
  Benjamin F., 106
  Gaylord, 106, 107
  Gaylord G., 91
TADMAN
  Thomas, 41
TALBOT
  John, 48, 101
TALBOT MILL
  ---, 100, 101, 105
TALMADGE
  Isiah, 55
TANEY
  Roger B., 70
TANNERY, The
  (Eddy's), 79
TAPPENDEN
  William, 59
TARSENEY
  Andrew, 128
  James, 128
  John, 128
  Thomas, 128

Bean Creek Valley, Michigan

WHITE continued
  Charles, 44
  Curran, 36
  Curren, 27
  David, 20
  Horace, 24, 27
  Ira, 53, 113
  Robert, 21
  Sylvester, 48, 54
  Theron, 53
WHITEHORN
  R. H., 36, 106
  Robinson H., 56, 106, 107
WHITING
  Cyrus, 53
WHITMAN
  Ephraim, 39
  Japheth, 118
  Jeptha, 53
  --- (Mr.), 118
WHITNACK
  John, 137
WHITNEY
  Bowen, 55
  Chauncey, 36
  (DeGolyer) (Mrs.), 79
  Elizabeth, 135
  George, 54
  James, 16, 18
  L. P., 85
  Lemuel P., 97
  Loren, 128
  Nathan, 54, 90
WHITMORE
  Oren, 84
WHITNEY
  Orlando, 112, 114
  Richard H., 53
  Susan B. (Cobb), 97, 98
  William A., 79, 97
WHITNEY & CO.
  ---, 79
WIGGINS & TUCKER
  ---, 77, 78
WILBUR
  Albert, 116
  Alvin, 117
  Easton, 124
WILCOX
  Collins, 128
  Felix A., 101
  Henry N., 124
  J. N., 122
  Lyman, 53
  Margaret, 84
  Stephen, 27
  W. S., 16
WILDER
  Levi B., 112, 52
WILEY
  David, 18
WILKINS
  L. P., 117
WILL
  Thomas, 50
WILLETT
  Cornelius, 39
WILLEY
  --- (Rev.), 37
WILLIAMS
  Coleman (Prof.), 95
  George, 55

WILLIAMS continued
  Ira, 128
  John, 55, 106, 128
  Joseph R., 53, 59
  Thomas, 51
  Thos. C., 116
  Zebulon, 45, 46, 54, 104,
    106
WILLIS
  Edward, 118
  John R., 50, 118
WILSON
  Charles B., 54
  George W., 118
  Horatio, 41
  James, 39, 41, 120
  --- (Mrs.), 119
  Philo, 114, 116
  Simon D., 39, 51, 54,
    110, 118, 119
WILSON GROVE SCHOOL
  ---, 90
WILSON & SWINDLE
  ---, 119
WINANS
  Ed. H., 67
  --- (Mr.), 73
  William, 72
WINEGAR
  R. D., 108
WING
  Austin E., 11, 14, 133,
    136, 137, 138
  --- (Mr.), 12
  Warner, 118
WING, EVANS & BROWN
  ---, 134, 137, 138, 139
WINSLOW
  William, 32
WINTER
  E. Conant, 17, 20
WIRTS
  John R., 96
  Mary, 98
  S. M. (Dr.), 72, 78
  Stephen M., 97
  Stephen M. (Dr.), 97, 98
WIRTS STEAM MILL
  ---, 114
WISCOTT
  David, 36
WISNER
  Daniel A., 123
WITHERELL
  Edson, 54, 103
WOLCOTT
  Horace, 136, 139
  Lawrence (Esq.), 8
  Newton C., 109, 110
  --- (Rev. Mr.), 50
  William (Rev.), 50, 51,
    52, 53
WOLCOTTS
  ---, 138, 139
WOLF
  John D., 114
WOLVERTON
  E., 79
WOOD
  Brother, 93
  Charles, 117
  Jackson M., 96

WOOD continued
  John, 18
  Marvin, 117
  N., 36
WOODBRIDGE
  William, 8, 47
WOODRUFF
  Lewis, 55
WOODS
  Albert, 54
  William, 66
  Willis, 128
WOOD'S MILL
  ---, 108
WOODSTOCK
  (Chapter VI), 101-103
WOODSTUCK HOTEL
  ---, 21
WOODWORTH
  Erastus C., 53
  Orville, 41, 42, 43, 112,
    115
  William M., 51
WORDEN
  Asa, 55
  Dudley, 34, 35, 36, 50, 97,
    98
  Dudley (Mrs.), 34, 35
  Phebe, 98
  Robert, 6, 34, 37, 56, 96,
    106, 108
  Robert (Mrs.), 34
WORTH
  Moses S., 118
WORTHINGTON
  Henry (Rev.), 90
  --- (Mr.), 91
  Nicholas, 124
WRIGHT
  B., 95
  Benjamin, 67, 96
  Brother, 93
  Elizabeth, 100
  Uriah E., 41, 52
WRIGHT (XII)
  (Chapter XII), 119
WRIGHT & SOLOMON
  ---, 49

YERRINGTON
  Ezekiel, 50
YERKS
  William, 39, 41
YORK
  Phebe, 110
YOST
  ---, 128
  Emery, 128
YOUNG
  W., 128
  William, 22, 23, 128
YOUNGLOVE
  Joseph, 101
YOUNGS
  William, 128

-22-

MAP OF
LENAWEE COUNTY
Michigan

N. Friend Engr. Plate.

Drawn & Compiled by F. KRAUSE, C.E. Ann Arbor, Mich.

Kelley's Corners

WOODSTOCK

CAMBRIDGE

Cambridge

Springville P.O.

FRANKLIN

Tipton P.O.

Franklin Foster

Clayton

CLINTON

Newburg

TECUMSEH

Tecumseh

Macon

Lake Ridge P.O.

MACON

ROLLIN

Geneva

Rollin

ROME

Rome Center

ADRIAN

RAISIN

Ridgeway

RIDGEWAY

Church Crossing

Little Hope

Ogden Center

DEERFIELD

Deerfield

HUDSON

son

Clayton

DOVER

RICH

MADISON

Lenawee Junction

Wellsville

PALMYRA

Palmyra

Blissville

Blissfield

BLISSFIELD

Lyon

Fairfield

Medina

Canandaigua

MEDINA

SENECA

Weston

FAIRFIELD

Jasper

West Ogden P.O.

Ogden Center

OGDEN

Riga

RIGA

RANGE 1 EAST   RANGE 2 EAST   RANGE 3 EAST   RANGE 4 EAST   RANGE 5 EAST